C000125944

Postcolonial Brittany

Cultural Identity Studies

Volume 2

Edited by
Helen Chambers

PETER LANG
Oxford · Bern · Berlin · Bruxelles · Frankfurt am Main · New York · Wien

Heather Williams

Postcolonial Brittany

Literature between Languages

PETER LANG

Oxford · Bern · Berlin · Bruxelles · Frankfurt am Main · New York · Wien

Bibliographic information published by Die Deutsche Bibliothek
Die Deutsche Bibliothek lists this publication in the Deutsche National-
bibliografie; detailed bibliographic data is available on the Internet at
‹http://dnb.ddb.de›.

British Library and Library of Congress Cataloguing-in-Publication Data:
A catalogue record for this book is available from The British Library,
Great Britain, and from The Library of Congress, USA

ISSN 1661-3252
ISBN 978-3-03-910556-4
US-ISBN 978-0-8204-7583-7

© Peter Lang AG, European Academic Publishers, Bern 2007
Hochfeldstrasse 32, Postfach 746, CH-3000 Bern 9, Switzerland
info@peterlang.com, www.peterlang.com, www.peterlang.net

All rights reserved.
All parts of this publication are protected by copyright.
Any utilisation outside the strict limits of the copyright law, without the permission
of the publisher, is forbidden and liable to prosecution.
This applies in particular to reproductions, translations, microfilming, and storage
and processing in electronic retrieval systems.

Contents

Acknowledgements

This project began when I was Kathleen Bourne Junior Research Fellow at St. Anne's College, Oxford. I am grateful to the Principal and Fellows of St. Anne's for allowing me to embark on this project in 1999–2000. I am also grateful to the University of Wales, Aberystwyth for granting me sabbatical leave to write up the project in 2004–2005.

For financial support I am indebted to the British Academy for a Small Grant which enabled me to pursue the project at the Bibliothèque nationale in Paris in 2002.

For practical advice and assistance I am particularly grateful to librarians at the Taylor Institution Library, Oxford, the Bibliothèque nationale, Paris, and the National Library of Wales, Aberystwyth.

It is a pleasure to acknowledge the help, support and interest received from a number of friends and colleagues, from the worlds of both French Studies and Celtic Studies. Thanks are due to Malcolm Bowie, Aude Campmas, Helen Chambers, Mary-Ann Constantine, Sharif Gemie and other members of the Brittany study group, Charles Forsdick, Jacqueline Gibson, Nigel Harkness, Katherine Lunn-Rockliffe, Patrick McGuinness, Gwenno Piette, David Trotter, David Willis.

Special thanks to Nic, and to Steffan for sleeping.

Introduction: Is there a Francophone Brittany?

Is the epithet 'Francophone' possible for a part of mainland France? Overwhelmingly, the term has come to be associated with the literature produced in countries colonized by France and written in the language of the oppressor. Qualifying Brittany as 'Francophone' gives, on one level, a simple and accurate indication of the official and majority language in that region today, but its application to a place that is part of the *République une et indivisible* also calls into question the position of the French language in Brittany. Through its association with issues of postcoloniality,[1] the term 'Francophone' simultaneously conceals and affirms the existence of the region's indigenous language, the Breton language. If there is a Francophone Brittany, then this is not simply a Brittany that happens to speak French because it is part of a nation whose identity is predicated on linguistic unity. Rather it is a Brittany that speaks French over and in combination with Breton. The history of Breton and its persecution, the resulting bi-cultural situation, and impact on the politics of identity, all point to the relevance of a postcolonial framework for the study of Brittany.

The use of the word Francophone to refer to a part of mainland France serves as a reminder that 'Frenchness' was only achieved surprisingly recently, and at the expense of France's other indigenous languages.[2] A full history of the gradual eclipse of Breton by French

---

1   For a recent discussion of this word's 'heavy baggage', see Charles Forsdick and David Murphy, 'Introduction: the case for Francophone Postcolonial Studies', in *Francophone Postcolonial Studies: A Critical Introduction*, ed. by Charles Forsdick and David Murphy (London: Arnold, 2003), pp.1–14 (p.7), and Charles Forsdick, 'Between "French" and "Francophone": French Studies and the Postcolonial Turn', *French Studies*, 59:4 (2005), 523–30.

2   There exists a rich variety of accounts of the demise of Breton, to which I am indebted. General surveys can be found in Jorj Gwegen, *La Langue bretonne face à ses oppresseurs* (Quimper: Nature et Bretagne, 1975), and part one of Maryon McDonald, *'We are Not French!': Language, Culture and Identity in*

would have to go back as far as the middle ages, via the Renaissance pride in and promotion of French, as manifested culturally in Du Bellay's poetic manifesto of 1549 the *Défense et illustration de la langue française*, and legally in the Villers-Cotterêts decree of 1539, by which François I made French the language of official records. However, it was only after the Revolution of 1789 that the eradication of France's indigenous regional languages was pursued as a political ideal, when these were initially tainted by association with counter-revolution, and later became synonymous with backwardness and superstition. Real pressure was brought to bear on regional languages in the wake of the Abbé Grégoire's survey carried out between 1790 and 1794, tellingly entitled *Sur la nécessité et les moyens d'anéantir les patois et d'universaliser la langue française*, and Barère's *Rapport*, also published in 1794, which contains the infamous claim:

> Le féderalisme et la superstition parlent bas-breton; l'émigration et la haine de la République parlent allemand; la contre-révolution parle italien et le fanatisme parle basque. [...] Chez un peuple libre, la langue doit être une et la même pour tous.[3]

The development of state education was key in bringing Brittany, like the other provinces of France, into Frenchness, and calls by administrators for the active suppression of the Breton language as a

---

Brittany (London, New York: Routledge, 1989). Possibly the most reliable and detailed is part two of Fañch Broudic, *La Pratique du breton de l'Ancien Régime à nos jours* (Rennes: Presses universitaires de Rennes, 1995). An account which focuses on the Revolution is found in Michel de Certeau, Julia Dominique and Jacques Revel, *Une Politique de la langue. La Révolution française et les patois: l'enquête Grégoire* (Paris: Gallimard, 1975). For a detailed discussion of the attitudes and actions of the French administrative machine towards the Breton language, specifically in the nineteenth century, see Valérie Lachuer, *L'État face à la langue bretonne* (Rennes: Klask, 1998). For a general historical survey of France's attitude towards her own indigenous languages, including Breton, see Dennis Ager, *Identity, Insecurity and Image: France and Language* (Clevedon: Multilingual Matters, 1999).

3   *Rapport et projet de décret présentés au nom du Comité de Salut Public sur les idiomes étrangers et l'enseignement de la langue française (8 pluviose an II).* Cited in Jorj Gwegen, *La Langue bretonne face à ses oppresseurs* (Quimper: Nature et Bretagne, 1975), p.33.

sure way of 'improving' Brittany are common in the first part of the nineteenth century. Typical is the following extract from a letter of 1831 from the préfet of Finistère to the Minster for Education, assuring him that he has no sentimental attachment to the language, and outlining the strategy that he favours:

> [il faut] par tous les moyens possibles, favoriser l'appauvrissement, la corruption du breton, jusqu'au point que d'une commune à l'autre on ne puisse pas s'entendre. [...] Car alors la nécessité des communications obligera le paysan d'apprendre le français.[4]

A similar view on the need for Breton to disappear in order for Brittany to be 'improved' is found in a series of four articles published in the *Revue de Paris* between 1829 and 1831 by Auguste Romieu, who was sous-préfet of Quimperlé, Finistère.[5] Another sous-préfet in 1845 tells primary school teachers: 'Surtout, rappelez-vous messieurs, que vous n'êtes établis que pour tuer la langue bretonne'.[6] This same attitude underpinned the educational reforms of Jules Ferry in 1880–1883, which saw the establishment of a French-language state school in every *commune*, and the Waldeck-Rousseau/Combes legislation in the first decade of the twentieth century, which banned the use of regional languages in religious instruction.[7] Well into the twentieth century children who were heard speaking Breton in school were forced to wear the 'symbole' to mark them out for punishment.

The result is that today, in sociolinguistic terms, there is indeed a Francophone Brittany. Though in Upper Brittany this has been so since the middle ages, in Lower Brittany the more recent and gradual

---

4   *Annales de Bretagne*, 1917, pp.4, 8; cited in *Histoire générale de la Bretagne et des Bretons*, 2 vols, ed. by Yannick Pelletier (Paris: Nouvelle Librairie de France, 1990), II, 556–57.

5   Auguste Romieu, 'La Basse-Bretagne, ses mœurs, son langage et ses monuments', *Revue de Paris*, 2 (1829), 155–67; 'La Basse-Bretagne', *Revue de Paris*, 22 (1831), 13–20, 274–81; 'La Basse-Bretagne', 30 (1831), 145–54.

6   Cited in *Histoire générale de la Bretagne et des Bretons*, II, 557.

7   For a detailed account of the extreme reactions to the Combes legislation in Brittany, including armed resistance and public demonstrations, see Caroline Ford, *Creating the Nation in Provincial France* (Princeton: Princeton University Press, 1993), esp. pp.135–69.

changes to the balance of French and Breton can be traced in the centralizing regime of post-Revolutionary France, and later the educational reforms of the nineteenth century. It is ironic that these were all undertaken in the name of 'égalité; as Mona Ozouf puts it: 'L'égalité scolaire, en réalité, était une égalité meurtrière, puisqu'elle dissimulait un génocide culturel'.[8] In this respect the reforms were not dissimilar to educational policy in France's overseas colonies. As Louis-Jean Calvet argues in his critique of the concept of *Francophonie*, there was essentially no difference between the linguistic policy of the French Revolution in the Hexagon, and that of the Third Republic in the colonies.[9]

Though the decline of Breton continued throughout the twentieth century, this same century saw concerted efforts, involving more energy than ever before, to secure a future for the language. And with some measure of success: to take education as an example, a campaign that can be traced back as far as the end of the nineteenth century culminated in the establishment of the *Diwan* schools, though these are under constant legal and financial threat.[10] Also, the twentieth century saw more publishing in the Breton language than ever before, and some radio and television provision has been secured. Today the private television company TV Breizh broadcasts around twenty hours a week of Breton programmes, in addition to about sixty-five hours a year broadcast by the state France Ouest/France 3 Iroise.[11] The situation for radio is better, with the private company

---

8   Mona Ozouf, *L'École de la France: essais sur la Révolution, l'utopie et l'enseignement* (Paris: Gallimard, 1984), p.21. For a collection of Breton speakers' memories of schooldays in Brittany in the twentieth century, see Klaoda an Du, *Histoire d'un interdit: le breton à l'école* (Lesneven: Hor Yezh, 1991).

9   Louis-Jean Calvet, *Linguistique et colonialisme: petit traité de glottophagie* (Paris: Payot, 1974), p.15. 'Hexagon' refers to the geographical France without its overseas colonies.

10 For a detailed history of the Breton-medium schools movement, see Jean-Charles Perazzi, *Diwan: vingt ans d'enthousiasme, de doute et d'espoir* (Spézet: Coop Breizh, 1998).

11 The situation of TV Breizh is in constant flux due to financial pressures. For example in summer 2005 the Breton-language news programme was reduced

Radio Kreiz Breizh on air twenty-four hours a day, broadcasting in both Breton and French, and the state Radio France Ouest/Radio Breizh Izel providing somewhere around fifteen hours a week in Breton. Without official status, though, the numbers of Breton speakers will continue to decline. Statistics relating to Breton are notoriously difficult to establish as censuses in France do not take account of linguistic data; however it has generally been accepted that Breton is still practised by up to 500,000 people.[12]

It is not only because the native language is still spoken that Brittany today provides arguably the most striking and distinct example of internal difference in France. What makes Brittany's case unique is the concertedness and strength of attempts to revive and protect its language, in all spheres, from education and politics to literary criticism. The resulting bicultural situation has been investigated to show that Francophone identities in Brittany are far from straightforward, and that the relationship between language and identity can be paradoxical. For example Mari Jones has examined how the death of the language is curiously offset by the birth of an identity. She argues that for traditional native speakers of Breton, who

---

from seventeen to eight minutes, and seven members of staff were made redundant.

12 The most recent authoritative survey (1997) was carried out by Fañch Broudic, who found that 31% of respondents, which would correspond to 370,000 individuals, claimed to 'understand Breton'. For a breakdown and full discussion of these results, see his *Qui parle Breton aujourd'hui? Qui le parlera demain?* (Brest: Brud Nevez, 1999). This research was a refinement of his 1990/91 work, using a bigger sample and modified questions. See also Marianne Renate Berger, *Sprachkontakt in der Bretagne: Sprachloyalität versus Sprachwechsel* (Tübingen: Niemeyer, 1988); her stated aim is to compensate for the lack of official census figures by investigating bilingual competence (p.7). She gives a detailed breakdown in percentage terms of the results for different communes chosen in the Pays bigouden, Tréméoc, Loctudy and Île Tudy (pp.44–5). Her research also differentiates between active and passive use, written and spoken, and so forth. See also Fañch Broudic's earlier *La Pratique du breton de l'Ancien Régime à nos jours* (Rennes: Presses universitaires de Rennes, 1995); part one reviews all previous attempts at establishing numbers up to and including his own TMO-Ouest survey in 1990/91, in which he calculated that 250,000 people could express themselves in Breton.

speak one of the four main dialects of Breton rather than a stand-ardized language, there is no such thing as a Breton identity. Such a homogenized identity, she contends, is the invention of a new generation of speakers, the *néo-bretonnants* who have learnt a pan-Brittany variety of Breton, usually via the education system. And it is this latter group that is mainly responsible for promoting Breton as a language of and for the modern world, producing the ironic situation 'that the future of the language and the cultivation of the notion of a separate Breton identity should be left largely in the hands of people who speak French as their mother tongue.'[13] In similar vein, Jean-Pierre Simon has explored how a positive idea of Bretonness or 'néo-Bretonnité' has grown from what he terms an 'identité négative', and asks how it is that the language has been made to seem that of the whole of Brittany, proposing that this was ultimately the achievement of nineteenth-century enthusiasts.[14] For him it is not Brittany, or even the Breton 'people', that is responsible for creating the Breton movement, but rather it is the other way around:

> C'est celui-ci [le mouvement breton] qui [...] a produit et d'une certaine manière inventé la Bretagne et la bretonnité telles que nous les connaissons aujourd'hui.

He further argues, after Bourdieu, that: 'le discours régionaliste est un *discours performatif*.[15] In sociolinguistic work similarly focused on

---

13 Mari C. Jones, 'Death of a Language, Birth of an Identity: Brittany and the Bretons', *Language Problems and Language Planning*, 22 (1998), 129–42 (139). See also her 'At what Price Language Maintenance?: Standardization in modern Breton', *French Studies*, 49 (1995), 424–38. The classic study of modern Breton identities and the 'néo-bretonnants' is Maryon McDonald, *'We are Not French!': Language, Culture and Identity in Brittany* (London, New York: Routledge, 1989), though this work is highly controversial and has been criticized by both néo-breton militants (the author's term), and the academic community. For details of the former see the author's own discussion in the book, for the latter see D. Ellis Evans, 'Celticity, Celtic awareness and Celtic Studies', *Zeitschrift für celtische Philologie*, 49–50 (1997), 1–27 (16).
14 Jean-Pierre Simon, *La Bretonnité: une ethnicité problématique* (Rennes: Terre de Brume, 1999), pp.162–63.
15 Ibid., pp.195, 198.

the question of identity, Rachel Hoare has even shown how the association between Breton identity and Breton-accented French can actually be stronger than that with the Breton language itself.[16]

Nevertheless, the main chapter in the history of the demise of the Breton language, and therefore the key to understanding the curious contradictions of Breton identity, is the nineteenth-century one. At the beginning of the nineteenth century the average citizen of the new *République* had little or no sense of national identity, but by the end of the century a sense of 'Frenchness' existed, and perhaps paradoxically, so did 'regional' identity, and 'Breton identity' in particular. A shared, standardized language is generally considered a prerequisite for the creation of a feeling of group identity, as language is so much more than a simple means of communication. France is considered the paradigmatic example of this tendency, as to a greater extent than in any other country, notions of nationality are based on linguistic uniformity, as confirmed recently in the addition of the Article that 'the language of the Republic is French' to the Constitution in 1992. This was not so before the Revolution, as Anne-Marie Thiesse states:

> la monarchie française, même si elle avait imposé précocement l'usage du français dans les actes administratifs et créé une Académie chargée de veiller à la pureté et au rayonnement de la 'langue du roi', n'avait pas jugé utile de la faire pratiquer par l'ensemble de ses sujets.[17]

The sense of national identity, shared heritage, and homogeneity necessary to the idea of 'Frenchness' was largely the achievement of the nineteenth century, and it is at least in part because of the symbolic

---

16   'il semble y avoir une association plus forte dans les esprits des auditeurs-juges entre l'identité bretonne et le français parlé avec l'accent breton qu'entre l'identité bretonne et la langue bretonne', Rachel Hoare, *L'Identité linguistique des jeunes en Bretagne* (Brest: Brud Nevez, 2003), p.131; see also her 'Linguistic Competence and Regional Identity in Brittany: Attitudes and perceptions of identity', *Multilingual and Multicultural Development*, 21:4 (2000), 324–46; and 'An Integrative Approach to Language Attitudes and Identity in Brittany', *Journal of Sociolinguistics*, 5:1 (2001), 73–84.

17   'Des fictions créatrices: les identités nationales', *Romantisme*, 110 (2000), 51–62 (54).

importance of language that 'more than half the population of France may be asserted to have changed language, to French, since 1789'.[18] Both Breton and French identities were achieved only gradually, and were the result of a process that has recently been analysed by Anne-Marie Thiesse in *La Création des identités nationales: Europe, XVIIIe–XXe siècle*.[19] Far from being in straightforward opposition, Thiesse has argued, the interplay between the 'petite patrie' and the development of national identity is complex and paradoxical. This interplay is what makes Brittany such a rich test case to add to the study of Francophone identities.

The term 'Francophone' also has a special resonance when used as a label for literature. Wherever the label is used there is another language in the equation, and it is the tensions between these languages that have in recent years drawn the attention of critics to literatures produced in bicultural and multicultural situations, particularly those brought about by colonialism. Postcolonial criticism looks at these literatures for what they can tell us about politics, personal and party, and texts are investigated for the verbal manifestations of inter-cultural friction. Francophone studies is the branch that looks at cultural situations in parts of the world where one of the languages caught in such tension is French. Thus the label 'Francophone literature' not only indicates that the literature is in the French language, but simultaneously draws attention to and questions this Frenchness, and as such it suggests an attitude. Until now Francophone studies have been fascinated by the degrees of difference offered by farther-flung parts of *la Francophonie*, and have neglected

---

18   Ian J. Press, 'Breton Speakers in Brittany, France and Europe: constraints on the search for an identity', in *The Changing Voices of Europe: Social and Political Changes and their Linguistic Repercussions, Past, Present and Future*, ed. by M. Mair Parry, Winifred V. Davies, and Rosalind A. M. Temple (Cardiff: University of Wales Press, in conjunction with the Modern Humanities Research Association, 1994), pp.213–26 (p.215).

19   Anne-Marie Thiesse, *La Création des identités nationales: Europe, XVIIIe–XXe siècle* (Paris: Seuil, 1999), and more recently her 'Des fictions créatrices: les identités nationales', *Romantisme*, 110 (2000), 51–62. On this question see also Stéphane Gerson, 'La représentation historique du "pays", entre l'État et la société civile', *Romantisme*, 110 (2000), 39–49.

to scrutinize the Frenchness against which this 'difference' is defined. Brittany as a result is accepted as an unproblematized part of this Frenchness, despite having a culture that is Francophone in all senses of the word. French and Francophone studies have largely ignored the existence of this literature. For instance a recent *Encyclopaedia of Contemporary French Culture*[20] contains entries on regionalism, and even regional writing in Breton and Occitan, but there is no category 'Francophone writing: Brittany'. Another recent volume, *Contemporary French Cultural Studies*,[21] is far more concerned with 'non-territorial' languages, and external differences than with 'internal' ones, although it makes brief mention of Brittany.

Postcolonial studies have shown no more interest than French studies, indeed one of the seminal works in the field excluded the Celtic peripheries of Britain from its study with the claim that:

> While it is possible to argue that these societies were the first victims of English expansion, their subsequent complicity in the British imperial enterprise makes it difficult for colonized peoples outside Britain to accept their identity as post-colonial.[22]

Subsequent criticism has shown, though, how the very length of a given 'colonial' situation can make it an important addition to the portfolio of case-studies. Robert Crawford in *Devolving English Literature* argues the case for Scotland as offering the longest continuing example of a substantial body of literature 'produced by a culture pressurized by the threat of English cultural domination'.[23] Brittany has been considered too close to home to fit the postcolonial criticism paradigm, although a closer look shows that there is a comparable postcolonial situation. The way in which French writers and administrators especially from the Revolution of 1789 to the middle of the nineteenth century used the vocabulary of colonialism, and a

---

20   ed. by Alex Hughes and Keith Reader (London: Routledge, 1998).
21   ed. by William Kidd and Siân Reynolds (London: Arnold, 2000).
22   *The Empire Writes Back: Theory and Practice in Post-colonial Literatures*, ed. by Bill Ashcroft, Gareth Griffiths, and Helen Tiffin (London: Routledge, 1989), p.33.
23   *Devolving English Literature* (Oxford: Clarendon Press, 1992), p.8.

colonializing discourse, of Brittany is discussed in my first chapter. The adoption of a 'colonial' framework and terminology in the 1960s and 1970s in particular by the Breton movement itself is discussed in chapter 3. It follows that the cultural situation here is also comparable to that found in any other country that has been colonized by France. Perhaps the most fruitful way of answering the question 'Is there a Francophone Brittany?' is by asking whether there is a Breton Brittany. The answer is an unqualified yes: there is a Breton-language literature, which took off in the twentieth century.[24] The definiteness of this answer hardly conceals the fact that it is neglected and a minority pursuit, but its existence is nevertheless undisputable. Literature in French, on the other hand, while all too real in terms of numbers of potential readers, or print runs, is the more precarious of

---

24   There has been relatively little sustained work in English on Breton literature, though a notable exception is the recent book-length study by William Calin, *Minority Literatures and Modernism: Scots, Breton, and Occitan, 1920–1990* (Toronto: University of Toronto Press, 2000). Other accounts include Yves-Marie Rudel, *Panorama de la littérature bretonne des origines à nos jours: écrivains de langue bretonne & de langue française* (Rennes: Imprimerie Bretonne, 1950), Abeozen, *Istor lennegezh vrezhonek an amzer-vreman* (Brest: Al Liamm, 1957), Per Denez, 'Modern Breton Literature', in *Literature in Celtic Countries*, ed. by J. E. Caerwyn Williams [Taliesin Congress Lectures] (Cardiff: University of Wales Press, 1971), pp.113–36; Jean Le Dû, and Yves Le Berre, 'Un siècle d'écrits en langue bretonne: 1790–1892', in *Histoire littéraire et culturelle de la Bretagne*, 3 vols, ed. by Jean Balcou and Yves Le Gallo, Centre de recherche bretonne et celtique (Paris/Geneva: Champion-Slatkine, 1987), II, 251–91, and Fañch Morvannou, 'La littérature de langue bretonne au XXe siècle', in *Histoire littéraire et culturelle de la Bretagne*, III, 175–249, Lukian Raoul, *Geiriadur ar skrivagrerien ha yezheurien vrezhonek aet da annen a-raok mis Meurzh 1992* (Brest: Al Liamm, 1992). The most authoritative recent reference is a projected four-volume anthology by Francis Favereau, *Anthologie de la littérature bretonne au XXe siècle*. Vols 1 and 2 are already published: *Le premier 'Emzao' 1900/1918*, vol. 1 (Morlaix: Skol Vreizh, 2002), *Anthologie de la littérature bretonne au XXe siècle: Breiz Atao et les autres en littérature 1919/1944*, vol. 2 (Morlaix: Skol Vreizh, 2003), these contain detailed bibliographies. See also his *Littérature et écrivains bretonnants depuis 1945* (Morlaix: Skol Vreizh, 1991), translated into English as *Breton Literature and Writers since 1945* (Morlaix: Ar Falz, 1992).

the two, in that it is disputed, sometimes to the point of being denied. This 'other' literature is the object of my study.

It has frequently been argued that this literature does not exist, or in other words that there is nothing to distinguish it from French literature. This is the view expressed by Gwennolé Le Menn in his overview of literature in Breton in the second volume of Yannick Pelletier's *Histoire générale de la Bretagne et des Bretons*, devoted to 'cultures et mentalités bretonnes'. In this he explains that he is excluding Haute-Bretagne from his survey because its culture and dialect (Gallo) are variations on French, and he says of literature produced in French from any part of Brittany: 'si elles sont parfois inspirées par la Bretagne, [elles] font partie intégrante de la littérature française'.[25] The view that there is only French literature and Breton literature and nothing in between is implicit in Hémon's reply to accusations that *Gwalarn*'s literature was not 'Breton' as it did not correspond to reader expectations in terms of subject-matter:

> Qu'ils accusent notre littérature de n'être pas bretonne, d'être antibretonne! Elle n'en a cure. *Elle est écrite en breton*. […] Ah, ces braves Bretons francisés qui, de confiance, admirent la littérature en langue bretonne comme ils admirent le Kreiz-Ker et les broderies bigoudenn – qu'ils seraient navrés s'ils savaient à quel point notre littérature se soucie peu de 'faire breton', combien, au contraire, elle s'efforce de rechercher l'universel et répugne à toute entreprise de terroir.[26]

This same view was expressed in the case of Welsh by Saunders Lewis in his seminal essay 'Is there an Anglo-Welsh literature' of 1939. Even if the existence of work written in the language of the 'oppressor' is undeniable on a pragmatic level, this argument has had the merit of keeping questions of definition to the fore. What makes literature 'Breton' today if it is not the language in which it is written?

---

25 *Histoire générale de la Bretagne et des Bretons*, II, 405. See Pascal Rannou, 'De "l'histoire littéraire et culturelle de la Bretagne" à "l'histoire générale de la Bretagne et des Bretons', series of 5 articles in *Le Peuple breton*, issues 324–28 (1991).

26 *Kornog*, 1929. Cited in Morvan Lebesque, *Comment peut-on être breton?: essai sur la démocratie française*, preface de Gwenc'hlan Le Scouëzec (Paris: Seuil, 1970), p.175.

How far should we rely on geography, birth, citizenship, subject matter? Is it Breton literature just because it is written by somebody born in Brittany, such as Villiers de l'Isle-Adam who hardly wrote anything about Brittany? What about outsiders who deliberately and publicly adopt Brittany as their *patrie*, such as Saint-Pol-Roux from Marseille? And should the Brittany-based works of such a canonical writer as Balzac form part of 'Francophone Breton literature'? The way in which Brittany's Francophone literature is both loudly denied by Breton militants and quietly ignored by critics and historians of French literature[27] only makes it more compelling. Its situation is more precarious than that of its much smaller neighbour, making it the 'minor' of the two literatures in the sense put forth by Deleuze and Guattari in their study of Kafka.[28]

Brittany's Francophone literature is also interesting because it has, for the length of its history, been overshadowed and contaminated by its neighbours: French literature proper and Breton literature proper. Literary criticism in general has largely moved beyond the idea that literatures evolve in a vacuum. Today we see cross-fertilization in more places than just the obvious interface between two different national literatures with translation, in its restricted sense, as the bridge between them. Eagleton has argued in *Exiles and Emigrés* for a pluralist view of literature, in which the presence of the 'exile' and the 'alien' creates rich cultural situations. He shows how such alienation is not clear-cut, and is at its most fruitful when the borderline is not clear, as is the case for Lawrence, who, coming from a working-class background, was both insider and outsider to English literature:

> Lawrence's achievement was to bring to bear on the disintegrating order of his time, the rich values of a working-class experience: to generalise from this

27 Anne-Marie Thiesse describes the French-language texts produced in the provinces in the nineteenth century as a missing chapter in histories of French literature, *Écrire la France: le mouvement littéraire régionaliste de langue française entre la belle époque et la libération* (Paris: Presses universitaires de France, 1991), p.10.

28 Gilles Deleuze and Félix Guattari, *Kafka: pour une littérature mineure* (Paris: Minuit, 1975).

basis, a critique of England which seemed at times as alien as the judgement of a foreigner, yet as intimately acquainted with its real issues as a native.[29]

Eagleton sums up the rich possibilities of a bicultural situation:

> great art is produced, not from the simple availability of an alternative, but from the subtle and involuted tensions between the remembered and the real, the potential and the actual, integration and dispossession, exile and involvement.[30]

The word 'translation' itself is no longer used in literary criticism without at least an awareness of its wider senses, those explored by a new generation of theorists of translation such as Bassnett and Cronin.[31] Their work focuses on cultural cross-currents in literary texts, and is less interested in actual translation. It is the conflicts and failures of fit between cultures and systems, as manifested in literature, that inform us about the identity of one or other of these cultures. According to Homi Bhabha: 'it is in the emergence of the interstices – the overlap and displacement of domains of difference – that the intersubjective and collective experiences of *nationness*, community interest, or cultural value are negotiated.'[32] What he here calls the 'interstices' are particularly interesting, and even more urgent, in work explicitly battled over, or caught in real linguistic conflict. Drawing on Bhabha's work M. Wynn Thomas undertakes a groundbreaking reading of the literatures of Wales, in which he aims to 'explore ways in which these two cultures have to some extent developed in tandem, and share certain unnoticed common features that show them to have been the products (and producers) of the same history'.[33] His more recent book *Corresponding Cultures*[34] is based on

---

29 Terry Eagleton, *Exiles and Emigrés* (London: Chatto and Windus, 1970), p.17.
30 Ibid., p.18.
31 See, for example, Susan Bassnett and Harish Trivedi, eds, *Post-colonial Translation: Theory and Practice* (London: Routledge, 1999), and Michael Cronin, *Across the Lines* (Cork: University of Cork Press, 2000).
32 Homi K. Bhabha, *The Location of Culture* (London: Routledge, 1994), p.2.
33 M. Wynn Thomas, *Internal Difference: Twentieth-century Writing in Wales* (Cardiff: University of Wales Press, 1992), p.xiv
34 *Corresponding Cultures: The Two Literatures of Wales* (Cardiff: University of Wales Press, 1999).

the idea that the two literatures of Wales demand to be considered together. That is, we cannot fully understand one without the other, for even if they were in conflict, they were still 'corresponding' with one another.

It is clear that the French-language literature of Brittany is a 'Francophone' literature in more than the most restricted, linguistic sense. Attempts to define it as such began with the founding of the review *Bretagnes* by Paol Keineg and Kristian Keginer in Morlaix in 1975. It was in the columns of this publication that the question of the specificity of, indeed the existence of, a French-language Breton literature was systematically tackled for the first time. As Keginer observed:

> la francité et la bretonnité se manifestent précisément sur deux plans radicalement distincts: ce qui y est français c'est la langue, et ce qui y est breton, c'est la création. Il s'agit donc d'une création bretonne de langue française [...] ou plutôt de mots français, ou à partir de mots français.[35]

Never far from controversy, its nine issues debated the question as it related to language and literature, but was also highly politicized, as Keineg and Keginer, having close links with the Union Démocratique Bretonne, pursued a policy of decolonization. Definitional work on the literature was inseparable from the political fervour, and as a result Keginer, and Keineg in particular, have become a privileged point of reference in the work of postcolonial literary critics in Brittany.

The question 'is there a Francophone Brittany?' is today being asked by Plurial, the journal of the Centre d'Études des Littératures et Civilisations Francophones at the University of Rennes. The journal combines revisionist work on the contribution of precursors to the definitional debate, such as the poets who wrote in *Bretagnes*, with discussion of present-day debates in Francophone writing from around the globe. An issue devoted to 'métissage', contains criteria set out by

---

35   Kristian Keginer, *Bretagnes*, 6, p.22. Cited in Pascal Rannou, 'Approche du concept de littérature bretonne de langue française', in *Métissage du texte: Bretagne, Maghreb, Québec*, ed. by Bernard Hue (Rennes: Presses universitaires de Rennes, 1994), pp.75–86 (p.79). While *Bretagnes* was the major forum for discussion, the debate can also be traced in a special number of *Europe*, 625 (1981), ed. by Jean-Marie Le Sidaner.

Pascal Rannou in a short but ambitious article: 'Approche du concept de littérature bretonne de langue française', which is the culmination of years of work on the question.[36] In it Rannou quickly moves beyond the argument about whether this literature exists, lamenting the way critics consider both literatures in isolation from each other. He singles out two recent, and significant, volumes on Brittany, the *Histoire littéraire et culturelle de la Bretagne*, and the *Histoire générale de la Bretagne et des Bretons*, to show how anthologies and reference works exemplify the problem. He is disappointed by Gwennolé Le Menn's exclusionary gesture in the latter, and castigates both editorial teams for failing to address the definitional problems. The works display: 'aucune interrogation conceptuelle, une démarche qui reste purement compilatoire,'[37] relying instead on what he dismisses as the 'droit du sol' (geographical criteria) and 'droit du sang' (ethnic origin).

Rannou grasps the nettle, and his suggested criteria for the definition of Francophone Breton literature are bolder, and are set out here in three main parts. The first is based on what he describes as the alienation of the writer – 'l'aliénation propre à tout écrivain breton francophone' – and which is the legacy of the cultural genocide suffered by Brittany. This need not be explicit in the text, and may be

---

36 'Approche du concept de littérature bretonne de langue française', as above. See also his earlier 'Littérature et bretonnité', *Le Peuple Breton*, issues 278–279 (1987). And his unpublished DEA thesis, *Approche du concept de littérature bretonne francophone à travers des textes de Villiers de l'Isle-Adam, Yvon le Men, Kristian Keginer et Youenn Coïc*, (Université de Haute Bretagne, Rennes, 1991).

37 'Approche du concept de littérature bretonne de langue française', p.76. See also his series of short articles 'L'*Histoire Culturelle et Littéraire de la Bretagne* à la loupe', in *Le Peuple Breton*, issues 293–297 (1988), and his 'De "l'histoire littéraire et culturelle de la Bretagne" à "l'histoire générale de la Bretagne et des Bretons', a series of 5 articles in *Le Peuple breton*, issues 324–328 (1991). Similar treatment is given to Le Quintrec's *Littératures de Bretagne* (Rennes: Ouest France, 1992), by Yannick Lemaire, who condemns it for making no attempt at definition, and having produced nothing more than a series of disclaimers: 'nous ne voyons pas l'intérêt d'un tel ouvrage. Œuvre de circonstance? Plaisir personnel? Lagarde et Michard de la littérature bretonne?', also in *Le Peuple breton*, 351 (1993), p.20.

symbolic or present between the lines. The second has to do with the relationship of the text to past clichés of Bretonness. Rannou advocates avoidance of the 'picturesque' and 'folkloric' in favour of what he calls a 'linear' description of a Breton setting – 'linéarité de la description du paysage breton'. Further criteria relate to the piece's form, the example suggested is the incorporation of the Celtic motif of the double spiral into the structure; and he also discusses lexical peculiarities which are the result of borrowings, or calques. He ends by putting forward the 'métisse' idea, which is further developed in his work on Hélias, where he shows how the latter's *Le Cheval d'orgueil* can only be properly understood as part of a 'littérature métissée'.[38] His work on Tristan Corbière is equally pioneering; in the collection *Visages de Tristan Corbière*, extensive analysis of Corbière's notoriously heterogeneous language, reveals him to be the first 'écrivain aliéné' in the sense explored in Rannou's more theoretical work.[39]

Thierry Glon's work inevitably comes up against this central problem of definition, through the twin concerns of 'alienation' and 'recouvrance'. He identifies 'recouvrance' as a key characteristic of Breton writing in French,[40] defining it as: 'cette convocation magique et culpabilisée d'un temps meilleur dont les écrivains bretons se sentent exilés comme de nouveaux Romantiques',[41] and ends by asking whether this might not be traced right back to the nineteenth century. The question is explored further in a later piece on 'recouv-

---

38 Pascal Rannou, *Inventaire d'un héritage: essai sur l'œuvre littéraire de Pierre-Jakez Hélias* (Relecq-Kerhuon: An Here, 1997).

39 *Visages de Tristan Corbière*, ed. by Pascal Rannou and Pierre Bazantay (Morlaix: Skol Vreizh, 1995).

40 'il me semble que la littérature bretonne en français possède une réelle spécificité littéraire qui n'est pas liée à une hypothétique *âme bretonne*, ni même à une thématique trop souvent normative de la mélancolie ou de la pastorale. À mon avis, elle tient son originalité du fonctionnement de la *Recouvrance*', Thierry Glon, 'Écrivains de la "recouvrance" (de 1960 à 1980)', in *Écrire la Bretagne 1960–1995*, ed. by Bernard Hue and Marc Gontard, *Plurial 5* (Rennes: Presses universitaires de Rennes, 1995), pp.33–52 (p.52).

41 Ibid., p.51.

rance' with specific focus on Xavier Grall,[42] who used the term himself with the meaning 'se retrouver soi-même', or 'se désaliéner' in his *Cheval couché*.[43] Another key contributor to the debate is Marc Gontard, who produced a survey article 'Pour une littérature bretonne de langue française', published in *Écrire la Bretagne 1960–1995*, and a discussion of hybridity in 'Effets de métissage dans la littérature bretonne'.[44] Gontard has pushed his interest in the question to extremes, writing an experimental novel, *De Sable et de sang*, which he describes as a Breton novel, but in which that adjective itself is never used.[45]

Though it has received little critical attention, the existence of this literature has been acknowledged, and it is now increasingly being investigated. If Brittany had been invisible to all but Celtic scholars for so long, this is now changing in some areas. What might be called a *centralizing* way of looking at France has been challenged in recent years in the discipline of history. Caroline Ford has shown how the nation was 'made' in provincial France, challenging the traditional discourse of centralizing history. In tracing the growth of national identity she rejects the traditional investigation of it as something imposed by the centre on the periphery, arguing that 'the creation of national identity is a process continually in the making rather than the imposition of a fixed set of values and beliefs'.[46] Her case-study of Finistère shows how

political change and national awareness were effected not through the wholesale importation of urban values, Parisian political movements, and the assimilation of the periphery into the center, but through an indigenous

---

42 Thierry Glon, 'Xavier Grall et la recouvrance', in *Bretagne: l'autre et l'ailleurs*, ed. by Marc Gontard, *Plurial* 8 (Rennes: Presses universitaires de Rennes, 1999), pp.58–75.

43 Xavier Grall, *Le Cheval couché: réponse au cheval d'orgueil* (Paris: Hachette, 1977). This was, as the title suggests, a direct reaction to Hélias's book.

44 In *Métissage du texte: Bretagne, Maghreb, Québec*, ed. by Bernard Hue, *Plurial* 4 (1994), pp.27–39.

45 (Paris: L'Harmattan, 1982).

46 *Creating the Nation* (Princeton: Princeton University Press, 1995), p.5.

movement that emerged in the countryside and ultimately came to represent the periphery at the center.[47]

A similar non-centralizing view is found in Robert Gildea's *The Past in French History*; he asserts that 'there is no single French collective memory but parallel and competing collective memories elaborated by communities which have experienced and handle the past in different ways'.[48] From Brittany Jean-Yves Guiomar has argued that the Breton movement comes from the periphery, which has made itself the centre.[49] However, in other disciplines, especially literary studies, Brittany remains invisible. In fact Brittany suffers two layers of neglect. Firstly postcolonial studies have been rather slow in giving serious attention to Francophone material, and this despite relying heavily on French theory.[50] Secondly postcolonial studies on the whole exclude 'ancient' colonizations, as demonstrated above in my comparison of Brittany with the Celtic peripheries of Britain. It is hardly surprising that postcolonial studies have only recently begun to have an impact on the study of the literatures of Brittany. Critics at the Centre d'Études des Littératures et Civilisations Francophones at the University of Rennes are at the forefront in adapting the framework to the particular bicultural situation in modern Brittany, and have studied Brittany in parallel with other better-publicized examples of 'métissage', for instance the Maghreb and Québec.

Presumably because their other culture is Anglophone, postcolonial studies made their mark on the other Celtic countries much earlier, in the form of 'Celticism'. Just as 'Orientalism', after Said,[51] describes a discourse composed of blanket statements about other cultures classed as 'Oriental', so 'Celticism' is composed of blanket statements made from a particular point of view, about Celts. The new criticism to which it gave rise saw a similarity between the way

---

47 Ibid., p.9.

48 (London/New Haven: Yale University Press, 1994), p.10.

49 *Le Bretonisme: Les historiens bretons au XIXe siècle* (Mayenne: Imprimerie de la Manutention, 1987), p.88.

50 For a recent discussion of this problem see Charles Forsdick and David Murphy, 'Introduction', in *Francophone Postcolonial Studies*, pp.1–14.

51 Edward W. Said, *Orientalism* (London: Penguin, 1995), first published 1978.

nineteenth-century European Orientalists wrote about Eastern themes in homogenizing terms and from a eurocentric perspective, and the approach of two of the founding fathers of Celtic Studies as we know it today, Ernest Renan and Matthew Arnold. Criticism of Anglo-Irish literature showed the way, and Mc Cormack was the first to deliberately model 'Celticism' on 'Orientalism' in order to describe the discourse inaugurated by Renan and Arnold.[52] Malcolm Chapman later described Arnold's work in embellishing and interpreting Renan as 'arguably the most influential piece ever written in the field of Celtic studies',[53] and went further, summing up Renan's 'Celt' thus:

> A conflation of the domesticity and femininity of Renan's childhood; of the emotionality that he felt his intellectuality had lost him; all the supposed characteristics of primitive literature, *naïveté*, spontaneity, and simple unaffected truth.[54]

For Mc Cormack Anglophone Celtic literature must not be seen in isolation, and can only be properly understood as interacting with other literatures. The literature produced in Ireland, then, must be seen as a whole:

> No account of Anglo-Irish literature can be complete without some attention to the question of its relation to Gaelic culture, the nineteenth-century decline of Gaelic as a vernacular, and the movement to revive it (p.219).

Venturing further afield, when the emergence of English- or French-language literatures in Celtic regions is considered in the context of European Romanticism, Renan's influential essay 'La Poésie des races celtiques' of 1854 can be seen as very much the product of its time, representing a

---

52 In his *Ascendancy and Tradition in Anglo-Irish Literary History from 1789–1939* (Oxford: Clarendon Press, 1985); see especially p.220. See also Declan Kiberd, *Inventing Ireland: The Literature of the Modern Nation* (London: Vintage, 1996), p.6.

53 *The Celts: The Construction of a Myth* (London: Macmillan, 1992), p.215.

54 Malcolm Chapman, *The Gaelic Vision in Scottish Culture* (London: Croom Helm, 1978), p.84.

meeting point between the high sophistication of comparative philology as developed in Germany, France, and Britain from the initiative of Herder, and the popular perception of a Celtic fringe as an aesthetic survival in the industrial age.[55]

Despite the key role played by Renan's essay, Brittany has not received attention either from the direction of French Studies or that of 'Celticism'. The influential collection of essays *The Invention of Tradition* includes chapters on Wales and Scotland, but not Brittany.[56] Similarly Terence Brown's collection *Celticism* neglects Brittany *per se*, though it does cover French Romanticism.[57] This Francophone Brittany, then, has yet to be studied in a sustained way within a framework that takes account of analogous debates in postcolonialism and Celticism.

My first chapter looks at the invention of Brittany. The idea that all places are invented in literature is expressed by Proust in an essay on Nerval's *Sylvie*: 'c'est que ces noms, nous les avons lu dans *Sylvie*'.[58] Literature creates for us, or in other words blinds us to, the real landscape. The motif is developed in *Du côté de chez Swann*, where Proust discusses the relationship between real landscapes and those that exist through reading. He describes the latter type thus:

> venait ensuite, à demi projeté devant moi, le paysage où se déroulait l'action et qui exerçait sur ma pensée une bien plus grande influence que l'autre, que celui que j'avais sous les yeux quand je les levais du livre.[59]

The meaning of 'inventing Brittany' in chapter 1 is based on the idea that any literary work is written partly in reaction to previous literary works. As Michael Riffaterre has argued, the relation of poetry to the world is always and irreducibly intertextual, because poetry articulates

---

55   Malcolm Chapman, *The Gaelic Vision*, p.224.
56   ed. by Eric Hobsbawm and Terence Ranger (Cambridge: Cambridge University Press, 1983), reprinted Canto, 1992.
57   (Amsterdam: Rodopi, 1996).
58   Marcel Proust, *Contre Sainte-Beuve*, (Paris: Gallimard, 1954), p.189.
59   Marcel Proust, *A la recherche du temps perdu*, ed. by Jean-Yves Tadié, Bibliothèque de la Pléiade (Paris: Gallimard, 1987), 4 vols, I, 85.

'reality' only by way of its reworking of prior literary and linguistic forms.[60]

Reading can also be a deliberate preparation for travel. Stendhal, in his *Mémoires d'un touriste*, is quite open about seeing the Breton landscape through the filter of his reading of Walter Scott.[61] Literature can affect real life, and real landscapes can be changed because of the influence of literature, as when Botrel 'returns' to Brittany, and starts a pardon that attracts tourists,[62] or the fact that tourists can now visit a 'roche de Velléda' at Plancoët, thanks to Chateaubriand.[63] In the Romantic period even the landscape represented in the visual arts was born from literature rather than from observation of the real thing, and was largely based on the poetry of Brizeux's *Marie*, La Villemarqué's *Barzaz Breiz*, and the prose of Balzac's *Béatrix*.[64]

Many of these issues have naturally been addressed in critical work on travel literature. A passion for travel had been born with the Napoleonic wars, and travel within France was linked to the discovery

---

60   See Michael Riffaterre, *The Semiotics of Poetry* (Bloomington and London: Indiana University Press, 1978). See also Paul Zumthor's lexically-based history of 'space' *La Mesure du monde* (Paris: Seuil, 1993).

61   He mentions the writer by name, *Mémoires d'un touriste*, 2 vols (Paris: Calmann-Lévy, 1854), II, 6, 7, and later describes people and conversations as 'tout à fait dans le genre de celles de *Waverley*', II, 10.

62   Discussed in Thiesse, *Écrire la France*, p.174.

63   See Yannick Pelletier, *La Bretagne chez Chateaubriand* (Spézet: Coop Breizh, 1998), p.18.

64   See Denise Delouche, 'Le Mot et l'image dans la vision romantique picturale de la Bretagne', in *Ouest et romantismes*, actes du colloque des 6,7,8 et 9 décembre 1990, ed. by Georges Cesbron (Angers: Presses de L'Université d'Angers, 1991), pp.253–63; 'Trois ouvrages ont eu un écho privilégié chez les peintres: *Les Chouans*, *Les Martyrs*, et *Marie*', p.256. See also Denise Delouche, 'Rencontres de peintres et de poètes en Bretagne au XIXe siècle', *Cahiers d'Iroise*, 22e année, No 4 (Nouvelle Série), Octobre–Décembre 1975/4, pp.175–83. The reaction to *Marie* is a delayed one: 'Cependant, alors que "Marie" a fait l'enthousiasme unanime des critiques, l'écho près des peintres n'est pas immédiat: ceux-ci ont d'abord vu la Bretagne âpre et sauvage évouquée par Chateaubriand dans "Les Martyrs"; c'est lentement, après 1848–50, que la Bretagne agreste et souriante chantée par Brizeux séduit et s'impose, favorisée par le courant général qui porte les artistes vers le monde paysan', p.176.

of history and identity. The extent to which these travellers were describing, or even seeing, the real landscape has been a matter for debate. In the case of the Pyrenees the real landscape was obscured by the fashion for soul-searching, as well as by other literature.[65] In Chateaubriand literal and metaphorical travel are inseparable, as seen for example in *René*: 'Heureux ceux qui ont fini leur voyage, sans avoir quitté le port'.[66] Travel as framework or simply as metaphor is particularly common in Francophone Breton writing not just because of the influence of real travel accounts, or the real journey that had to be made up to the capital by any ambitious writer, but also because it conveys the insurmountable distance between cultures that is implicit in this writing.[67]

So this book makes no new claim in arguing for a literary bias in an investigation of the construction of an identity. The importance of literature for the study of postcolonial situations is accepted because literature, in the words of *The Empire Writes Back*, 'was made as central to the cultural enterprise of Empire as the monarchy was to its political formation'.[68] But in the case of Brittany, literature has received scant attention, even though, as Guiomar has argued, literature is where the whole Breton movement begins: 'Je suis depuis long-temps convaincu que la question bretonne se joue et se comprend

---

65   Anne Lasserre-Vergne says: 'Les Pyrénées n'ont d'intérêt, d'existence, de réalité que dans la mesure où elles renouvellent sans cesse les impressions du voyageur', *Les Pyrénées centrales dans la littérature française entre 1820 et 1870* (Toulouse: Éché, 1985), p.92.

66   (Geneva: Droz, 1947), pp.22–3. For discussion of this aspect see M. Granet, 'La Nostalgie de l'Ouest dans le livre IV des *Mémoires d'outre-tombe* de François de Chateaubriand, une figure de l'intellectuel', in *Ouest et romantismes*, pp.371–80; Granet explores the paradox that: 'Il voyage physiquement vers l'Est, mais sentimentalement vers l'Ouest' (p.371).

67   See Heather Williams, 'Le voyage transculturel de Brizeux', in *Seuils et traverses: enjeux de l'écriture de voyage*, 2 vols, ed. by Jean-Yves Le Disez (Brest: CRBC, 2002), I, 275–85, and Eugène Bérest, 'Les voyageurs français en Bretagne', in *Histoire littéraire et culturelle de la Bretagne*, II, 177–218.

68   *The Empire Writes Back*, ed. by Ashcroft, Griffiths, Tiffin, p.3.

d'abord sur le terrain de l'histoire littéraire [...]. Tout est parti des années 1820–1840'.[69]

In the French-language literature of Brittany the matters of intertextuality, bi-culturality and postcolonialism meet, producing a complex case of internal cultural difference. The 'space' between languages, or distance implicit in the juxtaposition of 'Brittany' and 'Francophone', needs to be characterized. A reading method like that developed by Jean-Pierre Richard in which 'pa(ysa)ges' collapse into 'pages' is needed. Richard's method in *Pages/Paysages*[70] is close reading that he describes in terms of a balance between 'pages', or the words on the page, or their disposition, and paysage, which is the version of reality produced by a given *œuvre*:

> une lecture qui se fonderait à la fois sur l'essence verbale des œuvres littéraires (ce qui les constitue en *pages*), et sur les formes, thématico-pulsionnelles, par où s'y manifeste un univers singulier (ce qui les organise en *paysage*).[71]

In chapters 2 and 3 the space between languages is investigated through a series of close readings of literary texts that represent Brittany or Bretonness in the French language. This is the space that is negotiated by translation, be it a smooth translation of Breton scenes and themes into a French fit for the *salons* of the capital, or a foreignizing translation of Breton motifs into a French that writhes and struggles to accommodate them. It is also the space negotiated by the bilingual author who writes in the shadow of the other language: the literary conventions of one may permeate his work in the other, or the idioms and syntax of one may make their ghostly presence felt in the other. It can equally be a space of violence as in the case of the writer whose whole community has lost its mother tongue, and writes under protest in the language of the cultural oppressor. As the first sustained analysis of the literature produced between French and Breton, this book will show us something about the way literary

---

69   Guiomar, *Le Bretonisme: les historiens bretons au XIXe siècle* (Mayenne: Imprimerie de la Manutention, 1987), p.254

70   *Pages/Paysages: Microlectures II*, (Paris: Seuil, 1984).

71   Avant-propos to *Pages/paysages*, p.7.

French is affected by such intercultural tensions, and it will also be a book about what it can mean to be caught between two cultures.

Although interest in cultural differences, especially those generated by postcolonial situations, has steadily increased within French studies over the last decade or so, the linguistic and cultural minorities in the French regions, and particularly their literary outputs, have, until now, received only limited attention from literary scholars. As I have shown, Brittany is no exception. This book accepts that the term 'Francophone' and the postcolonial framework are useful in discussions of Brittany, and further suggests that the case of Brittany has something to offer postcolonial studies. The French-language literature of Brittany is written in reaction to, and always in dialogue with mainstream French literary representations of Brittany. Chapter 1 shows how true this was at the time when this literature was born in the 1830s, and argues that Brittany was invented in these texts. Chapters 2 and 3 then show how subsequent literature, up to the present day, is still reacting to the moment of its invention. In chapter 2 I compare the work of two Breton-born poets, Auguste Brizeux and Tristan Corbière, and in chapter 3 I discuss the renewal of the Breton movement in the 1960s and 1970s, which stemmed from a realization on the part of Bretons, led by the 'poets of decolonization', that their country was, and had been, in a 'colonial' situation.

This study charts the development of a French-language literature of and for Brittany against a backdrop of language change from overwhelmingly Breton to overwhelmingly French. The French-language literature of Brittany will be traced from its beginnings in the wake of European Romanticism to its encounter with postcolonial ideas and criticism, as it is in these texts that the image and self-image of Brittany is made. In sum, this book asks what makes literature Breton today if it is not the language in which it is written. The literary texts selected for study here are French, but they draw attention to and question this Frenchness on various levels. My analysis of this literature exposes the cultural heterogeneity concealed beneath the surface of one of the most centralized administrations in Europe. The challenge presented by Brittany to the notion of Frenchness will be an instructive case study of intercultural conflicts and how these are negotiated in literature.

Chapter 1: Inventing 'Brittany'

Brittany was invented in the nineteenth century. Or rather the Brittany we know today is largely the product of the textual practices and representations of the nineteenth century, and it is to texts, and later to visual representations of Brittany from the nineteenth century that we owe our ideas of what constitutes Bretonness. By the end of the century the connotations and associations of Bretonness were unmistakable, and ripe for exploitation by the mass tourist industry, but there is a world of difference between texts from the early decades of the century and those from the fin-de-siècle and beyond, as during the course of the nineteenth century the stereotype of Brittany flips from mainly negative to mainly positive. A typical early description of Brittany is the following complaint about Brittany's physical difficulty of access by Jacques Cambry, author of the hugely influential, not to say plagiarized, *Voyage dans le Finistère*:

> Les chemins de traverse sont des abîmes impracticables dans l'hiver: les voitures s'y brisent; des chevaux, des bœufs, des hommes y sont tous les jours estropiés (1798).[1]

A generation later nothing has changed, as we find similar complaints in Balzac: 'Là, le génie de la civilisation moderne s'effraie de pénétrer à travers d'immenses forêts primordiales'(1829).[2] But by the 1870s we find Brittany recommended as a holiday destination in fashionable Parisian magazines, such as Stéphane Mallarmé's *La Dernière mode*, where the poet who has briefly become a fashion writer refers to: 'le littoral fashionable de la Normandie et celui de Bretagne', but recommends Brittany as the option of the traveller in the know,

---

1 Jacques Cambry, *Voyage dans le Finistère, nouvelle édition*, ed. by M le Chevalier de Fréminville (Brest: Lefournier, 1836), p.25.
2 Balzac, *Les Chouans*, ed. by Pierre Gascar (Paris: Gallimard, 1972), p.39. Page references will hereafter be given in the text, to this edition, unless stated otherwise.

already the choice of 'les amateurs, artistes ou gens épris des grands sites et de solitude', Normandy being too popular.[3] A little later again, and Proust's seaside scenes were originally to be set in Brittany. In the final version of his *A la recherche du temps perdu* the construction of Balbec, his quintessential seaside town on the Normandy coast, still owes something to Brittany. The narrator, Marcel, is enchanted by its proper names, and dwells on the literal meanings of the Breton 'Penn-ar-bed' (the end of the earth) and 'Armor' (the sea):

> Balbec! La plus antique ossature géologique de notre sol, vraiment Ar-mor, la Mer, la fin de la terre.
> [...]
> Alors je cherchais à retrouver dans Balbec 'le pays des Cimmériens'.[4]

What accounts for such a complete turnaround in attitudes? By what process does Brittany trade its connotations of backwardness and darkness for those of leisure and light? Or how was the 'Brittany' we know today invented? This chapter will investigate the astonishing shift from negative to positive by identifying some key moments and issues in the development of French-language representations of Brittany. First an overview of the early nineteenth-century context will suggest why and how Brittany became a popular choice for so many writers.

Brittany victim of fashion

In order to trace the making of the myth, we may first ask why there is an explosion in writing about Brittany in the early nineteenth century. Post-revolutionary France had its state, but had yet to forge the nation that would fit it. The people who were to benefit from 'égalité' of

---

3   Stéphane Mallarmé, *La Dernière mode*, September 6, 1874, in *Œuvres complètes II*, ed. by Bertrand Marchal (Paris: Gallimard, 2003), p.503.

4   Marcel Proust, *A la recherche du temps perdu*, I, 129, 251. In Greek mythology the 'Cimmériens' are those who live at the edge of the earth.

rights had different backgrounds and histories, and did not even speak the same language. In fact they had little in common beyond this political bond, and so a sense of collective, national identity had, in effect, to be forged or invented.

In so far as the Revolution of 1789 represented a rebirth and a new beginning, the new France as a whole had to re-think its own identity. The necessary self-analysis entailed in particular a redefinition of France's relationship to the past, as the pre-revolutionary period represented all that had been escaped and negated. National history that had chronicled the rise and fall of monarchs was replaced by a new historiography, which sought instead to identify the roots of the Republic, and the forefathers of the 'peuple'; thus began a golden age of history writing.[5] One clear consequence of this was a more urgent working out of the relationship between the Gauls, who were seen as the ancestors of the people, and the Franks, who were considered to be the ancestors of the aristocracy. This was already discussed before the Revolution, as Dietler has shown: indeed the popularization of the idea can be traced to the historical writings of the Comte de Boulainvilliers (1727), who

> repeatedly asserted that France was composed of two races of people: the nobility, who were the descendants of the Franks, and the Third Estate, who were descended from the Gallo-Romans.[6]

---

5   See Ceri Crossley, *French Historians and Romanticism: Thierry, Guizot, The Saint-Simonians, Quinet, Michelet* (London: Routledge, 1993), which takes the following as its guiding question: 'Why did the legacy of the Revolution entail a reconstruction of the past?'. See also Dakyns, who argues that Romanticism's feel for the past is 'immeasurably more profound' than that of the eighteenth century, Janine R. Dakyns, *The Middle Ages in French Literature 1851–1900* (Oxford: Clarendon Press, 1973), p.2. She also gives some attention to the overlap between enthusiasm for things Celtic and things medieval, pp.11, 59. See also Charles Rearick, *Beyond the Enlightenment: Historians and Folklore in Nineteenth-century France* (Bloomington and London: Indiana University Press, 1974).

6   Michael Dietler, '"Our Ancestors the Gauls": Archaeology, Ethnic Nationalism and the Manipulation of Celtic Identity in Modern Europe', *American Anthropologist*, 96 (1994), 584–605 (587). See also Annie Jourdan, 'The Image

The Revolution led to Gauls being proposed as potential ancestors for the whole new nation, and gave rise to the memorable slogan 'nos ancêtres les Gaulois'. This leads, quite neatly, to unprecedented levels of interest in the people who were perceived to be France's remaining link with the Celtic people of Ancient Gaul: the Bretons. The terrible irony is that, as Dietler puts it:

> republican enthusiasm for establishing a nation with claims to authenticity rooted in the ancient Celtic past should have nearly succeeded in wiping out the one surviving link to Celtic identity that had a reasonable claim to continuity: the language spoken by the people of Brittany.[7]

So although there had been a slowly increasing scholarly interest in Celts and Celtic languages in particular before the Revolution (Pezron 1703, and Pelloutier 1740), this coveted connection with Ancient Gaul was the catalyst that transformed what was no more than a minority scholarly interest into 'Bretonism' in due course.

Evidence of how valorized the Celts were in France at this time is found in the very title of the Académie celtique, established under Napoleon in 1805, with the purpose of elevating the study of France's own distant past to the position of a new Classics. Founded by Éloi Johanneau, Jacques Cambry, and Michel-Ange de Mangourit, and with the Empress Josephine for a patron, the Académie celtique further fuelled the debate on France's Celtic ancestry, but in fact had more to do with French nationalism than with Celtic studies proper, or even with Brittany. Though this connection launched Bretonism, the latter is in no way a continuation of the Académie. Indeed the historian of Bretonism, Jean-Yves Guiomar, shows how Bretonism really came into its own only when it left Gaul, or Gaulomania, behind; something which was made possible by borrowing some of the glory of the Welsh tradition.[8] Later in the century, the Gaulish connection

---

of Gaul during the French Revolution: Between Charlemagne and Ossian', in *Celticism*, ed. by Terence Brown (Amsterdam: Rodopi, 1996), pp.183–206.

7   Dietler, ibid., p.593.

8   'Quand les bretonistes répudièrent la Gaule (1840–1850)', in *Nos ancêtres les Gaulois*, actes du colloque international de Clermont-Ferrand, ed by Jean Ehrard and Paul Viallaneix (Clermont-Ferrand: Association des Publications de la Faculté des Lettres et Sciences Humaines, 1982), pp.195–201.

could even be written out of history, as it was by Renan, who omits discussion of the Celtic ancestry of the French from a revised version of his essay on the poetry of the Celts.[9] So rather than lead smoothly into 'Bretonism', the Académie is entirely revamped in 1814 under the rather safer title: the 'Sociéte royale des Antiquaires de France', because of the over-enthusiasm of a number of its members for all things Celtic.

What the Académie was supposed to be about was France's nationalist need to document itself. Its 'questionnaire', a series of fifty-one questions, split into four categories, covering the seasons, birth and death, 'monuments', legends and folk beliefs,[10] was sent to all parts of France, and is widely regarded as marking the birth of French ethnography. In this there was an element of France wishing to keep up with its neighbours near and far, and envy of London and Calcutta, who already possessed such ethnographical institutions.[11] The relationship with French nationalism was uncomfortable to say the least, as this interest in provincial differences was in a sense part of a project to eliminate them. The men behind the questionnaire were not just pro uniformity, but, as administrators, sought to engineer this uniformity. Their over-use of the word 'monument', not just for archaeological remains, but also for beliefs, and even dialects, is telling. Differences were being collected and documented so as to be made into attractive postcards, and any talk of the preservation of regional languages meant in the museum. In her study of the Académie Nicole Belmont characterizes its stated aim thus: 'recueillir

9   'La Poésie des races celtiques' was first published in the *Revue des Deux Mondes*, n.s. 5 (1854), 473–506. For discussion of textual variants see René Galand, *L'Ame celtique de Renan* (New Haven: Yale University Press, 1959 [c. 1958]), p.83. On the point when Gaulomania gives way to Bretonism, see the contributions of Guiomar and Tanguy to the collection *Nos ancêtres les Gaulois*, and especially Joseph Rio, *Mythes fondateurs de la Bretagne: aux origines de la celtomanie* (Rennes: Editions Ouest-France, 2000), for a thorough investigation up to the end of the eighteenth century.

10   Reprinted in Nicole Belmont, ed., *Aux sources de l'ethnologie française: l'académie celtique* (Paris: Éditions du CTHS, 1995), pp.23–37.

11   See Mona Ozouf, *L'École de la France*, p.351.

les traditions, les coutumes, les usages, les langues locales en raison de leur intérêt propre et avant leur disparition supposée proche'.[12]

Proof that the academy had never been there in the service of Brittany, or even Celtic culture more generally, comes in the story of the demise of a society which was feared to be based on a 'système plus séduisant que solide'.[13] The preface to the 'Mémoires' of the new society explains that it wishes to be more scientific than its pre-decessor, and claims that much of the recent glorification of the Celts, and the Bretons, had been misguided, if not blindly pro-Celtic wishful thinking. Keen to distance itself from claims such as that by La Tour d'Auvergne that Celtic was *the* original human language, and that of Johanneau, the Académie's most outspoken member, that nearly all the peoples were descendants of the Celts, the new society is extra cautious, going as far as to suggest that 'bas-breton' might not even be the language of the Celts. Later on Raynouard even declared Breton to be a dialect born in the fifteenth century. The coining of the term 'Celtomanie', a retrospective and pejorative label, defined in the *Trésor de la langue française* (TLF) as an 'esprit de système qui caractérise les (savants) celtomanes', around 1838, shows to what extent this fashion and enthusiasm had also given rise to a certain Celtoscepticism.

This interest in collecting and documenting derived also in part from the ideas of Herder, which spread with Romanticism. For Herder popular literature and songs were nothing short of the archives of the people, containing their whole history, their whole way of life. He published his own *Volkslieder* in 1778–1779, and called on intel-lectuals far and wide to collect the basis of their own cultures in order

---

12 *Aux sources de l'ethnologie française,* pp.9–10. This paradox of increased interest in them coinciding with a desire to eliminate regional particularities is also pointed out by Mona Ozouf.

13 Extract from the *Mémoires* of the new society, cited in Tanguy, *Aux origines du nationalisme breton,* 2 vols (Paris: Union générale d'éditions, 1977), I, p.275. The *Mémoires* of the new society set out the reasons why the Académie was disbanded and reinvented as the 'Société Royale des Antiquaires de France' in 1814. On this question see Mona Ozouf, *L'École de la France,* esp. p.354; also Nicole Belmont, in *Aux sources de l'ethnologie française,* who puts it down to: 'la celtomanie outrancière de certains membres', pp.15–16.

to produce a true popular history. Although there were calls, even in France, for such collections before the Revolution, it was the new France that had rejected the history of a succession of crowned heads that fully realized the need for a popular history, not least because, as was the case with the Académie celtique, it had an eye on its neighbours, and knew that it lagged behind Germany in this respect.[14] Not only did Brittany provide something that could compete with Germany, but also its medieval past could challenge France itself. The Académie celtique marked the first systematic attempt at collecting songs, then Michelet, for instance, had plans for an 'Encyclopédie des chants populaires', modelled on Herder, around 1828, and by 1848, popular poetry enjoyed 'une sorte de faveur générale'.[15] Herder's influence was profound, indeed Raymond Schwab goes as far as to claim that: 'Tous les chers préjugés sur lesquels, aujourd'hui encore, repose notre idolâtrie de l'enfantin et du primitif, on peut, à vue cavalière, en tenir Herder pour responsable'.[16]

Brittany benefited from this vogue for 'primitivism' and native material, which was then championed in the works of Senancour and Mme de Staël. As far as literature was concerned, subject matter which was specific to and native to France found favour, and Breton material seemed to be quintessentially French. For Michelet – probably the greatest nineteenth-century historian – the history of Brittany quite simply *is* the history of France, because it is at its core. In his *Tableau de la France* he aimed to show how the unity of France grew out of the rich mosaic of provinces: 'Évoquer la Bretagne primitive, c'est, en fait, écrire le mythe de nos origines. Retracer les étapes de la transformation de la Bretagne, c'est retracer les étapes mêmes du

---

14   For a detailed historical survey see Charles Rearick, *Beyond the Enlightenment*, p.17, and for further disussion see Mary-Ann Constantine, *Breton Ballads* (Aberystwyth: Cambrian Medieval Celtic Studies, 1996), p.9.

15   Paul Bénichou, *Nerval et la chanson folklorique* (Paris: Corti, 1970), p.51. Bénichou also lists extracts from contemporary writers to show in what sense France was felt to 'need' such a tradition: 'La France est moins riche que d'autres pays en chants primitifs', p.90.

16   *La Renaissance orientale* (Paris: Payot, 1950), p.225.

développement de notre patrie'.[17] The same interest in the national heritage is evident in a grand undertaking like that of Taylor, Cailleux and Nodier, in the *Voyages pittoresques dans l'ancienne France* (Brittany volumes published 1843–6), in which Brittany occupies a similarly formative place. In his introduction to this work Taylor claims that his first visit to Brittany thirty-five years previously had given him the idea for the whole series of 'voyages'. In short, Brittany was understood as a paragon among the provinces; in the words of Anne-Marie Thiesse: 'Mais la position particulière de la Bretagne, parangon des provinces et en même temps région ayant gardé une identité forte, donne une forme extrême à l'opposition Paris/Province'.[18]

So 'Bretonism', launched by Gaulomania, continued to benefit from other Parisian fashions of the early nineteenth century that took over from it, albeit as an example of the primitive/savage rather than directly for its prestigious cultural heritage. Often we have the sense in these projects that regional differences needed to be recorded, *precisely* because they were about to be extinguished in the name of progress and democracy. The authors of the *Voyages pittoresques* describe their project thus:

> Nous devons nous hâter de reproduire les ruines de la Bretagne, car la civilisation va y entrer par la Normandie, le Maine, l'Anjou et le Poitou qui la bornent sur les autres points. Chaque jour maintenant va effacer davantage ce que sa physionomie a d'original et de caractéristique.[19]

The more threatened something seemed, the more it appealed to another Romantic taste, that for the near extinct. In the 1820s, across Europe, there was a fashion for what Fiona Stafford has called the 'myth of the last' of a race, or a type.[20] This fashion influenced Balzac in *Les Chouans*, where Brittany represents the last bit of primitivism

---

17   Cited in Jacques Landrin, 'La Bretagne de Michelet: mythe et réalité', *Ouest et romantismes*, pp.391–404 (400).
18   Anne-Marie Thiesse, *Écrire la France*, p.46.
19   Justin Taylor, Charles Nodier and Alphonse de Cailleux, *Voyages pittoresques et romantiques dans l'ancienne France*, 2 vols (Paris: Didot, 1820), I, 3.
20   See Fiona Stafford, *The Last of the Race: The Growth of a Myth from Milton to Darwin* (Oxford: Clarendon Press, 1994), pp.200, 232–42, also Malcolm Chapman, *The Celts*, p.139.

within France; indeed one of his earlier titles puts the emphasis on 'the last': *Le Dernier Chouan ou la Bretagne en 1800*. The same fashion fed into Souvestre's most famous work: *Les Derniers Bretons* (1836).[21]

There was something more important than the renewed interest in 'nos ancêtres les Gaulois', however, and even than the Romantic interest in ideas of extinction. More than anything it was the shift in sensibility that came with Romanticism that accounts for the attention Brittany enjoyed. It was the reaction against the hyper-cultured, over-sophisticated life of the leisured classes in the eighteenth century that led to a valorization of the simple, the natural, the untainted by society, including peasants, children, and nature. Jean-Jacques Rousseau, the eighteenth-century *philosophe*, and father of Romanticism, founded a literature of the flight from Paris, whose most influential practitioners in nineteenth-century France would include Chateaubriand, Senancour, Lamartine, Vigny, George Sand, and Nerval. His call 'fuyez les villes' is explicit in the preface to his moralizing epistolary novel *Julie ou la Nouvelle Héloïse* (1761), where the rural community of Clarens represents an antidote to the evils of Paris, a refuge that poor Saint-Preux returns to after his trip to the dangerous and corrupting French capital.[22] However it is the botanizing Rous-

---

21   There is an echo of another famous novel in this: *The Last of the Mohicans* by Fenimoore Cooper, or in the French title that Balzac would have known: *Le Dernier des Mohicans: histoire de mil sept cent cinquante-sept* (in the translation by Defauconpret). This is part of the same 'fashion', and perhaps it is because he was aware of his debt to Cooper that Balzac changed his title from 'Le Dernier Chouan' to 'Les Chouans'. This change of date from 1800 to 1799 was made in the interest of historical accuracy, but the change in the wording is more intriguing. Helen Elcessor Barnes argues in *A Study of the Variations between the Original and the Standard Editions of Balzac's 'Les Chouans'* (Illinois: The University of Chicago Press, 1923) that: 'the Cooperesque touches indicate no tendency to break away from the influence of the American author, but rather zealous efforts to maintain the atmosphere of *The Last of the Mohicans*', p.35.

22   Jean-Jacques Rousseau, *Julie ou La Nouvelle Héloïse* (Paris: Garnier Frères, 1960). Saint-Preux's impression of Clarens is found in the form of a complete portrait in a letter to Mylord Édouard: 'Quelle retraite délicieuse! Quelle charmante habitation! Que la douce habitude d'y vivre en augmente le prix!

seau of the *Rêveries du promeneur solitaire* (written between 1776 and 1778), especially the famous fifth 'promenade' on the 'Île Saint-Pierre', whose influence on subsequent literary depictions of nature as well as on the 'récit personnel' was decisive.

While one explanation for the predilection for solitary scenes shown by Rousseau might have been his paranoia about escaping from his enemies: 'mes puissants oppresseurs', 'injustes ennemis',[23] and their plots against him: 'le plus affreux complot qui jamais ait été tramé contre la mémoire d'un homme',[24] the real reason why it was so influential was that Rousseau was not alone. His work crystallized a tendency, and others were affected by the landscape in this new way, like Diderot's Dorval in *Entretiens sur 'Le Fils naturel'*, as early as 1757:

> Le lendemain, je me rendis au pied de la colline. L'endroit était solitaire et sauvage. On avait en perspective quelques hameaux répandus dans la plaine; au delà, une chaîne de montagnes inégales et déchirées qui terminaient en partie l'horizon. On était à l'ombre des chênes, et l'on entendait le bruit sourd d'une eau souterraine qui coulait aux environs. [...] Dorval s'était abandonné au spectacle de la nature. Il avait la poitrine élevée. Il respirait avec force.[25]

The aesthetic revolution in the way outside reality, or nature, was described, was memorably characterized by Abrams as a shift from a mirror to a lamp:

[...] on y trouve partout des cœurs contents et des visages gais' (part 5, letter II, p.447). Paris, in contrast, is false and corrupt: 'Jusques ici j'ai vu beaucoup de masques, quand verrai-je des visages d'hommes?' (letter to Julie, part 2, letter XIV, p.185), and the corruption extends as far as the Parisians' language: 'que penses-tu qu'on apprenne dans ces conversations si charmantes? [...] on y apprend à plaider avec art la cause du mensonge, à ébranler à force de philosophie tous les principes de la vertu, à colorer de sophismes subtils ses passions et ses préjugés, et à donner à l'erreur un certain tour à la mode selon les maximes du jour', (letter to Julie, part 2, letter XIV, p.182).

23 *Les Confessions*, 3 vols, ed. by Ad. Van Bever (Paris: Garnier Frères, 1952), II, 237.
24 *Les Confessions*, III, 112.
25 *Œuvres esthétiques*, ed. by Paul Vernière (Paris: Garnier Frères, 1968), p.96.

The work ceases then to be regarded as primarily a reflection of nature, actual or improved; the mirror held up to nature becomes transparent and yields the reader insights into the mind and heart of the poet himself.[26]

So poetry was no longer thought to have developed from man's instinct to imitate nature, but rather to have originated in the cries of primitive man. A sense of nostalgia for this pure variety of poetic expression permeates descriptions of nature, and changes modern man's relationship to it. The experience of nature sought out by French writers is more and more extreme, as demonstrated by the disappointment of Senancour's protagonist Oberman in the countryside at Fontainebleau:

> J'ai bien une terre libre à parcourir; mais elle n'est pas assez sauvage, assez imposante. Les formes en sont basses; les roches petites et monotones; la végétation n'y a pas en général cette force, cette profusion qui m'est nécessaire; on n'y entend bruire aucun torrent dans des profondeurs inaccessibles: c'est une terre de plaines. Rien ne m'opprime ici, rien ne me satisfait. Je crois même que l'ennui augmente: c'est que je ne souffre pas assez.[27]

Sainte-Beuve, along with Nodier and George Sand, was responsible for promoting and republishing Senancour's *Oberman* in 1833, at around the time when he was praising Brizeux in the *Revue de Paris*.[28]

The enthusiasm for the peasant inhabitants of the rural idyll was also a measure of the Parisians' fear of the more threatening urban proletariat.[29] At a time when intellectuals were convinced that

---

26   Meyer H. Abrams, *The Mirror and the Lamp: Romantic Theory and the Critical Tradition* (Oxford: Oxford University Press, 1953), p.23. A study on French writing, inspired by Abrams's approach is Marguerite Iknayan, *The Concave Mirror: From Imitation to Expression in French Esthetic Theory 1800–1830* (Stanford: Anma Livre, 1983).

27   *Oberman*, ed. by Béatrice Didier (Paris: Livre de poche, 1984), letter XVIII, pp.88–9.

28   See *Revue de Paris*, 34 (1832), 210–22. On Sainte-Beuve's Joseph Delorme and his enjoyment of ordinary, quiet countryside, see the discussion in Christopher W. Thompson, *Walking and the French Romantics: Rousseau to Sand and Hugo* (Bern: Peter Lang, 2003), p.49.

29   On the politics behind Sainte-Beuve's attitude, or that of Romanticism generally, Fausta Garavini says: 'Les collaborateurs de la *Revue des Deux Mondes* refusent les frémissements de révolte qui agitent la poésie ouvrière et

literature really could make a difference, they promoted the wholesome way of life of the provinces, and saw it as their duty to create reviews and to diffuse Romantic ideas in the local press.[30] Eugène Fromentin sums up what he calls the 'incroyable influence des chefs d'école':

> Les petits poètes servent de réflecteurs aux grands. Leur nombre s'accroît en raison des ressources poétiques et des besoins des localités. Nous avons dans ce moment en Languedoc, en Provence, en Bourgogne, en Bretagne des pléiades poétiques au service de M. de Lamartine et de M. Victor Hugo.[31]

Brittany's inventors

I turn now to the writers who can be numbered among Brittany's inventors. The starting point of such a survey is necessarily open to debate, as such points can always be traced further and further back. However, important work in Breton studies across a number of disciplines has established the 1830s as a crucial decade in the evolution of representations of Brittany. Historian Jean-Yves Guiomar sees in this decade 'une sorte d'explosion culturelle en Bretagne, préparée par des écrivains comme Le Gonidec, Brizeux, Emile Souvestre et La Villemarqué', or the beginning of a period that he

---

quarante-huitarde, mais ils voient dans le "bon paysan" un antidote, précisément, contre l'esprit de 48 et l'exaltation du prolétariat urbain', Fausta Garavini, 'Province et rusticité: esquisse d'un malentendu', *Romantisme*, 35 (1982), 73–89 (76).

30 Anne Martin-Fugier in *Les Romantiques: figures de l'artiste 1820–1848* (Paris: Hachette, 1998), demonstrates the unique excitement and optimism of this time in French literary life through a survey of the memoirs written by those who were young at the time, see esp. p.298.

31 Fromentin, Eugène, *Œuvres complètes*, ed. by Guy Sagnes, Bibliothèque de la Pléiade (Paris: Gallimard, 1984), p.916.

calls the 'création de la Bretagne'.[32] Art historian Denise Delouche in *Peintres de la Bretagne: découverte d'une province* agrees.[33] Catherine Bertho, in a seminal paper in the social sciences, is one of the first critics to concentrate on identifying this shift. Her 'L'invention de la Bretagne' argues for 1830 as the turning point which sees 'l'aimable supplanter le sauvage et le bucolique détrôner l'étrange'.[34] From then on the stereotypes were fixed; her discussion of these focuses in particular on the 'jeune fille en coiffe':

> La Bretagne devient la province par excellence où l'opinion conservatrice projette l'utopie réactionnaire d'une société agraire vivant sans conflits sous la houlette de ses maîtres traditionnels. Le personnage le plus typique devient alors féminin: c'est la jeune Bretonne en coiffe, symbole transparent, quoique inlassablement commenté, de l'innocence, agenouillée au pied d'un calvaire.[35]

In 1830 the negative, 'savage' stereotype of Brittany had already begun to give way to the positive, pure and feminized version of their *petite patrie* that subsequent generations of writers struggled to subvert.

---

32 Guiomar, *Le Bretonisme*, pp.116, 87. Tanguy, in *Aux origines*, goes for a slightly earlier date: 'Car il est indéniable que depuis les années 1820, on s'acheminait vers le *Barzaz Breiz* de 1839 et même de 1845', I, 321.

33 (Paris: Klincksieck, 1977).

34 'L'invention de la Bretagne: Genèse sociale d'un stéréotype', *Actes de la recherche en sciences sociales*, 35 (1980), 45–62 (58). This highly inflential paper was the result of much broader work in her thesis, *La naissance des stéréotypes régionaux en Bretagne au XIXe siècle* (1979).

35 Ibid., p.49. This crystallization of stereotypes, she says, explains the success of Brizeux's *Marie* because: 'En 1836 [sic], dans le poème d'Auguste Brizeux, *Marie*, la jeune fille bretonne en coiffe, pieuse et soumise, rassemblait toutes les qualités de la Bretagne en général. Les poupées bretonnes des boutiques de souvenirs remplissent à peu près le même rôle', p.62.

Chateaubriand

The first literary writer who can lay any claim to being the starting point is Chateaubriand, as Cambry is prehistory for our purposes because though immensely influential, his work does not set out to be literature. Indeed in the *Histoire littéraire et culturelle de la Bretagne* it is argued that a passage from the Velléda episode of Chateaubriand's *Les Martyrs* constitutes Brittany's 'véritable entrée en littérature' in 1809, because it is shown to contain already all the elements of the French-language stereotype that subsequently established itself, that is the 'vieux arbres', 'landes', 'bruyère et fougère, rochers informes, océan redoutable, ciel bas'.[36] The key passage reads:

> J'arrivai enfin chez les Rhédons. L'Armorique ne m'offrit que des bruyères, des bois, des vallées étroites et profondes traversées de petites rivières que ne remonte point le navigateur, et qui portent à la mer des eaux inconnues; région solitaire, triste, orageuse, enveloppée de brouillards, retentissante du bruit des vents, et dont les côtes hérissées de rochers sont battues d'un océan sauvage.
>
> Le château où je commandais, situé à quelques milles de la mer, était une ancienne forteresse des Gaulois, agrandie par Jules César lorsqu'il porta la guerre chez les Vénètes et le Curiosolites. Il était bâti sur un roc, appuyé contre une forêt, et baigné par un lac.
>
> Là, séparé du reste du monde, je vécus plusieurs mois dans la solitude. Cette retraite me fut utile. Je descendis dans ma conscience; je sondai des plaies que je n'avais encore osé toucher depuis que j'avais quitté Zacharie; je m'occupai de l'étude de ma religion.[37]

Whether or not this focus on Brittany was just an accident of birth, Chateaubriand is important for our purposes because he is a canonical figure, and indeed considered one of the fathers of Romanticism. Though he did not devote a whole work to his homeland (in the manner of say Renan with *Souvenirs d'enfance et de jeunesse*),

---

36 Louis Le Guillou, ,'Romantisme et christianisme bretons', in *Histoire littéraire et culturelle de la Bretagne*, II, 17–78 (20, 21).

37 Chateaubriand, *Œuvres romanesques et voyages*, 2 vols, ed. by Maurice Regard, Bibliothèque de la Pléiade (Paris: Gallimard, 1969), II, 251.

Brittany comes in at key points in his career.[38] It also permeates the rest of his work, so that we can see *René* as a 'première esquisse d'*un certain* paysage breton',[39] and it is well known that his composition process involved borrowing ideas from his own earlier texts.

His *Mémoires d'outre-tombe* had gained almost mythical status by the time of his death when he left its manuscript at the foot of his bed. Extracts had already been published, private readings had been given, and he had kept rewriting and changing it. 'Œuvre de presque toute une vie', says Jean-Claude Berchet in his preface to the Garnier edition;[40] and this long gestation produced a polyphonic text. The author's early years receive much attention, and Chateaubriand begins by tracing his lineage, and then describing his birth, in the middle of a storm. While talking of his earliest childhood, he provides a description of his own grave, explaining that '*be*, en breton, signifie *tombe*' (I, 140), so that the end is contained from the outset. Soon comes the much anthologized passage 'Le printemps en Bretagne':

> Le printemps, en Bretagne, est plus doux qu'aux environs de Paris, et fleurit trois semaines plus tôt. Les cinq oiseaux qui l'annoncent, l'hirondelle, le loriot, le coucou, la caille et le rossignol, arrivent avec des brises qui gébergent dans les golfes de la péninsule armoricaine. La terre se couvre de marguerites, de pensées, de jonquilles, de narcisses, d'hyacinthes, de renoncules, d'anémones, comme les espaces abandonnés qui environnent Saint-Jean-de-Latran et Sainte-Croix-de-Jérusalem, à Rome. Des clairières se panachent d'élégantes et hautes fougères; des champs de genêts et d'ajoncs resplendissent de leurs fleurs qu'on prendrait pour des papillons d'or. Les haies, au long desquelles abondent la fraise, la framboise et la violette, sont décorées d'aubépines, de chèvrefeuille, de ronces dont les rejets bruns et courbés portent des feuilles et des fruits magnifiques. Tout fourmille d'abeilles et d'oiseaux; les essaims et les nids arrêtent les enfants à chaque pas. Dans certains abris, le myrte et le laurier-rose croissent en pleine terre, comme en Grèce; la figue mûrit comme en Provence;

---

38 The relevant passages from the *Mémoires d'outre tombe*, as well as some extracts from earlier works, are conveniently grouped in Yannick Pelletier, *La Bretagne chez Chateaubriand.*

39 Louis Le Guillou, 'Romantisme et christianisme bretons', in *Histoire littéraire et culturelle de la Bretagne*, II, 17–78 (20).

40 Chateaubriand, *Mémoires d'outre-tombe*, 2 vols, ed. by Jean-Claude Berchet (Paris: Classiques Garnier, 1989), p.xxix. References are to this edition, and hereafter given in the text.

chaque pommier, avec ses fleurs carminées, ressemble à un gros bouquet de fiancée de village (I, 162–63).[41]

Like so many portrayals Chateaubriand's owes something to Cambry. Louis Le Guillou claims: 'Chateaubriand se souviendra si bien de la description par Cambry de la campagne idyllique de Plougastel-Daoulas qu'il en décalquera littéralement son "Printemps."'[42] Chateaubriand carries more influence than Cambry because of his position in the mainstream of French culture. Other motifs that will become staples of writing on Brittany are also found here, for instance the emphasis on the sadness of his family's seat: 'Si la tristesse était grande sur le bruyères de Combourg, elle était encore plus grande au château' (I, 209), or on Brest as the end of the earth: 'après ce cap avancé, il n'y avait plus rien qu'un océan sans bornes et des mondes inconnus; mon imagination se jouait dans ces espaces'(I, 199).

We may ask how 'Breton' this writing is. Apart from the fact that many of its features can be explained by looking to the literary fashions of the day, Chateaubriand is upfront about the fact that he has based these descriptions on his memories of his exotic travels. In this way his representations of Brittany owe more to the moods induced by foreign landscapes than to views of the real Brittany: 'Maintes fois, en voyant le soleil se coucher dans les forêts de l'Amérique, je me suis rappelé les bois de Combourg: mes souvenirs se font écho' (I,187). His reading also informs his portrait of his native Brittany, the privileged reference points being Scott: 'Dans les bruyères de la Calédonie, Lucile eût été une femme céleste de Walter Scott, douée de la seconde vue; dans les bruyères armoricaines, elle n'était qu'une solitaire avantagée de beauté, de génie et de malheur' (I, 216),

---

41 This passage has been the object of much re-writing, and has been expanded from the earlier version in *Mémoires de ma vie* version, and was included in *Lectures* (1834). For details of variants see ed. Berchet, I, 162.

42 Louis Le Guillou, 'Romantisme et christianisme bretons', in *Histoire littéraire et culturelle de la Bretagne*, II, 13–4. The passage in Cambry describing the pointe de Plougastel reads: 'où règne un printemps éternel. Vous n'êtes plus dans la Bretagne; les fraises, la framboise, la rose, la jonquille, la violette et l'églantier, couvrent les champs chargés d'arbres fruitiers […]. Tous les légumes y croissent avec abondance et devancent de six semaines l'époque qui les voit naître ailleurs', *Voyage dans le Finistère*, pp.268–69.

48

and Macpherson's Ossian, which Chateaubriand himself translated. Though Chateaubriand's work is undeniably important in the evolution of representations of Brittany, he cannot be considered a deliberate 'inventor' of Brittany. Balzac, in contrast, did devote entire works specifically to Brittany.

Balzac

One reason why Chateaubriand's texts stand out is that so much of what was being written about Brittany in his day, and well beyond it, was negative. It was not until the 1830s that the dominant picture of Brittany in literary texts began to change. The difference between what went before the 1830s and what came afterwards is demonstrated strikingly by the case of Balzac, whose three Breton novels, that is those based in Brittany or dominated by Breton characters – *Les Chouans* (1829),[43] *Béatrix* (1839), and *Pierrette* (1840) – show strikingly different ideas of Brittany and Bretonness. The earliest of these three is nevertheless responsible for Balzac's reputation as one of Brittany's worst enemies.

Les Chouans displays an unmistakably 'colonializing' attitude in its comparison of Breton counter-revolutionary soldiers to the primitive inhabitants of France's overseas colonies:

> Une incroyable férocité, un entêtement brutal, mais aussi la foi du serment; l'absence complète de nos lois, de nos mœurs, de notre habillement, de nos monnaies nouvelles, de notre langage, mais aussi la simplicité patriarcale et d'héroïques vertus s'accordent à rendre les habitants de ces campagnes plus

---

43 Dating *Les Chouans* is problematic because Balzac appears to have attempted to suggest an earlier date for it, see Barnes, *A Study of the Variations*, p.5. He began the novel in September 1828 in Fougères itself, where he was staying with a family friend; he published it in 1829 under the title: *Le Dernier Chouan ou la Bretagne en 1800*, then brought out a new version in 1834 under the title: *Les Chouans ou la Bretagne en 1799*, and then made some further changes for its incorporation into the *Comédie humaine* in 1845.

pauvres de combinaisons intellectuelles que ne le sont les Mohicans et les Peaux rouges de l'Amérique septentrionale, mais aussi grands, aussi rusés, aussi durs qu'eux (39).

The paternalism implied by such descriptions is confirmed in the preface, where Balzac calls for 'l'amélioration physique et morale de la Bretagne'. So primitive are these men that they are routinely compared to animals. We are told from the opening page that the men seem to fuse naturally with the animal skins they wear as protection: 'Les mèches plates de leurs longs cheveux s'unissaient si habituel-lement aux poils de la peau de chèvre [...] on pouvait facilement prendre cette peau pour la leur [...]'. (22) And Marche-à-Terre is frequently described as an animal:

> Cet inconnu, homme trapu, large des épaules, lui montrait une tête presque aussi grosse que celle d'un bœuf, avec laquelle elle avait plus d'une ressemblance. [...] Enfin l'absence complète des autres caractères de l'homme social rendait cette tête nue plus remarquable encore. [...] Les peaux de biques, pour parler la langue du pays, qui lui garnissaient les jambes et les cuisses, ne laissaient distinguer aucune forme humaine (34–5).

The primitive and the animal often go together; 'animalisms' are also found in *The Last of the Mohicans*, and such comparisons with Bretons are not unique to Balzac. Merimée, who was sent to Brittany on a Government mission, writes in a letter shortly after the pub-lication of *Les Chouans*: 'On voit dans les villages les enfants et les cochons se roulant pêle-mêle sur le fumier…Mais les bêtes ont plus d'esprit que les Bretons'.[44] Indeed barbarity and animalism have long been associated with descriptions of Celts, and especially in the context of war.[45] Renan's condemnation of Chrétien de Troyes in 'La

---

44 Mérimée, letter to Jaubert de Passa, 8 October 1835, *Correspondance générale*, ed. by Maurice Parturier, 14 vols (Paris: Plon, 1934), VI, 463–64.

45 See R. R. Davies, *The First English Empire: Power and Identities in the British Isles, 1093–1343* (Oxford: Oxford University Press, 2000), pp.121, 125. See also Patrick Sims-Williams on 'sauvage' in 'The Invention of Celtic Nature Poetry', in *Celticism*, pp.97–124 (p.105). For a survey of pre-Romantic references to Brittany, see Ronan Le Coadic, *L'Identité bretonne* (Rennes: Terre de Brume, 1998), p.118.

poésie des races celtiques' focuses on the latter's use of animal comparisons:

C'est bien à Chrétien de Troyes, par exemple, qui passa sa vie à exploiter pour son propre compte les romans bretons, qu'il appartient de dire:
'Les Gallois sont tous par nature
Plus sots que bêtes de pâture.'[46]

In *Les Chouans* this is more than an occasional comparison. Here the 'corne' used to call the men's attention is described as resembling that used to gather flocks (34), and Balzac makes special capital out of the name 'chouan' itself, making the 'cri de chouette' function as a leitmotif in the novel. First of all its use and meaning is explained (49), then the 'cri de chouette' has a part to play in the plot (52, 65, 118–20), which culminates in Marie Verneuil using the call herself (263, 373). Another reason why Balzac was so focused on animality is that under the influence of recent ideas in the natural sciences, he believed that the different 'types' of person grow out of their social circumstances, just as a zoological species evolves in accordance with its geographical context. *Les Chouans* was written before he had conceived of the 'Comédie humaine' structure, but plays a key part in the development of the ideas later collected in the famous 'Avant-propos' to the latter,

Le créateur ne s'est servi que d'un seul et même patron pour tous les êtres organisés. L'animal est un principe qui prend sa forme extérieure, ou, pour parler plus exactement, les différences de sa forme, dans les milieux où il est appelé à se développer ('Avant-propos').

Thus the peculiarities of the Bretons, and the whole history of Brittany, can be explained by the physical reality of its landscape:

---

46 'La poésie des races celtiques', *Revue des Deux Mondes*, n.s. 5 (1854), 473–506 (505). Renan's opinion of him is clearer in this passage: 'Le bavardage des imitateurs français et allemands du moyen âge, de Chrétien de Troyes et de Wolfram d'Eschenbach par exemple, ne peut donner une idée de cette charmante manière de raconter', (ibid., p.482).

> Ce malheur s'explique assez par la nature d'un sol encore silloné de ravins, de torrents, de lacs et de marais; hérissé de haies, espèces de bastions en terre qui font, de chaque champ, une citadelle; privé de routes et de canaux (39).

Balzac's scientific enthusiasm for the peculiarities of the landscape gives extra resonance to descriptions, familiar since Cambry, of the hostility of the terrain, such as: 'Là, le génie de la civilisation moderne s'effraie de pénétrer à travers d'immenses forêts primordiales' (38). For Balzac the novelist, features of the Breton landscape could also be used as symbols. By this time the prevalence of 'ajoncs' (gorse) and 'genêts' (broom) – as used by Chateaubriand in *Mémoires d'outre-tombe* – was well-established as one of the commonest clichés in descriptions of Brittany. In *Les Chouans* a description centring on the ajoncs/genêts is used to characterize Brittany as a mixture of the beautiful and the dangerous, because Chouans hide behind the bushes:

> les Chouans se cachaient derrière ses touffes d'un vert sombre. Ces talus et ces ajoncs, qui annoncent au voyageur l'approche de la Bretagne, rendaient donc alors cette partie de la route aussi dangereuse qu'elle est belle (104).

In Balzac these bushes become a synecdoche for the region, in that they signal to the traveller that he is entering Brittany.

At the other end of the spectrum, Balzac the interpreter of Breton peculiarities sometimes seems to be recording detail as if for posterity:

> Deux énormes *pichés*, pleins de cidre, se trouvaient sur la longue table. Ces ustensiles sont des espèces de cruches en terre brune, dont le modèle existe dans plusieurs pays de la France, et qu'un Parisien peut se figurer en supposant aux pots dans lesquels les gourmets servent le beurre de Bretagne, un ventre plus arrondi (300–1).

This explanation, addressed to a hypothetical Parisian reader, is typical of Balzac's later novels. More than in the detail, the young Balzac was interested in progress, specifically the progress that France herself has made through the Enlightenment to democracy. Counter-revolutionary Brittany was one of the new Republic's greatest internal contradictions, and the greatest challenge to progress. Brittany in this novel represents an earlier stage in France's development, with the opening sentence setting up an opposition between pre- and post-revolutionary calendars: 'Dans les premiers jours de l'an VIII, au commencement de vendémaire, ou, pour se conformer au calendrier actuel, vers la fin du mois de septembre 1799, une centaine de paysans...'(21). Entering Brittany, then, would be equivalent to visiting France's past. This is indeed the experience of the characters in the novel who arrive from Paris. For instance the Polytechnicien thinks that the people he sees in Brittany are 'retardés', and that everything around him is inferior:

> Ces gens-là m'ont l'air d'être bien retardés en fait de civilisation. – Ah! Reprit-il en soupirant, il n'y a qu'un Paris au monde, et c'est grand dommage qu'on ne puisse pas l'emmener en mer! (124).

Marie de Verneuil, similarly has difficulty believing that human beings can live in such muddy conditions: 'Mademoiselle de Verneuil se demandait s'il était possible que des êtres humains vécussent dans cette fange organisée' (299). The Breton language, when mentioned at all, is used as a further example of the clock having been turned back a few hundred years, and is even linked with animality when Marche-à-Terre is described as emitting first a 'cri bestial', and then, in the next sentence as speaking 'bas-breton' (67). This famous description of 'Marche-à-Terre' combines animality and pastness:

> Des sabots énormes lui cachaient les pieds. Ses longs cheveux luisants, semblables aux poils de ses peaux de chèvres, tombaient de chaque côté de sa figure, séparé en deux parties égales, et pareils aux chevelures de ces statues du Moyen Age qu'on voit encore dans quelques cathédrales (35).

Here the result is that he is not only made to belong to a different kingdom – the animal kingdom – but to a different era altogether: the middle ages.

Pierrette, published over a decade later, could hardly be more different. In this novel Bretons come across as good patriots, as when Brigaut's father's past as a Chouan is glossed over, and when Brigaut even writes to Pierrette that she should be proud that her father was 'mort pour la France'. The only mention of the much-feared 'Chouans' by name in this novel is when their infamous war-cry is hijacked and used to the good. Whereas in Les Chouans this imitation of an owl's cry is connected with the animalisms used of the Bretons, in

Pierrette the only time a comparison is drawn with animals is when the non-Breton characters Sylvie and her brother are described as 'bêtes sauvages' in a cage in the Jardin des plantes. Indeed it is difficult to see the Breton characters in *Pierrette* as anything but reversals of those in *Les Chouans*. The way in which the Chouan soldiers themselves are redeemed in the novel is evidence enough, as it is Brigaut's use of the owl's cry that he has learnt from his father's chouan skills that enables him to save Pierrette. Other familiar symbols of Brittany also seem to have undergone reversal. In *Les Chouans* the gorse and broom was used to emphasize that the land was poor, and poorly-kept, and that the country was dangerous as these bushes grew so high that they could stop you in your tracks, or even conceal Chouans who might be out to kill you. In the later novel these same shrubs are invariably pretty and innocent, and used as a reminder of an idealized childhood.

The positive attention given to costume, especially the 'coiffe', in *Pierrette* contrasts with the emphasis on 'costumes bizarres' and animal skins in the *Chouans*. The 'coiffe' or traditional headdress is an obvious feature that marks a woman out as Breton, before being an individual. Whereas to outsiders 'coiffes' just designate 'Bretonness' – whatever that homogenized idea may be – to insiders they are invested with meaning, as the style of 'coiffe' can provide information about which part of Brittany somebody comes from, or whether they are in mourning, for instance.[47] For Balzac here the 'coiffe' is merely a picturesque and convenient pointer to Bretonness. The sense of distance suggested by this use of symbols is even clearer in the way Balzac constantly refers to main characters as 'la Bretonne', 'le courageux Breton', and so forth, presenting them as types, or repre-sentatives of Bretonness rather than individuals.

Over-schematic images can be problematic even when they are positive. There is an element of this in *Béatrix*, where the opposition set up between the innocence of the young Calyste in his idyllic province and the corrupting force of Paris is reminiscent of Rousseau's *Julie ou La Nouvelle Héloïse*. Like *Les Chouans*, *Béatrix* is also infused by ideas borrowed from the sciences. In the opening

---

47   This is an issue discussed in Lebesque, *Comment peut-on être breton?*, p.108.

pages, the family that forms the focus of the plot are described as if they had evolved as part of Brittany's landscape:

> Vieux comme le granit de la Bretagne, les Guaisnic ne sont ni francs, ni gaulois, ils sont bretons, ou, pour être plus exact, celtes, Ils ont dû jadis être druides, avoir cueilli le gui des forêts sacrées et sacrifié des hommes sur les dolmens.[48]

Bretonness is something that can be explained by the landscape, and also discerned in an individual's physiognomy, as in the case of the main character Calyste. When he is first introduced, we are told that there are 'signes de […] sa résistance bretonne' in the shape of his nose (652). Balzac is happy to re-use comparisons that had long since become clichés, such as that of stone: 'le granit fait homme' (of the Baron du Guénic). However, his interest in the natural sciences adds an extra layer of meaning to the emphasis on the famous stones of Brittany, as he uses archaeology as a metaphor for the special type of social science in which he as a novelist is engaged. He is an 'archéologue moral', whose business it is to 'observer les hommes au lieu d'observer les pierres' (638).

The colonializing attitude that infused *Les Chouans* has come full circle, and the focus is now on the picturesque or 'poetic' aspects of Brittany's difference rather than its inferiority. For the older Balzac the area is like an African desert, and the paludiers 'font croire à des Arabes couverts de leurs burnous'. So keen is he to emphasize this that he adds a further exoticizing description to a later version of the novel, where he says of the paludiers: 'Il y avait je ne sais quoi d'oriental dans ce tableau, car, certes, un Parisien subitement transporté là ne se serait pas cru en France' (803). The exoticism of Brittany had already become a classic comparison,[49] and in this novel Brittany provides a heightened backdrop for passions beyond the ordinary, as confirmed by the well-travelled and sophisticated Béatrix: 'je n'ai rien vu qui peigne mieux l'ardente aridité de ma vie' (808). It

---

48 Balzac, *La Comédie humaine*, ed. by Pierre-Georges Castex et al., Bibliothèque de la Pléiade (Paris: Gallimard, 1976), II, 643. Hereafter page references to this edition will be given in the text.

49 Castex, in the Pléiade edition, lists examples from the 1820s, see p.1467.

seems that Balzac chose Brittany because it offered him an extreme. In the case of *Les Chouans*, he could just as easily have set his novel in the Vendée, and when he was intending to write a sister novel on the Vendée (which never materialized) he described the war there as 'la guerre civile régulière'. The Vendée would have offered a less extreme case of difference.

Certainly Balzac is not merely concerned with accurately depicting Brittany as it was in his day, his errors in *Les Chouans* show this. For instance the way he seems to think Basse-Bretagne extends all the way to Fougères, and right into Normandie at one point, and also his assumption that Breton is spoken in Haute-Bretagne.[50] It may be that he only uses 'Basse-Bretagne' and 'Bas-Breton' throughout in order to emphasize the distance and difference from normal civilization. The Vendée and Brittany are conflated as they are defined by counter-revolution, but it hardly needs pointing out that the idea of provincial counter-revolution was exaggerated as it suited the revolutionaries well. [51] Add to this Balzac's use of clichéd types and readymade character and ideas, and he seems to owe much to established writers of the day. Certainly he was working within a tradition. Like Chateaubriand, his descriptions in *Les Chouans* are extremely similar to Cambry's. Compare this passage from Cambry's *Voyage dans le Finistère*:

> Battus des vents et des orages, ils sont vêtus de toile au milieu des hivers; leurs cheveux noirs flottans sur leurs épaules, tombent sur le front et leur couvrent les yeux;... ils vivent de quelques panais, de quelques choux; leur demeure est un trou formé par les rochers (*Voyage dans le Finistère*)[52]

with the following from *Les Chouans*:

---

50   This is not the case, but it is no surprise that Balzac gets this wrong, as even Barère, the author of a government report, thought that all five Breton départements were Breton-speaking, as pointed out in Fañch Broudic, *La Pratique du breton*, p.270.

51   This is discussed in Robert Gildea, *The Past in French History* (New Haven: Yale University Press, 1994), pp.168, 199, and Caroline Ford, *Creating the Nation*, p.33.

52   Jacques Cambry, *Voyage dans le Finistère*, p.77.

Ses longs cheveux luisants, semblables aux poils de ses peaux de chèvres, tombaient de chaque côté de sa figure (35)

Les mèches plates de leurs longs cheveux s'unissaient si habituellement aux poils de la peau de chèvre [...] on pouvait facilement prendre cette peau pour la leur... (22).

If Balzac himself invites us to see his novel *Les Chouans* as a fusion of Fenimore Cooper's *Last of the Mohicans*, and Walter Scott, we might add Chateaubriand's *Martyrs*, and Cambry's *Voyage*.[53] The later novels, equally, are composed from within an identifiable tradition. Sabine, the woman who is eventually married to the Breton Calyste in *Béatrix*, tells her mother that Calyste reminds her of a character from Walter Scott (851).

It seems likely that Balzac chose Brittany as his focus in *Les Chouans* because the clichés of backwardness and difference were already well established, and this enabled him to embroider on them. A decade on, he chose Brittany as the antidote to the evils of Paris and modern French society generally because these positive clichés were by then also gaining ground. To some extent both the positive and the negative clichés originate in the first wave of writing about Brittany. Chateaubriand's writing, for instance, contains the positive, pretty aspects of Brittany as well as the brutality. There is an extent to which Balzac is leading the way in this turnaround from negative to positive.

---

53   Cooper was in Paris, or in the vicinity, from July 1826 to February 1828, and again from July 1830 to 1833, and this did much to enhance his popularity. In any case, Balzac has made the task easy for the critic, by himself declaring that his literary models were Cooper and Scott: 'Il y a là tout Cooper et tout Walter Scott, plus une passion et un *esprit* qui n'est chez aucun d'eux' (Balzac, Letter to Mme Hanska, 30 December 1843; cited in Regard's edition of *Les Chouans*, p.xiii). On the influence of *The Last of the Mohicans*, and *Les Martyrs*, see Jean Balcou, 'Les Bretons, ce sont nos indiens', in *Ouest et romantismes*, pp.43–51. For a systematic study of parallels with Fenimore Cooper, see Helen Elcessor Barnes, *A Study of the Variations between the Original and the Standard Editions of Balzac's 'Les Chouans'*, and the extensive notes to Maurice Regard's edition: *Les Chouans* (Paris: Garnier, 1957). See also Yann-Ber Piriou, 'Une lettre de L. Sauvé à Luzel', in *Études sur la Bretagne et les pays celtiques: mélanges offerts à Yves le Gallo*, Cahiers de Bretagne Occidentale 6 (Brest, 1987), pp.407–10.

His real interest, however, was in France, and he is even less a deliberate inventor of Brittany than Chateaubriand. Even the latter, who was born in Brittany, is not perceived at the time – say in the writing of Sainte-Beuve – nor in recent criticism, as anything but incidentally Breton, with Brittany being no more than an accidental backdrop to his Romantic musings.

Brizeux

However formative the texts produced by Balzac and Chateaubriand, the interest they showed in Brittany can always be explained away. For instance Balzac is really interested in France's progress and Chateaubriand is really a Romantic. This all changes with Auguste Brizeux (1803–1858), who first came to prominence in the early 1830s, and is the writer who is seldom mentioned without the qualification 'barde de la Bretagne', or some variation thereof. He was responsible for the dramatic entry of Brittany onto the literary scene in 1831, with his hugely successful volume of poetry *Marie*, addressed nostalgically, and in equal measure, to a childhood sweetheart and to a motherland. He was the first writer to stake his career on the description and discussion of Brittany, setting himself up as 'barde' and 'chantre de la Bretagne'. What makes Brizeux different from the earlier participants in the invention of Brittany is that he was in active pursuit of 'Bretonness'. He is important not only because of this level of commitment, but also because it gained him success, even if this was short-lived. Today he has ceased to warrant an entry in the *Oxford Companion to Literature in French*,[54] and his works are out of print,

---

54   In the first edition, by Paul Harvey and J. E. Heseltine (Oxford: Clarendon Press, 1959) he had an entry in his own right, whereas in *The Oxford Companion to Literature in French*, ed. by Peter France (Oxford: Clarendon Press, 1995) he is only mentioned, briefly, under 'Brittany'. We could also trace his demise by looking at editions of *The Oxford Book of French Verse*; the 1908 edition, contains three Brizeux poems, but in 1957 there is only one.

despite a recent facsimile edition.[55] This is all the more surprising given the recent explosion in such publishing with authors such as Anatole Le Braz, not to mention La Villemarqué, being re-edited by small Breton publishing houses such as Coop Breizh, and Terre de Brume. His demise, though, suggests the extent to which Brizeux said something to the France of his day, and in fact conceals a huge influence that lasted a century. The *Histoire littéraire et culturelle de la Bretagne* stresses that he was a privileged reference point for generations of poets: 'Peu de poètes bretons qui, pendant tout un siècle, ne doivent le prendre pour modèle, le vénérer comme une idole. Pas un collégien qui ne sache de ses vers, par coeur'.[56] By far his most influential works were *Marie* and *Les Bretons*, two poetry collections in which he paints a portrait of Brittany that struck a chord with critics at the time and that dominated Francophone Breton writing for decades to come.

The most striking thing about Brizeux's Brittany is the landscape. We see nature in all its glory: flower-filled, fertile, and peaceful. Marie, the eponymous heroine is herself a flower: 'fleur de blé noir'. The men have the strength of nature: they are as strong as oak trees in 'Le chant du chêne' (OAB, III, 12),[57] and in 'Les lutteurs' (OAB, II, 63). Such comparisons are of course the very stuff of poetry, but Brizeux's emphasis on nature goes beyond the adoption of language and imagery traditional to poetry. The Bretons' harmonious relationship with their environment is admired, and such admiration derives from the Romantic enthusiasm for nature. However in the case of the *menhirs* scattered across the land, we are not just told that Bretons are 'solid like them', but these stones are made to overflow with meaning, to the extent that it becomes possible to converse with them (OAB, IV, 73, 89). The people and their environment are one, as the stones take on human characteristics. This is a neat variation on

55   Auguste Brizeux, *Marie*, présenté par Joseph Rio (Quimperlé: La Digitale, 1980), facsimile of 1853 edition. *Marie* is available at www.gallica.fr.

56   Jacqes Vier, 'Le romantisme en Bretagne: dans le sillage des maîtres', in *Histoire littéraire et culturelle de la Bretagne*, II, 79–102 (97).

57   Unless stated otherwise page references are to *Œuvres de Auguste Brizeux*, ed. by Auguste Dorchain, 4 vols (Paris: Garnier Frères, 1910), hereafter abbreviated as OAB, and given in the text.

the idea that the Breton people have been formed and shaped by, or even seem to have grown out of their physical setting. This theme can be traced to Mme de Staël, who was responsible for popularizing the idea that there is a fundamental difference between the literatures of the north and the south, which can be explained in terms of climate and terrain. This idea had been applied to Brittany by a number of influential historians such as Jules Michelet, and Amédée Thierry, and is also found in the travel writing of Cambry, and of Taylor, Cailleux and Nodier. For instance, in the words of the *Voyages pittoresques*: 'C'est un sol de rochers, c'est une race de granit' (I, 4). This was further strengthened in Balzac by his appetite for the natural sciences, and he uses it to stress primitiveness, be this in a negative sense as in *Les Chouans*, or with admiration as in the case of the Breton family in *Béatrix*. Brizeux's emphasis on harmony with the environment has a different purpose, as he wishes to appeal to the Romantic love of natural scenes, untainted by city life. These scenes need not be empty and untouched by humans, because these pure people live in accordance with nature, and in that sense they do not live in the idyll, rather they actually constitute it. Brizeux's human Bretons are as natural as a buckwheat flower or an oak tree.

The Romantic hero of *Marie* is frequently moved to tears:

> [...] Sentant mon cœur se fondre,
> J'essuyais à l'écart mes pleurs pour lui répondre
> ('A ma mère', OAB, I, 8),

particularly during solitary walks:

> Je revis mon pays et ses genêts en fleurs,
> Lorsque, sur le chemin, un vieux pâtre celtique
> Me donna le bonjour dans son langage antique,
> [...]
> Je me voyais enfant, heureux comme autrefois,
> Et, malgré moi, *mes pleurs étouffèrent ma voix*.
> ('Marie', OAB, I, 22, my emphasis).

These descriptions might seem to be less about Brittany than about introspection, and the local colour provided by them might seem incidental to the Romantic project of exploring personal feelings of nostalgia. Evidence of Brizeux's Romantic ambitions is found in the concessions made in *Marie* to the literary conventions of the day. For instance, Brizeux's glorification of the Breton milieu of his childhood, before Renan's more famous treatment in the *Souvenirs d'enfance et de jeunesse* (1883), reflects the Romantic valorization of childhood. Similarly his love for the 'patrie' is explained by an idea popular with Romantic thinkers, that 'l'enfance renferme le vieillard' ('Les Batelières de l'Odet', OAB, I, 88). On the other hand, we are informed by Brizeux's contemporaries that Marie was real, and that the descriptions of her are truthful. However, the mere fact that she existed does not prove that Brizeux's project was 'genuine' or 'naïve', indeed the small changes that he made to 'the facts' in the poeticized version of the story themselves suggest even more clearly that he had a literary agenda. For instance pretending to be fifteen – 'l'âge canonique de l'amour', his editor Dorchain points out (OAB, I, xxv) – rather than thirteen, when he falls in love with Marie suggests that he is manipulating his material in order to fulfil literary expectations. Also the removal of all the poems devoted to a Parisian love from later editions of *Marie* has the effect of purifying the collection in order to conjure up a chaste Brittany in accordance with the stereotype (OAB, I, 253).

The influence of travel writing is heavy on *Les Bretons*, Brizeux's second collection, where he uses the idea of a journey as a framework to enable him to conduct a survey of the country's features. The collection opens with a journey from Paris, to show what would strike a traveller moving westwards. The first two Bretons that we meet are old men, busy reminiscing ('Les Quêteurs', OAB, II, 20), next Breton women are commended for their similarity to nuns ('Les Noces de Nona', OAB, II, 29), and the portrait of the community as a whole comes up to the high standards of Rousseau's idealized Clarens in *Julie ou La Nouvelle Héloïse* ('Les Quêteurs', OAB, II, 20).

We then meet Loïc and Anna, the two main characters whose fate we are to follow. An account of Loïc's early years allows Brizeux to dwell on the importance of religion and superstition among the people, as we are told of the way he was saved as a baby by being dipped into a sacred well by his mother. This episode is immediately followed by a reminder of the grandeur and cruelty of nature, in the form of a storm at sea ('Le Chasse-Marée', OAB, II, 68). He describes the storm in terms of its 'beautés sauvages', a collocation that is key to images of Brittany in the French imagination, and he then makes this storm serve a structural purpose in the book, as it forces the two survivors to embark on a *tro Breiz*, or a pilgrimage around their country. This traditional 'tro' around Brittany is a device to describe the country in all its variety. The travellers are made to point out regional differences in language and costume, and to stress the importance to their culture of story-telling, or 'veillées' ('La Nuit des morts', OAB, II, 142), amongst other customs and superstitions. Everyone gets a mention, from the 'Ankou', (in 'La Charrette-de-la-Mort', OAB, II, 119), and the 'Barde' (in 'La Nuit des morts', OAB, II, 142), to the homesick conscripts (in 'Les Conscrits', OAB, II, 158), and the weavers (in 'Les Fileuses', OAB, II, 166), and we even witness a traditional wedding (in 'Les Noces', OAB, II, 193).

Brizeux is at pains to describe ordinary people, who live in the real Brittany of the 1830s and 1840s, rather than conjure up historical or mythological heroes from the past. These individuals are only called on when Brizeux wants to stress the importance of the 'veillée', or storytelling and superstition generally in the lives of Bretons. The effect of this emphasis and the exhaustive detail is that *Les Bretons*, in particular, provides an encyclopaedic account of life in Lower Brittany. It seems that Brizeux may have imagined his role to be something like that of Mérimée, who was sent to Brittany on behalf of the French government to record details of any remains or ancient buildings before they disappeared in the name of 'modernization'. Brizeux's conservationist tone make his project seem surprisingly similar at times: 'Quand l'éternel oubli recouvre tant de races,/ Mon peuple dans mes vers aura-t-il quelques traces?' (*Les Bretons*, OAB, II, 193).

In a later work, which uses the similar framework of a 'friend' arriving from Paris to visit a Breton village, Brizeux describes the friend's experience thus: 'Il avait devant lui le monde primitif' ('Journal Rustique: Une visite', *Histoires poétiques*, OAB, IV, 80). In other words a Breton scene is like living history, more specifically France's ancient history which has survived. This explains why Brizeux notes all activities and characteristics so carefully, and why this was of such interest to the French readership. These are not individuals but historical types, as there was no need to discuss past heroes given that seeing Bretons of the day was just like stepping back through the centuries. Fundamentally Brizeux's work shares the attitude of the Académie celtique:

> ...et si tu dois mourir,
> Vois avec quel amour j'épanche de ma verve
> Ce miel de poésie, Arvor, qui te conserve:
> Comme autour de ton corps je construis un tombeau. ('Le Convoi du fermier', *Les Bretons*, OAB, II, 127)

The poetry becomes an elegy. Just as the Académie celtique questionnaire was only interested in France's colourful past because it was safely in the past, the way Brizeux writes here is directly appealing to a modern France that admits 'difference' on condition that it is dying. It is because of this underlying attitude that Brizeux has been rejected by Breton nationalists, and is today all but forgotten. The huge success that he once had however, and his subsequent influence, mean that he must not be written out of histories of Breton literatures. A closer look at the context in which he worked will allow us to better understand the choices that he made.

His choice of the French language for his main works is responsible for his dismissal by many, as this is taken as evidence of questionable motivation. Given that he was capable of writing in Breton (and indeed does so at a later point in his career), why did Brizeux write in a language that was foreign to most of his own people? Brizeux does not seem embarrassed about writing across his fellow Bretons, indeed he addresses this issue in the opening poem of *Marie*, where the heroine is introduced not by name, but, perversely, by a clause which tells of the book's irrelevance to her: 'Celle pour qui j'écris avec amour ce livre/ Ne le lira jamais', (OAB, I, 4), for she knows no French. Brizeux goes so far as to build the role of interpreter into his poetic scenario, when he imagines the monoglot Marie being told of the poetry she has inspired:

> Pourtant je veux poursuivre; et quelque ami peut-être,
> Resté dans nos forêts et venant à connaître

> Ce livre où son beau temps tout joyeux renaîtra,
> Dans une fête, un jour, en dansant lui dira
> Cette histoire qu'ici j'ai commencé d'écrire (OAB, I, 5).

The poetry's addressee is thus excluded from its readership, and with her the 'patrie' that she incarnates, for 'Ses yeux n'y trouveraient qu'une langue étrangère' (OAB, I, 5). In excluding the very people it purports to be about, this poetry has an eye on the tastes and fashions of Paris. Indeed, I shall argue that the success of *Marie* is explained by the fact that it was written across 'Marie', across Brittany, and *to* a Paris that was in some sense searching for a Breton poet.

To be fair to Brizeux, the language choice is something of a false issue. Jean Le Dû and Yves Le Berre, in a survey of Breton literature in the nineteenth century, have written of the sterility of the Breton-language literary milieu.[58] The state of cultural life in Brittany at the time meant that Brizeux was faced with a choice between French Romanticism and a 'fabricated' genuine Breton tradition which either admitted to itself that it was a recreation, or used folk or oral literature as a remnant or a pointer towards authenticity. In a sense La Ville-marqué is the one who made the right choice, because he is more remembered today, though perhaps for the wrong reasons. La Ville-marqué – Brizeux's rival for the position of poet of Brittany – took this alternative path, which was in its own way just as much aimed at the capital.[59] Also, in Brizeux's defence, his attitude towards the Breton language is far from typical of his day. Mérimée wrote to a friend in Provence that Breton was an ugly language, the language of the devil, and admitted that he had tried to get revenge on Brittany in his official report for the government because La Villemarqué had accused him of stealing a manuscript. Auguste Romieu, the sous-

---

58   'Un siècle d'écrits en langue bretonne: 1790–1892', in *Histoire littéraire et culturelle de la Bretagne*, II, 251–91.

59   'Nul ne soutient plus que le *Barzaz Breiz* est une œuvre *populaire*. Le recueil s'adressait au monde lettré de la capitale: le peuple bretonnant, celui qui parle quotidiennement breton, l'a dans son ensemble ignoré ou lui a préféré les versions moins policées que lui transmettait une robuste tradition', Donatien Laurent, 'Savoir et mémoire du peuple: Introduction', in *Histoire littéraire et culturelle*, II, 247–49 (249).

préfet of Quimperlé, argued in the *Revue de Paris* that the old Celtic language had restricted the Breton people, and prevented them from becoming part of the modern world.[60] Romieu's answer to the problem was to get rid of the language, through what he calls a 'régime colonial'.

While administrators were busy plotting the eradication of the language, Brizeux was lamenting its decline. Once he was established as a writer, he actually published in Breton: *Barzonek pe kanaouen ar Vretoned* (Quimper/Morlaix, 1836), *Telen Arvor: la harpe d'Armorique* (Paris: Duverger, 1839), *Furnez Breiz: Sagesse de Bretagne* (Lorient: Gousset, 1855).[61] Also it was he who made sure that the new edition of Le Gonidec's *Grammaire Celto-Bretonne* went to press after his friend's death. The ailing Le Gonidec himself named Brizeux, along with La Villemarqué, as a possible heir:

> Je crois vous faire plaisir en mettant en rapport avec vous deux messieurs de mes amis qui s'occupent avec beaucoup de zèle de la langue bretonne; l'un (M. Hersart de La Villemarqué), est un antiquaire très-studieux, l'autre, (M. Brizeux), est un poète aimable. Je leur ai donné votre adresse. Si je suis mis hors d'état de travailler pour notre littérature Bretonne, j'aurais le plaisir au moins de voir les jeunes gens s'y adonner avec fruit.[62]

It is also clear from a piece like 'Aux prêtres de Bretagne' (1840) that he is prepared to condemn the church for failing to show sufficient respect for the language, and says that the place of the language in the education system worries him.[63] Nonetheless, he does exploit the

---

60   'Tant que le vieux langage des Celtes confinera les paysans dans le cercle féodal que l'ancien seigneur et le curé ne leur permettent pas de franchir, il vous sera impossible de modifier la pensée de ces hommes, parce qu'il vous sera impossible la connaître.' Auguste Romieu, 'La Basse-Bretagne, ses mœurs, son langage et ses monuments', *Revue de Paris*, 30 (1831), 155–67 (153).

61   For further details of his Breton-language publications see Georges Mahé, 'Essai de bibliographie des œuvres bretonnes de Brizeux', *Cahiers d'Iroise*, 21 (1974), 214–20.

62   Letter to Thomas Price (Carnhuanawc), cited in Jane Williams 'Ysgafell', *Literary Remains of the Rev. Thomas Price, Carnhuanawc, Vicar of Cwmdû, Breconshire; and Rural Dean*, 2 vols (Llandovery: William Rees, 1854–55), II, 167–79.

63   Auguste Brizeux, *Aux Prêtres de Bretagne* (Paris: Dentu, 1840).

Breton language for Romantic purposes. Sometimes it is there merely as an item in what seems to be an inventory of Brittany, at other times it is mentioned for sentimental effect, as when 'celtique' is rather conveniently rhymed with 'antique'. Hearing the language moves him profoundly:

> ...un vieux pâtre celtique,
> Me donna le bonjour dans son langage antique
> [...]
> Et malgré moi, mes pleurs étouffèrent ma voix! ('Marie', *Marie*, OAB, I, 22).

The fact that he can speak Breton is also important to his project in another way. In his preface to *Marie* he claims that it is not possible to write reliably about Brittany without an understanding of the Breton people's language. In his narrative poems he describes himself talking to Bretons as a way of proving the authenticity of his descriptions of their lives, and he has no worries at all about the complex process of translating the experiences of one culture into the language of another. The language, then, is something that assists his research, and his knowledge of it is proof of the authenticity of his portrait.

More telling even than his language choice is the way he negotiates the world of Parisian tastes, and we might speculate that he turned to write about Brittany because it was 'fashionable'. Brizeux's first publications, a play called *Racine*, and a memoir novel *Mme de Lavallière*,[64] fell flat, and it was only after turning to writing about Brittany that he succeeded in attracting the attention of key critics. The trajectory of those provincial writers who failed in the Parisian mainstream suggests quite how fashionable Breton material was. As fellow-Breton Souvestre knew only too well, having strategically-placed friends in the capital helped,[65] but so too did transforming

---

64   A. Brizeux et P. Busoni, *Racine: Comédie en un acte et en vers* (Paris: Barba, 1828), first performed 27 December 1827. Auguste Brizeux, *Mémoires de Madame de La Vallière*, vol 2 of *Mémoires secrets et inédits sur les cours de France aux XVe, XVIe, et XVIIIe siècles* (Paris: Mame et Delaunay-Vallée, 1829).

65   In the opening pages of his seminal work *Les Derniers Bretons* Émile Souvestre recounts how he had no success with his manuscript play until enlisting the help of an influential Breton based in Paris, named Duval, though even then he is not

oneself into the poet of a particular region.[66] Even La Villemarqué's case suggests this, for instance Tanguy portrays a La Villemarqué who is converted to Brittany while in Paris, shortly after obtaining his bac.[67] Chapman is rather harsher in his telling of the same tale in *The Celts*.[68] Given that Paris was attracting ambitious artists from all parts of Europe at this time, it is hardly surprising that Paris salons were also the place to be as far as France's own provincial cultures were concerned. In any case, as Per Denez has put it: 'It is well known that Paris is the biggest Breton town in the world'.[69] The idea of Paris as 'capitale du monde' was already a cliché from the late eighteenth century, and the lure of the capital becomes an obsessive theme for the heroes of Balzac, Stendhal and Flaubert.[70] Going to Paris was inescapable. Centralization in France had increased under Napoleon, and by the 1830s it was felt to be oppressive. Tanguy goes over this

---

successful enough to stay in the capital: 'il y avait à soutenir un duel éternel pour lequel il fallait un caractère de fer ouaté de coton. Je compris que je n'étais point né pour une pareille existence', *Les Derniers Bretons*, 2 vols, ed. by Dominique Besançon (Rennes: Terre de Brume, 1997), p.31, first published in book form in 1836. La Villemarqué accuses him of packaging his descriptions to please the *Revue des Deux Mondes*, see 'La Renaissance bretonne', epilogue to *La Bretagne contemporaine: sites pittoresques, monuments, costumes, scènes de mœurs, histoire, légendes, traditions et usages des cinq départements de cette province* (Paris: Charpentier, 1865), p.5.

66 Anne-Marie Thiesse says: 'Ces littérateurs qui ont éprouvé durement leur provincialité se transforment peu à peu en écrivains de la province', *Écrire la France*, p.46. For a more detailed account see Catherine Bertho's comments on the young Bretons Souvestre, Brizeux, and La Villemarqué: 'Tous atteindront la notoriété à Paris en traitant de leur province d'origine. Certains d'ailleurs ne s'engagent dans cette voie qu'après avoir échoué dans les voies plus classiques de la réussite littéraire selon une trajectoire personnelle caractéristique, semble-t-il, des auteurs de romans rustiques et régionalistes dans leur ensemble', in 'L'invention de la Bretagne', p.58. For the suggestion that Hélias similarly chose to be a big fish in a small pond see Jean-Christophe Cassard, 'Comment peut-on être Pierre-Jakez Hélias?', *Le Peuple Breton*, 328 (April 1991), pp.21, 24, and also Xavier Grall, *Le Cheval couché*.

67 Tanguy, *Aux origines*, I, 35.

68 *The Celts*, p.138.

69 'Modern Breton Literature', in *Literature in Celtic Countries*, p.117.

70 See Christopher Prendergast, *Paris and the Nineteenth Century* (Oxford: Blackwell, 1996), esp. p.6.

ground, showing how even Victor Hugo felt that the young generation should not be forced to go to Paris.[71]

We can be certain, though, that Brizeux was aware that Brittany was popular, so much so that when his second collection *Les Bretons* was in preparation he feared that somebody might come along and steal his thunder. He asks Buloz, editor of the *Revue des Deux Mondes*, to advertize *Les Bretons* prior to its appearance, just in case somebody else gets there first.[72] This suggests not so much that people wanted to copy Brizeux because he was so original, as that Brizeux had chosen something obvious and fashionable by concentrating on Brittany. The importance of the *RDM* in Brizeux's story cannot be underestimated. Buloz, its editor, had met Brizeux, and was keen to promote *Marie* perhaps as a favour to his school friend Auguste Auffray, who had published it.[73] The importance of Sainte-Beuve, who took care of the poetry criticism for the *Revue des Deux Mondes*, is even greater. La Villemarqué too, and even Baudelaire, was keen to work to keep the powerful critic favourable to him.[74] If *Marie* went through several editions,[75] it is in large part thanks to Sainte-Beuve's 'coup de trompette'.[76]

---

71   Tanguy, *Aux origines*, I, 433–34.

72   Cited in Marie-Louise Pailleron, *François Buloz et ses amis: la vie littéraire sous Louis Philippe* (Paris: Firmin-Didot, 1930), p.122.

73   See Nelly Furman, *La Revue des Deux Mondes et le Romantisme (1831–1848)* (Geneva: Droz, 1975), p.66.

74   For instance, Baudelaire claimed that *Joseph Delorme* had pointed the way to *Les Fleurs du Mal*, see Rosemary Lloyd, *Baudelaire's World* (Ithaca: Cornell University Press, 2002), p.128, and Norman Barlow, *Sainte-Beuve to Baudelaire* (Durham, N.C.: Duke University Press, 1964).

75   *Marie: roman* (Paris: Auguste Auffray et Urbain Canel, 1832) [in fact published anonymously in 1831]; *Marie: poème* (Paris: Paulin et Eugène Renduel, 1836); *Marie, poème*, par Auguste Brizeux (Bruxelles: Sociéte Belge de Librairie, Hausnan, Cattois et Cie, 1837); on this and other unauthorized editions see René Maurice, 'Autour d'un Brizeux ignoré', *Cahiers d'Iroise*, 15 (1968), 145–53; *Marie*, par Auguste Brizeux, 3rd edn (Paris: Paul Masgana, 1840); *Marie - La Fleur d'or - Primel et Nola* (Paris: Garnier Frères, 1853).

76   When Sainte-Beuve comments on the work to be included in his five-volume *Portraits contemporains* of 1855, he says of his work on Brizeux and Barbier: 'C'étaient à proprement parler des articles d'annonce. Le coup de trompette y

But fashion can be fickle, as both Brizeux and La Villemarqué were to discover. It is easy to forget, as he is so well remembered compared to Brizeux, that La Villemarqué initially encountered problems when he attempted to publish his work. The *Barzaz Breiz* had to be published at the author's expense because the Comité Historique were fearful of endorsing a 'second Macpherson'.[77] In a passage from the preface La Villemarqué sensibly packages his subject matter as 'French', or necessarily of French interest:

> Il ne s'agit donc pas ici d'un intérêt purement local, mais bien d'un intérêt français; car l'histoire de la Bretagne a toujours été mêlée à celle de la France, et la France est aussi celtique par le cœur que l'Armorique est française aujourd'hui sous le drapeau commun.[78]

Earlier La Villemarqué's article 'Un débris du bardisme' had been refused by Buloz at the *Revue des Deux Mondes* on the grounds that the subject-matter was too obscure for his readership, and as a result La Villemarqué had to fall back on the *Écho de la Jeune-France*, finally publishing his piece on 15 March 1836.

La Villemarqué's failure to interest the *Revue des Deux Mondes* in Breton material makes the success of Brizeux all the more interesting.[79] Writers had to tread a tightrope, providing a certain degree of exoticism, or newness, while guarding against any real alienation that the French reader might feel. There are some hints that Brizeux was aware of the need to tread carefully. For instance the absence of all references to Ossian in his mature work is significant, if not strategic, given that his travel account from Venice in 1832, 'Une Ombre', indicates that he was a fan of both Walter Scott and Ossian. He recounts seeing the former in Venice:

---

domine', *Portraits contemporains*, II, 222, cited in Nelly Furman, *La Revue des Deux Mondes et le Romantisme*, p.65.

77   See Mary-Ann Constantine, *Breton Ballads*, p.13.

78   Théodore Hersart de la Villemarqué, *Le Barzazh Breizh: Trésor de la littérature orale de la Bretagne* (Spézet: Coop Breizh, 1997), p.36.

79   For an account of La Villemarqué's interaction with Sainte-Beuve, see Tanguy, *Aux origines*, I, 56.

un Anglais se découvrit et cria: 'Dieu vous garde, Sir Walter!' Comme un éclair, ce pieux salut dirigea mes yeux sur le front du noble barde. Hélas! Je pus les voir, ses traits souffrants et amaigris! Fantôme d'Ossian égaré sous le ciel bleu de Naples![80]

Paul Van Tieghem in his two-volume study *Ossian en France*, hints that this silence might be strategic: 'Brizeux, le Breton bretonnant, le chantre des celtes et de leurs traditions, ou ne connaît pas Ossian, ou le connaît trop bien et s'en défie'.[81]

Faced with this situation Brizeux attempts to present his own project as a break with earlier writing, claiming that he will be the first to truly paint a picture of Brittany: 'Bienheureux mon pays [...]/ Et qu'avec tant d'amour le premier j'ai chanté ('Le Retour', OAB, I, 107). As he will be the first to offer a reliable and authentic version:

> Le lieu où sont placées les douze idylles ou élégies qui donnent leur nom à ce livre ne se recommande ni par l'éclat des costumes, d'ordinaire si riches en Bretagne, ni par le dialecte pur de ses habitants. La partie méridionale du pays est même fort aride et sèche: ce ne sont que des bruyères et des landes, quelques ifs épars le long des fossés, ou de grosses pierres blanches lourdement couchées sur le sol. [...]
>
> Bien peu de gens ont des idées exactes sur la Bretagne. Pour apprécier les peuples simples, il faut avoir été élevé parmi eux, de bonne heure avoir parlé leur langue, s'être assis à leur table: alors se découvrent leur poésie intime et cachée, et la grâce native de leurs mœurs. (Preface to *Marie*, OAB, I, 1–2)

---

80   'Une Ombre: fragment d'un livre de voyage', *Revue de Paris*, series 4, vol 3 (1842), p.132, reprinted in OAB, IV, 365–74. Commentators have debated whether he had in fact read Ossian; see, for instance, A. Lexandre [pseudonym of Alexandre Tisseur], *Un Pèlerinage au pays de Brizeux: La Bretagne et son poète* (Paris: Dentu, 1879), p.60.

81   *Ossian en France*, 2 vols (Paris: Rieder, 1917), II, 354. This would not be surprising; Tanguy in *Aux origines* makes a similar point in telling how Macpherson had fallen in prestige by 1828: 'Que le succès croissant depuis 1820 de Walter Scott ait contribué à cette éclipse est indéniable. *Mais il n'est pas douteux non plus qu'Ossian est souvent ignoré de propos délibéré*' (I, 74, my emphasis). Similarly Brizeux steers clear of references to the folk-song collection projects that were underway in Brittany, thus clearly marking out the difference between himself and the other putative 'poet of Brittany', La Villemarqué.

70

This claim, in the preface to *Marie*, though something of a rhetorical stance, presents the collection as a new departure. In stressing his privileged vantage point it implicitly criticizes previous representations for their emphasis on the picturesque. Echoes of the vocabulary of earlier representations of Brittany betray a wish to challenge these. For instance Brizeux's claim that the picture he is about to paint will not concern itself with 'l'éclat des costumes...', recalls the opening page of Balzac's *Les Chouans*, where the ostensible bizarreness of Breton costume is stressed: '...une collection de costumes si bizarres et une réunion d'individus appartenant à des localités ou à des professions si diverses,' as a prelude to a description of peasants clad in goat hide, who can barely be distinguished from a state of animality.

It is difficult to believe his claims of authenticity if he was nevertheless writing to please Parisians' tastes. We have already identified some debts to mainstream Romanticism in terms of thematic influences, but a more clearly documented instance of Brizeux 'writing to Paris' is provided by his interaction with Sainte-Beuve, who had a direct and specific effect on the representation of Brittany that he finally produced. Orthographical changes made by Brizeux with each new edition of *Marie* provide clear evidence of a desire for packaging that would please the French eye. In fact the bully behind the changes was Sainte-Beuve, who, regretting the Breton spellings in the second edition, dismisses these, in print, as evidence of opportunism:

> le caractère breton prit le dessus, mais d'une façon un peu affichée. Tous les noms de bourgs, de fleuves et de montagnes, qui d'abord étaient à la française, revêtirent l'orthographe celtique, et purent paraître bizarres, d'harmonieux qu'ils étaient. C'est que dans l'intervalle l'auteur, comprenant quel parti il y avait poétiquement à tirer de cette contrée bretonne où un simple retour de cœur l'avait porté au début, s'y était enfoncé avec une sorte d'amour sauvage et d'ivresse impétueuse.[82]

---

82   Sainte-Beuve, 'Poètes et romanciers modernes de la France. XLV M. Brizeux (Les Ternaires, Livre Lyrique [Masgana])', *Revue des Deux Mondes*, 4: 3 (1841), 779–90 (782–83).

Needless to say, Sainte-Beuve approves of the re-Gallicization of the spelling in the third edition, describing this version as 'la perfection même'. Tanguy suggests that it was Brizeux's meeting with Le Gonidec, translator of the Bible into Breton, that prompted him to 'Bretonize' his work.

To take this a step further, we might even accuse Brizeux of being a fake, and of being in that sense no better than the La Villemarqué portrayed by Gourvil, or than Botrel, who invents himself as a 'barde', right down to the costume, and the learning of a smattering of Breton words. This was after all the age of hoaxes, the most famous example being *Ossian*. He was supposedly an ancient Gaelic bard, whose work was discovered in the eighteenth century by a Scot named Macpherson. Despite the fact that it was more exaggeration than truth, it captured the Romantic imagination, and its popularity spread through its influence on Goethe's *Die Leiden des jungen Werthers*, and on Chateaubriand, and endorsement by Napoleon, who was painted by Girodet in *Ossian Receiving Napoleon's Generals*; in short, it was at the core of European Romanticism. Its paradoxical success is nicely summed up by Malcolm Chapman: 'Macpherson's Ossian was largely inauthentic with respect to any genuine Gaelic verse tradition, but it was the very voice of authenticity for the developing sentiments of Romanticism in Europe'.[83]

Some people did accuse Brizeux of opportunism or even fakery in his day. Gourvil describes his language as fake, or as 'pseudo-léonais', and dismisses his claim to Bretonness: 'C'est à Paris, et non à Lorient ou à Scaër qu'il devint auteur bretonnant.'[84] An anecdote from 1832 shows how Brizeux may indeed have invented himself, in this spirit. In this year the young poet, fresh from a trip to Italy, invested in some new clothes. He bought 'ar braghou, ar chupen glaz, ar chupen gwenn, ar gilet gwenn, ar bodreo, ann tok', ready for his trip to Scaër. His aim was to blend in, but according to Tiercelin, who tells the story in *Bretons de lettres*, his efforts were wasted on the

---

83   Malcolm Chapman, *The Gaelic Vision*, p.42.

84   Francis Gourvil, *Théodore-Claude-Henri Hersart de La Villemarqué (1815–1895) et le 'Barzaz Breiz' (1839–1845–1867): origines, éditions, sources, critique, influences* (Rennes: Impr. Oberthur, 1959 [i.e. 1960]), p.27.

locals as they nicknamed him 'paôtr Paris' on account of his strange behaviour, working late into the night and rising even later.[85]

Be that as it may, a closer look reveals more subtle opportunism, such as his flirtation with the figure of the 'barde'. Its poetic nature is probably the most enduring cliché about Brittany; the language is poetic, the people are poetic, the landscape poetic. The authors of the *Voyages pittoresques et romantiques dans l'ancienne France*, Taylor, Nodier, and Cailleux, had stressed that the oral poetry heard in Brittany belonged to an unbroken tradition. Cambry could not resist digressions into the history of poetry in the middle of his descriptions of landscapes and scenery, and had claimed that poetry was the only medium of communication between lovers, because, as he argued,

> La poésie naquit avant la prose; elle est l'expression ardente des émotions de terreur, d'étonnement, d'admiration ou d'amour, que l'homme de la nature éprouve avec un sentiment plus vif que l'homme civilisé.[86]

Brizeux is happy to use the label 'barde' of himself, for example in 'Écrit en voyage' (OAB, I, 100), and again in 'Le Retour' (OAB, I, 107). He also uses the word to describe Walter Scott ('Une ombre' OAB, IV, 365–74), as well as for various other characters in his poems, but he is careful not to be arrogant, and so describes himself as a mere modern version:

> Où superbe il marchait, humble je me hasarde,
> Où sa harpe éclatait, mon cœur chante tous bas
> ('Journal rustique: de retour à Ker-Barz', OAB, IV, 85)

His rejection of the word 'poète' suggests that 'barde' offered some advantages. The fact that La Villemarqué changes the name of his collection from *Chants populaires de la Bretagne-Armorique*, or *Chants populaires de la Bretagne* to *Barzaz Breiz*, confirms this.[87] La Villemarqué was also happy to use the name 'barde' of

---

85   Details in Tiercelin, *Bretons de lettres* (Paris: Champion, 1905), p.265.

86   Cambry, *Voyage dans le Finistère*, pp.98–9.

87   When La Villemarqué first wrote to the ministre de l'Instruction publique, Salvandy, about his proposed publication, which he calls *Chants populaires de la Bretagne-Armorique*, he is rejected. He changed the title to *Chants*

himself. The first contact between him and Sainte-Beuve was in 1836 when Sainte-Beuve had come to rent a place in the same apartment block as La Villemarqué. Sainte-Beuve's aim was to be able to write in peace under the *nom de plume* Charles Delorme, and so cannot have been overjoyed when La Villemarqué pushed a piece of his own work under the door, a poem ending with the line: 'Ouvrez au barde bas breton!'.[88] La Villemarqué uses the word for Brizeux too, or to be more precise, calls him: 'Cher Prince des Bardes bretons'.

In La Villemarqué's case it is evident from his research work that he had a real interest in ancient bards. It is not so clear whether the role of 'barde' was more than a vague idea for Brizeux, or for his readers at the time. Given that things Celtic had enjoyed a period of unequalled fashionable status in the nineteenth century it comes as no surprise to find the word 'barde' in poems by Lamartine and Musset. This example is from Sainte-Beuve's novel *Volupté*, published in 1834, and thus contemporary with his articles on Brizeux in the *Reveu des Deux Mondes*:

> Arthur *notre jeune barde*, [...] je le trouvai sur la montagne, assis seul et les yeux en larmes vers la mer, sans qu'il me pût expliquer comment ni pourquoi il était là.[89]

Perhaps this was the ideal 'barde', and also what Sainte-Beuve wanted to see in Brizeux. Brizeux certainly seems to have recognized something of himself in Sainte-Beuve's fictional creations, or at least this is the burden of a poem sent by Brizeux to Sainte-Beuve with the following comments:

> Mais quels livres sont les vôtres, mon cher Sainte-Beuve!... *Volupté* a été plus forte que l'unité paisible de cette terre qui déjà me dominait, et j'ai retrouvé en

---

populaires de la Bretagne when it was published, at his own expense, in August 1839. Guiomar suggests that it was his trip to Wales that was responsible for the change to *Barzaz Breiz*, see 'Quand les bretonistes répudièrent la Gaule (1840–1850)', p.197.

88   See Sainte-Beuve, *Correspondance générale*, ed. by Jean Bonnerot, 15 vols (Paris: Didier, 1966), II, 60–1.

89   Author's emphasis. *Volupté* (Paris: Charpentier, 1919), p.252.

moi bien des choses qui s'allaient effacer. Un jour, je me réserve d'écrire tout ce que je pense d'un tel Traité de l'âme, mais à vous même je n'oserais. A vous je n'envoie que l'assurace d'une amitié bien vive et toute dévouée. [...]

> A DEUX MORTS
> Oh! Delorme, Amaury, qui d'un monde hideux,
> Voyageurs égarés, êtes sortis tous deux,
> L'un étreignant sa vie au creux de la vallée,
> L'autre enfermant au cloître une âme désolée,
> Mais tous deux expirant d'une si douce voix
> Que ma triste Armorique en agita ses bois:
> Oh! s'il est loin du monde un lieu sûr où l'on dorme,
> Dites-nous, Amaury, dites, Joseph Delorme,
> Où le lit est meilleur et le sommeil plus long!
> Est-ce à l'ombre du cloître? est-ce au creux du vallon?
> (Dans une lande.)[90]

Lamartine's use of the word 'barde' in 1835 is more exotic still, as his 'barde' actually sings in Arabic: 'des vers arabes'.[91] This suggests that 'barde' had lost its Celtic connotations for a while, or at least that the word had gained new meanings with Romanticism, and its taste for other cultures. Closer scrutiny of its use reveals that the word has evolved beyond its Celtic origin. A comparison of different editions of the *Dictionnaire de l'Académie française* will help us to understand its development. The word 'barde' is absent from the first edition of 1694. By 1798 we are informed that 'barde' means: 'poète chez les anciens Celtes', and the only reference to the present is an example given of how to use the word: 'Le célèbre Barde Ossian'. By the time of 'Celtomanie' in the 1835 edition, the dictionary's definition adds: 'Il se dit quelquefois, par extension, d'un poète héroïque et lyrique'. However, today's edition warns us that this meaning is 'rare'. It seems that something had changed in the first half of the nineteenth century. Although Lamartine, George Sand, and Sainte-Beuve were surely aware of the word's Celtic origin, more often than

---

90   Letter to Sainte-Beuve, 21 March 1835, cited in Sainte-Beuve, *Volupté*, pp.39–40.

91   'Jéricho', in *Souvenirs, impressions, pensées et paysages, pendant un voyage en Orient (1832–1833): ou, Notes d'un voyager* (Paris C. Gosselin, 1835), p.70. Cited in FRANTEXT.

not in their work it is used to mean 'Romantic poet', or even something along the lines of: 'young man who likes fleeing to nature to ponder God, life, the Universe'.

It is at least possible that Brizeux believed wholeheartedly that writing in a way that fitted Paris fashions was the best was of serving Brittany. It does not seem to have prevented him from also writing for his own people. He claims that Bretons sing his songs in public, and that he is welcomed home by people singing his poems, filling the village with song:

> Clairement imprimé sur une feuille blanche,
> Le chant par tout le bourg circulait, et cent voix,
> Ferventes, l'entonnaient aux marches de la croix
> ('Prières des laboureurs', *Histoires poétiques*, OAB, III, 270).

The people consider him one of their own, he insists, in 'Voix amies' ('Journal rustique', *Histoires poétiques*, OAB, IV, 162), and he is fond of adding that everybody knows his poems by heart. Although several of his poems describe the way he is perceived as a stranger when he returns to Brittany,[92] and despite the fact that it has also been argued that most Bretons did not know Brizeux during his lifetime,[93] it seems that he did make some contribution to cultural life in Brittany. For instance there is evidence that he sent a hundred copies of *Barzonek pe kanaouen ar Vretoned* to a book shop in Quimper in 1836 for distribution among 'colporteurs' and 'chanteurs de pardons', and there are similar stories about other works.[94] None the less Mona Ozouf's testimony in *L'École de la France* that the *Barzaz Breiz* is on the shelf in the family library, while there is no mention of Brizeux, sums up the relative status of Brizeux and his friend and rival La Villemarqué today.

---

92 These poems are additions to the 1836 edition of *Marie*, in *Œuvres de Auguste Brizeux*, ed. by Auguste Dorchain, 4 vols (Paris: Garnier Frères, 1910), for instance 'Le Chemin du pardon', I, 29, 'Rencontre sur Ar-Voden', I, 61.

93 'durant sa vie, son œuvre ne fut pas connue en Bretagne – hormis par un petit groupe de lettrés', René Maurice, 'Autour d'un Brizeux ignoré', p. 145.

94 See Georges Mahé, 'Essai de bibliographie des œuvres bretonnes de Brizeux', p.214.

Brizeux was caught between cultures in his attempt to make his mark in both simultaneously. His true inspiration is hinted at in a study of Brizeux's school books, by Maurice Souriau, who shows how central Virgil and Ovid were to Brizeux's early education. Brizeux translated passages from Virgil's *Georgics* and *Bucolics*, and part of Ovid's *Metamorphoses*, and was so well acquainted with the former that Souriau concludes: 'Sauf peut-être Victor Hugo, je ne connais pas de poète qui se soit uni plus intimement que Brizeux au génie de Virgile'.[95] According to his biographer Georges Mahé, his love of Virgil is the source of his ability to describe simplicity.[96] And according to his friend Auguste Barbier, in his autobiography, the greatest influences on Brizeux were La Fontaine, Racine and André Chenier, whose work he would constantly re-read. In Barbier's words, *Marie* was a rustic version of *Paul et Virginie*, Bernardin de Saint-Pierre's novel about innocence and closeness to nature.[97] Quite apart from this there is ample evidence, both thematic (nature, children, nostalgia) and lexical, that French Romanticism was the greatest influence of all. While ostensibly promoting his own rich cultural heritage as a Breton, he was heavily influenced by mainstream Romanticism. Analysis of Brizeux's output, and especially of the reception of his work in the capital, reveals that this Breton-born bilingual poet was packaging Brittany for a French market. This suggests that the French-reading public wanted to see in representations of Brittany a harmless, quaint exoticism, rather than any radical cultural difference or cultural autonomy.

With the benefit of analysis we can see Brizeux as an auto-ethnographic writer in the sense put forth by Mary Louise Pratt in *Imperial Eyes*:

> I use these terms [autoethnography, autoethnographic expression] to refer to instances in which colonized subjects undertake to represent themselves in ways that *engage with* the colonizer's own terms. If ethnographic texts are a

---

95   'Les cahiers d'écolier de Brizeux', in his *Moralistes et Poètes* (Paris: Vuibert et Nony, 1907), pp.197–225 (pp.205–6, 214).

96   *Brizeux: essai de Biographie (d'après des documents inédits* (Paris: Klincksieck, 1969), p.17.

97   *Souvenirs personnels et silhouettes contemporaines* (Paris: Dentu, 1883), p.235.

means by which Europeans represent to themselves their (usually subjugated) others, autoethnographic texts are those the others construct in response to or in dialogue with these metropolitan representations.[98]

One example from Brizeux will suffice: 'Tous jeunes paysans *aux costumes étranges,/* Portant de longs cheveux flottants, comme les anges' ('Marie', *OAB*, I, 19, my emphasis). He is quite aware that writing in French, with a Parisian audience in mind, makes him a stranger in his own land, but when he describes the clothes of his childhood classmates as 'costumes étranges' we must question his choice of adjective. Strange in whose eyes? – certainly not strange to somebody who was, as Brizeux claims elsewhere, 'élevé parmi eux'. It seems, therefore, that he is writing *as* a Parisian in order to appeal *to* Parisians. He seems to have imported not only Parisian lexis for descriptions of the countryside, but even their centralizing eyes for exoticism. He was practising self-invention in this way just as much as when he was donning the clothes of a Breton. Viewed in this light, his 'inventory' of Bretonness can be seen as sharing the attitude of the Académie celtique, and it is in this sense that he is seen by many Breton activists as harmful. However the issue of faking and authenticity is perhaps less interesting and informative for the purpose of exploring the 'invention' of Brittany than for what this tells us about contemporary attitudes and expectations. We can see through these how Brizeux bears a large part of the responsibility for the invention of the idea of Celticness, even if we would not go as far as the dictionary that gives Théodore Banville's eulogy for Brizeux as a definition of the word 'Celte': 'Dors, Celte aux cheveux blonds, honneur de la Cornouaille'.[99]

---

98 Mary Louise Pratt, *Imperial Eyes: Travel Writing and Transculturation* (London: Routldge, 1992), p.7.
99 Eulogy 'A Auguste Brizeux', of 1858, *Les Exilés* (Paris: Fasquelle, 1899), p.120.

Conclusion

How can the nineteenth century be a time when Brittany changed over from Breton to Francophone, but also a time when Bretonness was extremely fashionable? This is partly explained by the paradox identified by Thiesse in many of her works, and developed in her *Ils apprenaient la France*: that the affirmation of French national identity was arrived at *via* a celebration of local differences. The main organ was primary schools, where children were taught to love their 'petite patrie' as preparation for loving the 'grande', albeit through the medium of French. This acceptance of difference as long as it remained on the level of the picturesque was part of the nineteenth-century development of national identities. More generally, Thiesse lists comprehensively the elements required for this development:

> La liste des éléments que doit posséder une nation digne de ce nom est aujourd'hui bien établie: des ancêtres fondateurs, une histoire établissant la continuité de la nation à travers les vicissitudes de l'histoire, une galerie de héros, une langue, des monuments culturels et historiques, des lieux de mémoire, un paysage typique, un folklore, sans compter quelques identifications pittoresques: costume, gastronomie, animal emblématique.[100]

As we have seen, Balzac does not present a stable version of Brittany, rather his portraits contradict each other. Contained within one œuvre is the whole range of representations, and the question is where to position Balzac in the transition from predominantly negative, wild, male images of Brittany to positive, docile, female images. *Les Chouans* belongs to the first type, both by date and content, though even there we see hints of admiration for the Bretons' courage and sheer physical strength. By the time *Pierrette* is written there has been an explosion in writing about Brittany in French, and the positive, female image of Bretonness is exemplified in Brizeux's *Marie* of 1831. Pierrette, with her 'coeur d'une délicatesse presque sauvage', 'pas d'éducation que celle de la nature', is a direct descendant of Marie. These quotations are a particularly good indi-

---

100   Anne-Marie Thiesse, 'Des fictions créatrices', p.52.

cation of the contrast between the old, negative, chouan Brittany and the new one, as here the term 'sauvage' is used of a Breton character in an entirely positive, Rousseauist sense. In *Pierrette* 'sauvage' is only used negatively of or by the non-Breton characters. The pure, innocent love portrayed between Pierrette and Brigaut is exactly of the type that Brizeux has for Marie, and the grandmother figure in the novel corresponds to Brizeux's mother in his poems.

As far as Balzac is concerned, Brittany seems to be the best example of what the rest of France used to be, that is of how things were before the Revolution, how things would have been without the Revolution, or even how things were in the middle ages. If this is so, then his project is really about France and Frenchness. In *Pierrette* and *Béatrix*, the Bretonness of the positive figures in the plot seems to be a way of underlining their innocence, suggesting that they are unaware of the evil found in modern French society. It would seem that making characters Breton was for Balzac a shortcut for signalling purity, innocence, and all such qualities. In these novels he exploits and further popularizes ideas of Bretonness that had barerly existed a decade earlier.

How much closer have we come to understanding the invention of Brittany? We see a critical mass of representations in the early nineteenth century. We see 'Brittany' invented by a combination of insiders and outsiders, whose motives are varied, and we see that texts written in Brittany could nevertheless be written with Paris firmly in view. This tension between Brittany and Paris is an inseparable part of Breton Francophone writing. It might even be seen as the main source of Brizeux's success. Consider the comments by Georges Rodenbach, for whom Paris is the supreme creator of nostalgia, himself in Paris in voluntary exile from his native Belgium. He says of Brizeux:

> Pourquoi, à tout prix, se rendre à Paris, puisque c'est la Bretagne qu'il voulait peindre? C'est que Paris donne le recul, crée la nostalgie. [...] Pour bien aimer sa petite patrie [...], le mieux est qu'on s'en éloigne, qu'on s'en exile à jamais [...][101]

---

101 Georges Rodenbach, 'Paris et les petites patries', in *Évocations* (Paris: Renaissance du livre, 1924), pp.129–30, previously published in *La Revue*

There are waves of Brittany's popularity: the first major wave is popularity by association with Gaul, and the second is Bretonism proper. This took things further, but also had to combat scepticism, witness the fact that the pejorative term 'Celtomania' was coined in 1838. If Gaulomania was shown to be an ultimately French affair, Bretonisme too, on closer inspection, is rather Parisian. Brizeux's career has to be considered as part of the rise of Bretonism, which was itself part of mainstream French, and European, Romanticism.[102] Certainly, by the time Brizeux had published *Les Bretons* in the mid 1840s, the stereotypes of Brittany were fixed, and although it would be an overstatement to say that the Celts were 'invented' in the nineteenth century,[103] the Brittany that we know today, and certainly the 'Brittany' that is taken up or rejected by subsequent writers was formed at this time.

Renan is often referred to as the point of departure in any investigation of the dominant images of Brittany, indeed of Celticness, that we have today. Along with Arnold, whose *On Celtic Literature* is doubtless indebted to Renan's 'La Poésie des races celtiques', he is sometimes referred to as the origin of modern Celtic Studies. Renan's

---

encyclopédique, 1895; cited in Bernard Hue, 'De Bohême en Rennanie: L'aventure bretonne de Milan Kundera', *Écrire la Bretagne 1960–1995*, ed. by Bernard Hue and Marc Gontard (Rennes: Presses universitaires de Rennes, 1995), 57–61 (59).

102 What might be called the 'whole view' is already established in history writing on Brittany; 'Bretonism' is presented as a France-wide phenomenon by Bernard Tanguy in *Aux origines du nationalisme breton*; for him its history and evolution are to be understood against the growth of French nationalism, and as always entangled with currents in mainstream French culture. Guiomar takes the whole view further, showing how 'Bretonism' must be understood not just in a French, but in a European context, and stressing that the impetus actually comes from literature; of the *Barzaz Breiz* he says: 'Ce livre capital est un produit du romantisme littéraire français et en particulier de ses composantes venues d'Outre-Rhin', *Le Bretonisme*, p.254.

103 See the note of caution in D. Ellis Evans, 'Celticity, Celtic awareness and Celtic Studies', p.23. See also Sims-Williams, 'The Visionary Celt: the construction of an ethnic preconception', *Cambridge Medieval Celtic Studies*, 11 (1986), 71–96, who stresses that this is not *only* a Romantic invention, but also shaped by medieval Celtic literature, p.87.

autobiography *Souvenirs d'enfance et de jeunesse*, of 1883, emphasizes Brittany's isolation and difference: 'Une ville tout ecclésiastique,
étrangère au commerce, à l'industrie, un vaste monastère où nul bruit
du dehors ne pénétrait';[104] just as for Chateaubriand in his *Mémoires*,
Brittany is a retreat, both protected and a provider of protection. And
as it was for the Académie celtique, Brittany for Renan is a useful case
study that can teach us about the past, as time had stood still there:

> En Bretagne, avant 1830, le passé le plus reculé vivait encore. Le XIVe, le XVe
> siècle étaient le monde qu'on avait journellement sous les yeux dans les villes.
> L'époque de l'émigration galloise (Ve et Vie siècles) était visible dans les
> campagnes pour un œil exercé.[105]

The fusion of nature and psychology is one of the most striking
features of the Brittany eulogized in Renan's 'La poésie des races
celtiques': 'Chez les Kymris, au contraire, le principe de la *merveille*
est dans la nature elle-même, dans ses forces cachées, dans son
inépuisable fécondité'.[106] He implies that the Celts are poetic peoples
because of this privileged relationship with nature. None of this was
new, and the crystallization of these ideas can be seen already in the
crucial decade of the 1830s. It was during that decade that the old,
negative representation of barbarity and 'chouannerie' was replaced
by images of innocence and serenity most poignantly represented in
the person of a loving young peasant girl such as Marie, also seen a
little later in a figure such as Balzac's Pierrette. Brizeux's Marie had
struck a chord, and her descendants are many, including Balzac's
characters and even Renan's Celt.

---

104 Renan, *Souvenirs d'enfance et de jeunesse*, ed. by Jean Balcou (Paris: Presses
     Pocket, 1992), p.50.
105 Ibid., pp.89–90.
106 Renan, 'La Poésie des races celtiques', in *Essais de morale et de critique* (Paris:
     Calmann-Lévy, 1928), pp.375–456 (415).

Chapter 2: Language and authenticity

As we saw in the works of Proust and Mallarmé, perceptions of Brittany had changed dramatically by the latter half of the nineteenth century. Indeed, the level of expectation engendered by its now fashionable status is demonstrated in Mallarmé's reaction to Douarnenez, which he felt had short-changed him, as its scenery was not 'Wagnerian' enough for his liking.[1] The revolution in attitudes towards Brittany and Bretonness was the result of artists and writers working with, and manipulating, the representations that had become clichés thanks to Brittany's fashionable status. These representations and their story in the nineteenth century have been identified as 'le mythe breton',[2] or simply 'Bretagne' held in inverted commas. The previous chapter looked at how one literary representation can influence a later one, and how it can be just as important to know about earlier literary representations of Brittany as it is to know about the 'real' Brittany. This chapter shows how in the poetry of Brizeux, and those who came to 'le mythe' after him, the tensions implicit in such a project rise to the verbal surface. In the detail of their poetic textures

---

1   See Charles Chassé, 'Mallarmé dans le Finistère', in *Lueurs sur Mallarmé* (Paris: Editions de la Nouvelle Revue Critique, 1947), pp.79–84. On this trip, see also Auguste-Pierre Ségalen, 'Stéphane Mallarmé en Bretagne (Août–Septembre 1873)', *Cahiers d'Iroise*, 22e année, No 4 (Nouvelle Série), Octobre–Décembre 1975/4, pp.211–17, and the train section of *La Dernière Mode*, where Mallarmé presents the idea of chartering winter trains that would take jaded Parisians to the storminess of the Breton coast, *Œuvres complètes II*, 631.

2   As Anne-Denes Martin has called it. Her work traces the gradual shaking off of this myth in Breton-French poetry from Corbière onwards. 'Esquissé par Cambry à la fin du XVIIIe siècle, ce mythe, motif mélodique sur lequel les grands romantiques composèrent leurs variations, consacra dans le *Barzaz Breiz* les qualités poétiques du peuple breton, avant de trouver, au milieu du XIXe siècle, sa forme définitive dans "La Poésie des races celtiques" de Renan', *Itinéraire poétique: de Tristan Corbière à Xavier Grall* (Paris: l'Harmattan, 1995), pp.18–9.

we see that the 'Bretagne' we know is invented not so much in texts as in the relationship between texts.

The idea that a description of a landscape relies on previous descriptions of landscapes is not new. The set of terms, or pre-existent word group governing normal ways of describing a topic or a theme at a given historical moment has been memorably termed a 'hypogram' by Michael Riffaterre.[3] We are also familiar with the idea of the 'paysage' as fiction, an invention, or an 'objet construit', to use the words of Paul Zumthor, who tracks the evolution of the word 'pays'.[4] According to this approach, Tristan Corbière's poems about Paris, or about Brittany, should not be considered as merely describing a historical Paris or a 'real' Brittany. On the contrary these texts re-describe and transform previous descriptions of Paris or Brittany in unique ways. Such an approach informs the work of Christopher Prendergast in *Paris and the Nineteenth Century*, in which he sets out to investigate 'Paris' rather than Paris. He aims to study not the city *in* literature (as a theme), or the city *behind* literature (as backdrop, setting), but rather ways in which the city has been textualized, constructed in and by various writings: 'It is not about the referent "Paris", but about certain symbolic representations, various mani-festations of the discursive category "Paris"'.[5]

---

3   Riffaterre, *The Semiotics of Poetry*.

4   '*pays*, de sens peu précis mais toujours vigoureusement personnalisé', Paul Zumthor, *La Mesure du monde*, p.80. In his lexically-based history of 'space', he draws a crucial distinction between 'terroir' or 'territoire' and 'paysage': 'Invention moderne, le paysage n'existe pas en lui-même. Pourtant, il fait sens, grâce à nous qui le contemplons; et l'exaltation qui nous saisit alors provient du sentiment puissant et confus que nous avons de le faire être. Le paysage est pour nous un objet construit, mis en forme par une opération contrôlée des sens; [...] Il est fiction, et qui remet en cause la relation de l'homme avec le réel terrien [...] Il est survenu comme le font les rêves et, comme ceux-ci, subsiste désormais dans les mots par lesquels je l'évoque. Le paysage ne se dissocie donc pas d'un sujet auquel nécessairement il réfère', pp.86–7.

5   Christopher Prendergast, *Paris and the Nineteenth Century*, p.16.

Brittany and 'Bretagne'

My object of investigation, then, is less Brittany than its verbal representation; it is less a subject or theme than the construction of a place in and by literary language. As Prendergast argues, close textual analysis is the approach required, because,

> 'history' is not 'behind' the text, but *in* the text, in its sinews, textures, syntax, vocabulary, as process of articulation; and if that shift of preposition begs many questions, it at least moves us away from the positivist reduction of literary history to simple 'source' material towards a more active engagement with language and literature as themselves 'active' forms.[6]

What makes Brittany/'Bretagne''s case different from that of Paris/ 'Paris' is that this is a literature written across a cultural divide. French-language texts about Brittany are in a sense all 'translations', and 'Bretagne' is constructed in a language other than the native tongue of Brittany. The kind of tensions caused by this cross-culturality are most clearly observable in poetry, because it is ever the task of poetry to unsettle clichés, and to re-cast conventional ways of describing reality. In order to investigate the construction of 'Bretagne' or 'Brittany' as we know it today I shall focus first on the poetry of Brizeux, whose role in the crystallizing of clichés about Brittany is key, and then on Tristan Corbière, who violently rejected the clichés bequeathed by the Romantic generation. In investigating the quest for 'authenticity' that drove both poets in radically different directions, this chapter surveys how clichés can be shattered on various levels.

At the beginning of the 1830s the task facing proud Breton writers of Brizeux's generation was the correcting and replacing of negative clichés about Brittany. Initially the correction work was done mainly in a rather pedestrian way, for instance Brizeux politely reassures the reader in his preface that he is a true native, and therefore capable of correcting the mistakes of previous writers. There was, of course, some positive imagery mixed in to the 'Bretagne'

---

6   *Paris and the Nineteenth Century*, p.22.

inherited by Brizeux, notably that captured in the paradox of the noble savage, as glimpsed in Balzac's admiration for the strength of the chouan soldiers, and the Romantic communion with nature that we saw in Chateaubriand's 'printemps' passage. However, the overwhelming impression of Brittany was as backward and superstitious, or even dark and dangerous. It was only in the late 1820s and early 1830s that, little by little, positive images, heavily indebted to Romanticism's valorization of the rural and the primitive, supersede the negative ones.

By the mid-1830s, when Brizeux's *Marie* was already into its second edition, the clichés found in conventional representations of Brittany were unmistakable. The images that were established at this time live on to this day, peddled by the posters and pamphlets of the tourist industry, as well as in works of literature such as the controversially nostalgic *Le Cheval d'orgueil* by Pierre-Jakez Hélias. The touristy images of Marie types and poetic landscapes increased in direct relation to France's rural exodus, and the rise to prominence of Brittany as one of the more striking examples of internal difference (and one within easy reach of Paris), was part of a nationwide valorization of the picturesque possibilities of the provinces. While this provided a welcome change from negative images, such a reversal was no less an artistic construct, and no less a cliché than the older negative stereotypes. These patronizing generalizations were simply the other side of the coin, rapidly consumed by tourists and mainstream culture, but considered a curse by the Breton movement. As far as they are concerned, these patronizing positive images reached their apogee with Renan's 'La Poésie des races celtiques' (1854), and formed the basis for the Celticism that Renan (together with Arnold in Britain) propagated. This Celticism is on the one hand at the origin of the academic discipline of Celtic Studies, but also the Celtic equivalent to what Said has investigated in his groundbreaking work *Orientalism* (1978).

The dissatisfaction with Marie types, or with the positive stereotypes found in Brizeux, later Balzac, and Renan is not merely a game played out in modern literature departments, but is now well over a century old, and has spread well beyond the confines of the academy. What has united and motivated poets, critics and political activists in their dissatisfaction is a concern with authenticity. This chapter will trace how, in the course of the nineteenth century, authenticity ceased to be a matter of whether a writer was an insider or an outsider to a given culture, and increasingly came to depend on an attitude to language. At a basic level, and not unconnected to the insider/outsider issue, at least in the nineteenth century, the choice of language is a measure of authenticity. Brizeux's claim to authenticity relies heavily on reassuring the reader that he is fluent in the true language of Brittany, and therefore understands and represents the people and place properly, as he is able to use it as a research tool. Although he writes mainly in French, the fact that he knows Breton, and publishes in Breton, gives him credibility, marking him out as more reliable than Balzac, who demonstrated his ignorance in *Les Chouans* by making mistakes about the language. My interest here is in the flavour of the language used, as in the course of the nineteenth century authenticity was something that came to be bound up with the way language is used or abused. The question is not so much: is this text written in Breton or in French, but rather about the relationship between these two languages as it manifests itself in the detail of the French text. Is the French inhabited by Breton, or perceived to be by outsiders, or in other words is it 'foreign' enough? This chapter will demonstrate to what extent the drama of cross-culturality is really played out in the detail of the text and in textual inter-relations. The discussion of Brizeux will show that it is his choice of words, that is the textual detail, and not his choice of language, that ultimately betrays his lack of authenticity.

Brizeux

An anecdote about Brizeux recounted by La Villemarqué reveals the latter's confidence in translation as a smooth and unproblematic process. In his story of a trip – part pilgrimage, part detective work – that he made to the village of Moustier, where Brizeux's *Marie* is set,

La Villemarqué speaks, in Breton, to a number of locals, before tracking down a young girl named Fantik, who turns out to be Marie's cousin. He translates some of Brizeux's poetry into the girl's own language, for her to be able to exclaim: 'C'est pure vérité'.[7] With this climax to his story he protects Brizeux from any charges that his little peasant girl had been invented to please a Parisian audience. The way in which he brushes over the issue of translation, though, is telling. The fact that the Breton experience of these monoglot peasants had first been translated into French by Brizeux, and then back into Breton by La Villemarqué, is not even deemed worthy of comment, all of which makes the Breton language seem little more than a useful research tool that allows you to talk to peasants, and thus − it is implied − paint pictures that are reliable and authentic.

In his day Brizeux was considered by fans and detractors alike to excel in papering over the possible cracks between cultural contexts. The following comment by his editor Taillandier is typical:

> Brizeux n'est pas de ceux à qui la petite patrie fait oublier la grande. Au lieu de se battre dans les champs de Vannes, c'est lui qui nous le déclare, il serait allé à la frontière. Amour de la Bretagne, attachement à la France, ces deux sentiments, bien loin de se contredire, se soutiennent l'un l'autre.[8]

Similarly, Lexandre's study attempts to describe a tension in Brizeux, talking of 'cette lutte qui dut se livrer en lui, sans qu'il s'en doutât peut-être, entre les deux natures, entre le poète né celte et le poète français du XIXe siècle',[9] but only to reassure readers that Brizeux is a good patriot: 'Il ne faudrait pas croire cependant que dans cette portion du territoire national, l'attache à la petite patrie soit un signe qu'on ne tient pas des entrailles à la grande'.[10] The 'lutte' he refers to never seems to make much of an impression on the text, as smoothness was the aim of both Brizeux and La Villemarqué in all their

---

7   'C'est pure vérité, s'écria la jeune paysanne', 'La Renaissance bretonne', p.4.

8   Auguste Brizeux, *Œuvres complètes*, 2 vols, ed. by Saint René Taillandier, (Paris: Michel Lévy Frères, 1860), I, xxvii.

9   A. Lexandre [pseudonym of Alexandre Tisseur], *Un Pélerinage* (Paris: Dentu, 1879), p.70.

10   Ibid., pp.133–34.

writing, not just translation. To this end, Brizeux was keen that there should be no real alienation for the French reader, for example in Brizeux's case his attention to orthography, and in the case of La Villemarqué the choice of page layout[11] for the *Barzaz Breiz*, and the careful marketing of his material as necessarily of French interest is revealing.

However, this attitude depends on an understanding of translation as a smooth and politically innocent process, which it never can be. On a pragmatic level there is no simple answer to the problem of translating the 'culturally specific', or what have been called 'metonymic gaps'.[12] Brizeux's work is full of such gaps: words such as *ankou* (an incarnation of death) that cannot be adequately translated without a footnote, or at least a long paraphrase, words that as a result act as metonyms for cultural difference. More fundamentally, there is always an imbalance between two given languages, be it political, or simply socio-economic. Any writer presenting Brittany to a French-speaking readership is interpreting a culture with its own specific language, and is to a certain degree a translator. 'Translation', that is, in the sense that the whole of the Irish Renaissance has been described as a 'translation': 'The Irish Renaissance had been essentially an exercise in translation, in carrying over aspects of Gaelic culture into English, a language often thought alien to that culture'.[13] Translation being an imperfect process, Francophone Breton writing is infused with its problems. A writer's privileged position as an insider to the culture is therefore ultimately irrelevant. A representation of Brittany can still be inauthentic despite being produced by a native who speaks the language. This is because French-language texts produced in Brittany represent a rupture, which is either a linguistic shift – when material, motifs, conventions from an indigenous, non-French tradition are translated into the politically dominant language (French), or a cultural shift. Such a shift – when a poet describes a Breton

---

11 The Breton text is relegated to the bottom of the page, and the French translation given prominence.

12 On these 'gaps' between places and the language used to describe them, see *The Empire Writes Back*, ed. by Ashcroft, Griffiths, Tiffin, p.9.

13 Declan Kiberd, *Inventing Ireland*, p.624.

landscape or experience, but does so while submitting to a discourse alien in its conventions and motifs – is only incidentally linguistic. Ironically in Brizeux's case, the act of claiming authenticity and superiority positions him intertextually. From his privileged position of inside knowledge, then, Brizeux will choose the words with which to create a representation of Brittany with a difference. By the act of claiming the newness and accuracy of his own work he situates himself in a line of previous literary representations of Brittany, thus inviting an intertextual reading.

Even if the nineteenth century lacked the terminology of modern academic studies, a more sophisticated understanding of the relationship between the two languages was developing. Ideas of translation were broadening in the course of the nineteenth century. The idea of the Romantic as foreign, or non-French is presented by Mme de Staël, but as domestic (French) Romanticism developed, interest turned to the 'others' within, such as other social classes within the confines of Paris, or other regions. It has been claimed that 'Romanticism had in Staël's terms been almost characterized by its non-Frenchness',[14] and a growing preference for 'foreignizing' translation is seen in critical reactions to Brizeux and his contemporaries. There is a gradual valorization of a different type of translation, one that allows something of the original through, to create a disrupted or disruptive surface. Even Sainte-Beuve revises his opinion that Brizeux is too Breton, and decides that he is instead too adept as smoothing over the surface. The more mature Sainte-Beuve has come to associate a degree of alienation with authenticity, and condemns the poet he had once championed in these terms: 'cette gentille *Marie*, dans son premier costume, n'était qu'une petite paysanne à l'usage et à la mesure de Paris. Ce n'est que plus tard que Brizeux a songé tout de bon à se faire Breton'.[15]

---

14   Joep Leerssen, 'Outer and Inner Others: The Auto-Image of French Identity from Mme de Staël to Eugène Sue', *Yearbook of European Studies*, 2 (1989), 35–52 (42).

15   *Causeries du lundi, portraits de femmes et portraits littéraires*, 16 vols, ed. by Ch. Pierrot (Paris: Garnier, 1926–1949), xv, 14.

The type of translation practised by François-Marie Luzel grew in favour. His French in *Gwerziou Breiz-Izel*[16] appealed because it drew the reader back to the Breton by offering what has been described as a 'French made strange', or 'bent over backwards'.[17] This crooked French is the opposite of the smoothness of Brizeux, and even of La Villemarqué, of which Sainte-Beuve grows tired. He writes to Luzel to congratulate him on precisely this aspect of his French, citing his ability to allow something of the foreign language through as evidence of a more convincing 'Bretonness' than that of Brizeux:

> Brizeux, que vous chantez si bien, était un Breton qui l'était en quelque sorte redevenu après coup. Il semble que vous l'êtes plus naturellement. [...] vous y avez des accents qui nous atteignent même à travers la traduction et qui doivent mordre deux fois dans la langue natale.[18]

La Villemarqué tried to defend Brizeux against Sainte-Beuve's attacks by claiming that his friend was already 'très breton' at the time of publishing *Marie*, and had not sought to 'Bretonize' himself in response to some fashion or other.[19] But times had changed, and the growing expectation that poetry, especially that by a Breton, should be characterized by some degree of verbal exoticism or barbarity is expressed in Barbey d'Aurévilly's condemnation of Brizeux. He saw Brizeux as a lifeless figure who never evolved, and who was too Parisian. What he finds most unforgivable is his unimaginative, clichéd language:

---

16   François-Marie Luzel, *Gwerziou Breiz-Izel: chants populaires de la Basse-Bretagne*, 2 vols (Lorient: É. Corfmat, 1868–1874).

17   'Occasionally there appear half-defiant, half-apologetic justifications for his "crooked" French; his close though by no means unreadable translations are intended as a window onto the idioms and even the syntax of the Breton language', Mary-Ann Constantine, *Breton Ballads*, p.195. See also further comments in Mary-Ann Constantine, 'Ballads Crossing Borders: La Villemarqué and the "Breton Lenore"', *Translation and Literature*, 89:2 (1999), 197–216.

18   Letter to Luzel, 18 May 1865, Sainte-Beuve, *Correspondance générale*, XIV, 209–10.

19   'La Renaissance bretonne', pp.3, 5.

Il n'était pas assez poète pour se passer d'une langue toute faite, et celle qu'il a parlée purement, mais mollement en ces vers, est toute chargée des influences du temps et de l'heure où il les écrivit! Sa langue, à ce Breton, est, en définitive, la langue de tout le monde, – de tout le monde des poètes du XIXe siècle et sans exception! C'est celle que parlent, en échos, tous les écolatres qui s'amusent à ce jeu de raquette des vers.[20]

This reputation lasts to this day, and explains why Brizeux is out of both print and favour despite enormous success in his own day, and his literary historical significance. His success in his own day derived precisely from his facility in tapping into the tastes of his readership. His poems are infused by Romantic sensibility, and the valorization of the country (as opposed to the corrupt city) derived from Rousseau is felt at every turn: walks in the country, a sentimental attitude towards peasants, old people, and children, and being moved to tears. His debt to Romanticism is even clearer in his choice of words, in the opposition set up between the *paix, douceur, mollesse* of Brittany, peopled with characters who are always *nostalgique, simple, croyant*, and the harsh reality of Paris, for which he reserves words such as *plainte, gémissement, s'agiter*.

Brizeux's choice of lexis suggests something of his motivation, as words have histories. Keen not to alienate his French readers, his language presents them with a measured degree of exoticism. For instance place names are cited as evidence of the poetic nature of the Breton people and place, as in the case of Penn-Marc'h in 'Le Chasse-Marée', OAB, II, 68, and again in 'Les Noces de Nona', OAB, II, 29. As we saw in chapter 1, his choice of adjective can reveal the cultural distance inherent in his project of painting Brittany in French. The use of 'étrange' to qualify the costumes of his classmates makes of the poet a stranger in his own land, but Brizeux can never be a stranger in the same sense as a Parisian novelist, or a travel writer. The distance between this poetic voice and the monoglot Breton peasants he observes is at once less evident and less surmountable, as it is the distance that comes from borrowing new eyes, or a new language. It is

---

20   Jules Barbey d'Aurévilly, 'M. Brizeux', *Les Œuvres et les hommes*, III, *Les poètes* (première série), 26 vols (vol 3) (Geneva: Slatkine reprints, 1968), reprint of 1862 Paris edition, pp.75–98 (p.85)

more the distance of Proust's 'seul véritable voyage' than that of the travel account, and it is inherent in such a writing project, because previous descriptions live on as a virtual presence in the textual detail. This complexity is unavoidable, because French-language texts with a claim to 'Bretonness' are caught between cultures. On the one hand they are the heirs to previous representations in French written from the point of view of an outsider (often a traveller), and on the other hand to a genuine folk culture, which is connected to a lost indigenous poetic tradition stretching back to medieval times. French-language texts produced in Brittany thus represent an unavoidable rupture, and perhaps Brizeux's task was simply impossible. Once he had decided to write in French rather than in Breton he was trapped into having to forge a language from words that had pre-histories in the colonializing culture.

His search for an adequate language was also impossible in the sense that any primitivist writing must remain at a remove from the community it seeks to describe. The paradox is summed up by Fiona Stafford in a discussion of primitivism in English literature: 'Primitive poetry is, in a sense, a badge of respectability because it asserts the writer's membership of the non-primitive culture it ostensibly lambasts',[21] and there is no escape from this because 'had the poet remained part of his community and composed verse for a local audience, the results would not be primitivist'.[22] Brizeux belongs in the long line of writers who make local difference into mere local colour. Such levelling out is an inevitability when writers at the periphery seek to describe their home community in a way suited to the tastes of the reading public at the centre. The problem certainly was not unique to French-language Breton writing, and can be seen in writing about other regions of France, and indeed further afield.[23]

---

21 Fiona Stafford, 'Primitivism and the "primitive" poet: a cultural context for Macpherson's Ossian', in *Celticism*, pp.79–96 (90). 'Primitivism', as she investigates it, is certainly an element present in writing about the regions of France, it is another version of the centre-periphery relationship.

22 Ibid., p.91.

23 See Anne-Marrie Thiesse, *Écrire la France*, and Fiona Stafford, 'Primitivism and the "primitive" poet'.

Attempting to set oneself up as 'a Breton writer' is, as we have seen, beside the point. The issue of authenticity comes to be centred not so much around accidents of birth, or the possession of a skill such as Brizeux's vaunted 'avoir parlé leur langue', but is dependent on the particular use made of the French language, and can be observed at the micro-level of the text.

Corbière

Nothing illustrates this better than the case of Breton-born Tristan Corbière (1845–75), both in terms of his early reception history, and the way in which he has become a privileged point of reference in the work of a new generation of postcolonial Breton critics.

Corbière is widely acknowledged as the originator of Francophone Breton writing. Indeed the claim that this poet from Morlaix is the first authentic voice for, or of, a Francophone Brittany has become something of a critical commonplace, as casually repeated as the complaint that Brizeux is dull. However there is no external evidence that his project was intentionally Breton, despite his poetic work being peppered with references to cultural specificities. He never aligned himself with the Breton cause, and the work of subversion in his Brittany poems is no different from that found elsewhere his *œuvre*. His notoriety in the French capital is explained nevertheless in large part by his 'Bretonness'.

Corbière was almost unknown before Paul Verlaine included him as a case-study in his *Poètes maudits*, allowing him to rub shoulders with the likes of Arthur Rimbaud and Mallarmé. The *Amours jaunes* had had to be published at his own expense and had only received three (unfavourable) reviews, some ten years previously (1873),[24]

24   For details of the three reviews from 1873 see Jean-Louis Debauve, 'Autour de la publication des *Amours jaunes*', *La Nouvelle Tour de feu*, 11–3 (1985), 55–77. These reviews were: 'les Amours jaunes', in *La Renaissance artistique et littéraire*, II, no.38, 26 October 1873, p.304; reproduced in Francis F. Burch,

whereas now he had posthumously won his place. The price he had to pay, though, was to be presented as 'Breton':

Quel Breton bretonnant de la bonne manière! L'enfant des bruyères et des grands chênes et des rivages que c'était! Et comme il avait, ce faux sceptique effrayant, le souvenir et l'amour des fortes croyances bien superstitieuses de ses rudes et tendres compatriotes de la côte![25]

With this short but influential essay, Verlaine had established the dichotomy between Paris and Brittany as key to understanding Corbière's work, and this view held sway for the best part of a century, at least in France.[26]

The invocation of the biographical fact that Corbière was from Basse-Bretagne has been more of a hindrance than a help in the criticism of his poetry. First of all, his origins in a colourful province have done much to encourage the search for biographical explanations for his work, and his biography has acquired the status of myth. Albert Sonnenfeld's *L'Œuvre poétique de Tristan Corbière* (1960) was a landmark study. Sonnenfeld identified, and lamented, a split in Corbière criticism between those who argued that he was a great French poet, and others who attempted to claim him as a thoroughly Breton poet. For the former critics his 'ironic' poems, that is poems that engage with the French poetic tradition in order to comment on it, earned him a place in that tradition, making him a canonical author.

Sur Tristan Corbière (Paris: Nizet, 1975), pp.96–9; M. de Vaucelle, 'Chronique', *L'Artiste*, 1 November 1873; reproduced in Debauve, as above (pp.70–2); and '*Les Amours jaunes*, par Tristan Corbière', *L'Art universel*, 1 November 1873, reproduced in Debauve, as above 'Autour de la publication des *Amours jaunes*' (pp.72–6). On these early reviews see also Franck Stückemann, 'Tristan Corbière et la *Jeune Belgique*: ou le mystérieux auteur de la première critique des *Amours jaunes*', *Tristan Corbière en 1995: Lire 'Les Amours jaunes' 150 ans après la naissance du poète* (Morlaix: Comité Tristan Corbière et Bibliothèque Municipale de Morlaix, 1996), pp.122–29.

25   Paul Verlaine, *Les Poètes maudits*, ed. by Michel Décaudin (Paris: SEDES, 1982), p.22.
26   Corbière is unusual in having a different, and arguably more prestigious reception history outside France. See T. S. Eliot, *The Varieties of Metaphysical Poetry* ed. by Ronald Schuchard (London: Faber and Faber, 1993), and Ezra Pound, *Literary Essays of Ezra Pound* (London: Faber, 1934).

95

While the latter group, for whom the true interest of his work lay in its Breton aspects, dismissed his 'ironic' output in order to focus on re-establishing him as poet of that region. While attempting to end this dichotomy, arguing that it is precisely the fusion between, or the coexistence of, these two sides that we need to study, Sonnenfeld nevertheless perpetuated it by refining it, claiming that 'dans la structure des *Amours jaunes*, Paris signifie solitude et damnation, la Bretagne solidarité humaine et statut religieux'.[27] He argues that Paris is criticized by Corbière for isolating individuals while Brittany is idealized for its human solidarity and pervasive religion. This polar-izing view, unfortunately, became highly influential, and was thought to be reflected in the collection's 'architecture', which demonstrated some sort of balance, whereby the refuge in Brittany was a: 'monde authentique, fondateur de l'identité' (p.60). Worse than this, stressing his Breton origins was seen even by well-disposed critics as detracting from Corbière's value as an international poet, as this supposedly condemned him to the ghetto of regionalist writers (this current was inaugurated by Rousselot in his *Tristan Corbière* of 1951).[28]

The dichotomy was not finally erased until the work of Pascal Rannou, and other critics writing around the time of the 150th anniversary of the poet's birth. A collection published to mark this occasion: *Tristan Corbière en 1995: Lire 'Les Amours jaunes' 150 ans après la naissance du poète*,[29] shows how criticism has moved on. It contains an important contribution by Marc Gontard, who attempts to tease out the differences between the Celtic and the Breton in Corbière.[30] For him the pervasiveness of the theme of death is indicative of Corbière's position caught between Christian and Celtic cultures, and the turbulence of his poetry, concludes Gontard, can be attributed to this hybridity. Anne-Denes Martin, in the same volume,

27   Albert Sonnenfeld, *L'Œuvre poétique de Tristan Corbière* (Paris: Presses universitaires de France,1960), p.120.

28   *Tristan Corbière: un essai par Jean Rousselot* (Paris: Seghers, 1951).

29   (Morlaix: Comité Tristan Corbière et Bibliothèque Municipale de Morlaix, 1996).

30   'Tristan Corbière et l'imaginaire celtique', in *Tristan Corbière en 1995: Lire 'Les Amours jaunes' 150 ans après la naissance du poète* (Morlaix: Comité Tristan Corbière et Bibliothèque Municipale de Morlaix, 1996), pp.19–34.

also addresses the problem of the Breton angle in Corbière criticism, showing that his Bretonness has been underplayed because he was so rebellious: 'comme ils ne retrouvaient pas [...] la Bretagne pittoresque et conventionnelle que les poètes leur avaient appris à aimer, les critiques ne l'ont pas reconnue'.[31] In another anniversary volume Pascal Rannou begins by dismissing much previous criticism as 'anti-Breton' in that it assumes that qualifying Corbière as a 'Breton' poet is an insult, and is based on a limited understanding of Breton culture, themes and motifs. He then puts forward his 'métisse' hypothesis, that Corbière's work must be understood as the product of cultural hybridity (being a 'bourgeois francophone né en Bretagne'), and that he is an 'écrivain aliéné', and as such the initiator of Francophone Breton writing.[32] This view is shared by Anne-Denes Martin, who argues: 'Avec lui [Corbière] naissait la première expression originale d'un poète breton de langue française'.[33]

One reason why Verlaine stressed Brittany as a context was that this exotic background provided a reason for the 'strangeness' of Corbière's imaginary universe, but it is clear today that one need look no further than the history of mainstream French poetry in the 1870s to understand him, without resorting to his 'Bretonness' as an explanation for his difference. What Paul Bénichou has called a 'grande crise historique' – the nineteenth-century conflict between the poet and society – had radically changed the nature of the poetic vocation. The position of the artist had reached a new crisis, because a decline in

---

31 Anne-Denes Martin, 'Actualité de Tristan Corbière', in *Tristan Corbière en 1995: Lire 'Les Amours jaunes' 150 ans après la naissance du poète* (Morlaix: Comité Tristan Corbière et Bibliothèque Municipale de Morlaix, 1996), pp.94-101 (p.97).

32 Pascal Rannou and Pierre Bazantay, eds, *Visages de Tristan Corbière* (Morlaix: Skol Vreizh, 1995), p.72. The passage reads: 'Tristan Corbière est, de fait, l'initiateur d'une littérature bretonne francophone qui, sans se contenter d'exploiter une thématique, crée un langage inédit', back cover of ibid. See also Pascal Rannou, 'De Corbière à Tristan: La quête identitaire comme principe organisateur des *Amours jaunes*', unpublished doctoral thesis, Université de Haute Bretagne, 1998. Other recent critics such as Hugues Laroche in *Tristan Corbière ou les voix de la corbière* (Paris: Presses universitaires de Vincennes, 1997) reject the oversimplification of Sonnenfeld's dichotomy (see p.16).

33 *Itinéraire poétique en Bretagne*, p.96.

private patronage had brought about a situation where responsibility for the arts lay with the State's financial encouragement, but they were ultimately in the hands of market forces.[34] For Julia Kristeva there is an intimate connection between the exploitative structure of capitalism, the rejection of the poet by the bourgeois state, and the subversive textual practices of the intellectual avant-garde, and she has written of the 'revolution' in French poetic language in the late nineteenth century in her classic study of Lautréamont and Mallarmé.[35]

Corbière is much lauded by critics for his signal achievement in cutting through the picturesque clichés of Brittany. As Julien Gracq observed in the context of the 'Rapsode foraine', the poem is: 'peut-être le seul exemple [...] dans notre poésie d'une sublimation intégrale du pittoresque'.[36] In the last chapter a literary reaction against what were perceived as misleading, clichéd Romantic representations of Brittany was identified, and the case of Brizeux shows that there was a current claiming to paint the 'authentic' Brittany as early as the 1830s. Faced with negative clichés Brizeux sometimes exploits them, as when he subverts that of Brittany's difficulty of access. For instance in *Les Bretons* the physical and geographical obstacles that are condemned by the likes of Cambry and Balzac are actually called on

---

34 'A partir de 1850, dans le reflux du romantisme, [la crise] domine de plus en plus la situation de la poésie, stimulant puissamment un pessimisme qui semble désormais inséparable de la vocation poétique. La solitude du poète n'est qu'un autre nom de son ambition; c'est le revers du sacerdoce poétique plutôt que sa négation', Paul Bénichou, 'Mallarmé et le public', in *L'Écrivain et ses travaux* (Paris: Corti, 1967), pp.69–88 (p.79). For further discussion of this crisis, see Christopher Prendergast, *Balzac: Fiction and Melodrama* (London: Edward Arnold, 1978), Damian Catani, *The Poet in Society: Art, Consumerism, and Politics in Mallarmé* (Oxford: Peter Lang, 2003), John Lough, *The Writer and Public in France: From the Middle Ages to the Present Day* (Oxford: Clarendon Press, 1978).

35 Julia Kristeva, *La Révolution du langage poétique: l'avant-garde à la fin du XIXe siècle: Lautréamont et Mallarmé* (Paris: Seuil, 1974).

36 Julien Gracq, *En lisant en écrivant*, 2 vols (Paris: Corti, 1981), II, 746. Cited in Pascal Rannou, 'Julien Gracq: visiteur de la Bretagne', in Gontard, Marc, ed., *Bretagne: L'autre et l'ailleurs, Plurial* 8 (Rennes: Presses universitaires de Rennes, 1999), 129–43.

to protect the purity of Brittany: 'Arches des ponts, croulez! Poussez, bois défenseurs,/ Et fermez tout chemin à ces envahisseurs!'.[37] A far greater number of other clichés, though, are simply re-used by him, and we must wait for others to unsettle and recast them.

A key example is that of Brittany's stones. Where Brizeux describes stone relics as overflowing with meaning,[38] and where Balzac had used the same cliché of the importance of stone to the Bretons in *Béatrix*, Flaubert, the master of clichés, retorts: 'ce sont de grosses pierres', in his account of a walking tour of Brittany undertaken in 1847, *Par les champs et par les grèves* (1885, posth.). His build-up to this bold pronouncement on the Carnac stones covers several pages and is a sustained parody of the writings of the 'Celtomanes'. It culminates:

> Après avoir exposé les opinions de tous les savants cités plus haut, que si l'on me demande, à mon tour, quelle est ma conjecture sur les pierres de Carnac – car tout le monde a la sienne – j'émettrai une opinion *irréfutable*, irréfragable, irrésistible, une opinion qui ferait reculer les tentes de Monsieur De la Sauvagère, et pâlir l'égyptien Penhoët, une opinion qui casserait le zodiaque de Cambry, et mettrait le serpent Python en tronçons, et cette opinion, la voici: les pierres de Carnac sont de grosses pierres.[39]

While providing a bracing antidote to Romantic musings of the type found in Cambry and Brizeux, and the facile adoption of stoney imagery in Balzac, for Flaubert, this Celtomaniac obsession with hypothesizing on the meaning of relics simply provided another brilliant example of humanity's stupidity. It is a craze to which he returned in his unfinished parodic novel *Bouvard et Pécuchet*, which

---

37   *Les Bretons, Œuvres complètes*, ed. by Taillandier, I, 107.
38   'Les Celtes', OAB, III, 89.
39   Gustave Flaubert and Maxime du Camp, *Par les champs et par les grèves*, ed. by Adrianne Tooke (Geneva: Droz, 1987), pp.269–70. A version of the passage by Flaubert (not du Camp) that covers the visit to Carnac had been published during his lifetime as 'Les Pierres de Carnac et l'archéologie celtique', *L'Artiste* 1858.

he began writing in 1874.[40] Here he is mocking Celtomania rather than the Celtic peoples, ancient or modern, just as his travel book *Par les champs* acts out the insularity of the Parisian traveller in order for it to be ultimately parodied: 'Quoique ne parlant pas le français, et décorant leur intérieur de cette façon, on vit donc ici tout de même!'[41] By the beginning of the twentieth century it was becoming standard to complain about clichéd versions of Brittany. The Parisian naturalist novelist Henry Céard created a vicious portrait of Brittany in *Terrains à vendre au bord de la mer* (1906), which was appreciated by Karl-Joris Huysmans, who expressed his dissatisfaction with other, pervasive versions of Brittany in a letter to Céard where he concludes: 'Ça nous change des Souvestre et des Botrel'.[42] This vein could be traced further, right up to the modern full-scale parody of folklorist discourse in Yves Elléouët's, *Livre des Rois de Bretagne* (1974).

There is some evidence of direct parody of Romantic representations of Brittany in *Les Amours jaunes*, for instance in 'Le Phare', a poem that plays with erotic clichés about lighthouses. Katherine Lunn-Rockliffe draws attention to a specific source, arguing that this poem:

> exposes the inauthenticity of Breton Romantic poetry, by parodying 'Le Phare' by Hyacinthe du Pontavice de Heussey, which solemnly describes the lighthouse in inflated language such as: 'Il est seul dans son calme et sa virilité,/ Un contre tous, debout comme la vérité' [in *La Poésie Bretonne au XIXe siècle*, ed. by Joseph Rousse (Paris: Lethielleux, 1895), p.200].[43]

She shows how Corbière, on the other hand, seizes this tired imagery, putting it back to work:

---

40   *Bouvard et Pécuchet*, ed. by Jacques Suffel (Paris: Garnier-Flammarion, 1966), p.134 ff. See also Roger Ripoll, 'Bouvard et Pécuchet à la recherche des Gaulois', *Nos ancêtres les Gaulois*, pp.331–37.

41   Flaubert, *Par les champs et par les grèves*, p.253.

42   Cited by Louis Le Guillou, 'Images littéraires de la Bretagne au XIXe siècle: introduction', in *Histoire littéraire et culturelle de la Bretagne*, II, 7–15. He describes the novel thus: 'une étude au vitriol des mœurs de la Basse-Bretagne au début du XXe siècle', II, 8.

43   Katherine Lunn-Rockliffe, *Corbière and the Poetics of Irony*, p.82.

Il se mâte et rit de sa rage,
Bandant à bloc;
Fier bout de chandelle sauvage,
Plantée au roc!,[44]

and ending with the pun: 'l'érection du phare / N'y tiendrait pas...'
(ll. 59–60). Corbière is well known for such parody, and often composed more direct ones of mainstream poets, with targets including
Lamartine and Musset, Hugo and even Baudelaire. Further parodies of
less well-known Breton poets may well be waiting to be discovered,
as deliberately re-working the words of others is his *forte*. This would
not make him unusual in the history of representations of Brittany,
however; as we saw, the myth of Brittany was at this time ripe for
parody. Indeed it would have been surprising if he had not joined the
ranks of those writers who tackled clichés of Brittany head on.
However, the rest of this chapter will show, with the help of close-
reading, how radical Corbière's parody is, beginning with the refusal
of his poetic voice to be located at all, let alone to be pinned down as
'Breton'.

Just as *Les Amours jaunes* resists generic definition, hovering
between the *essais, étude, volume, copie, poème, livre, papiers,
album, bouts-rimés, ouvrage, chanson, vers*, all playfully put forth in
the opening poem entitled 'Ça' (Aj 24), so Corbière's poetry cannot
be tied to one or other of the two places it evokes most frequently, that
is Brittany or Paris. Despite frequent references to verifiable place
names, from Penmarc'h in remotest Brittany to the rue des Martyrs at
the foot of Montmartre, his poetry is no more about Brittany than it is
about Paris, as this is not a poetry of geographical place, any more
than it is a conventional volume of French poetry. The whole idea of a

---

44 'Le Phare' in *Tristan Corbière: Les Amours jaunes*, ed. by Élisabeth Aragon
and Claude Bonnin (Toulouse: Presses universitaires du Mirail, 1992), pp.426–
29, ll. 9–12; page references will hereafter be given in the main text, with the
title abbreviated to 'Aj'. I am greatly indebted in this section to the editorial
work of Aragon and Bonnin, and to previous Corbière editors and commentators. I have also benefited from Katherine Lunn-Rockliffe's *Corbière and the
Poetics of Irony* (unpublished doctoral thesis, University of Oxford, 2002),
which continues their work in identifying further intertextual references, see
p.6.

'Patrie' is mocked in 'Paria' (Aj 300), a poem about not belonging, and indeed non-locatability is arguably the most consistent feature of Corbière's work. A poetic persona appears to speak from beyond Paris in the cycle of eight sonnets entitled 'Paris' that opens the *Amours jaunes*. In the first two of these sonnets Paris is designated by an unceremonious 'là' (Aj 32, 34), but in the same cycle the conventional 'là-bas' of nostalgic lyric is used as an opposition for an 'ici' which must be Paris (unless it is the poetry itself referred to as a location) (Aj 38). Thus the voice has no stable location. Rather than use Paris as a setting, or describe Paris as a physical place, these sonnets present 'Paris' as a staging post in a poet's acceptance, or even a chapter in a poet's reception history. 'C'est la bohême' (Aj 40) conveys less a real place than a state of mind, an attitude. These Paris poems that set the scene for the whole collection point to and mock the prejudices of a capital that requires its poets to be a certain way, and for anything from outside Paris to conform to its own views of the world, including its views of 'otherness'.

Corbière is no more at home in or with Brittany than he is with Paris, presenting himself instead as a blend of otherness: 'Bâtard de Créole et Breton' (Aj 32). This is no simple matter of being half one and half the other, as 'Créole' already designates a hybrid. Similarly 'Breton', in a modern context where it describes an uneasy com-bination of Frenchness and Celticness, also already designates hy-bridity. It seems that the eight sonnets in the section entitled 'Paris' are not about Paris at all, but are primarily about cultural difference and exclusion, about being a non-Parisian (provincial, colonial, *naïf*, natural, 'enfant') and a poet pondering the routes towards acceptance into Parisian literary life. The poems are no more about Paris, or even 'Paris' or Parisness, than they are about Brittany or even 'Brittany'. They convey, rather, a poetic voice that refuses to be located. Outsider to one place as much as to the other, this voice's achievement is a text uniquely capable of unsettling accepted discourses on both from with-in.

It is clear from the outset that the poetic voice (or voices) in *Les Amours jaunes* is not easily locatable. Nevertheless Corbière appears interested in the opposition between Paris and his native province, and in the artistic hierarchy that pertained between the capital and the provinces generally, even if only because this, and its effect on a poor young unknown poet from the provinces, had become a topos of nineteenth-century literature. The Paris-province opposition is acted out explicitly in 'Ça' (Aj 40), where Paris is a bazaar, and a naïve writer ('enfant') from the provinces attempts to learn from a writer wise to the ways of the capital, much in the way that Brizeux learnt from Sainte-Beuve. There is no simple duality in this poetry however, as the ostensible dialogue between the Parisian and non-Parisian is blurred. He proposes opposing pairs only so as to undermine their neat opposition, extending his refusal to be bound by binary logic as far back as his birth, which, he claims, was neither breech nor cephalic: 'Il ne naquit par aucun bout' (Aj 48). He also plays on the pair 'presence' and 'absence', dodging categorization as either by claiming: 'C'est bien moi, je suis là – mais comme une rature' (Aj 152), in a poem whose title takes this idea further: 'le poète contumace', making of the poet a defendant of whom judgement of some kind has been passed in his absence.

'Le poète contumace' (Aj 146–61) is about the state of being a poet, and is at first glance brimming with nineteenth-century clichés on the issue. The long-suffering poet wallows in solitude and sadness ('triste'), as the naming of his trusty companion as 'Ennui' (l. 46) transports us directly to a Baudelairean context. The lonely ancient edifice – 'vieux couvent' – that he inhabits is reminiscent of the Gothic tale as perfected by Poe, and that had so caught the imagination of nineteenth-century France. Its coastal setting shows the same combination of ancient chambers and seascape as Mallarmé's roughly contemporaneous attempt at a Gothic tale, *Igitur* (c. 1869), and the Bretonness of Corbière's convent allows him to exploit Brittany's connotations of spirituality, just as fellow Breton Villiers de l'Isle-Adam had done by setting his own take on the Gothic tale in Basse-Bretagne in 'L'Intersigne' (1867). But rather than being allowed to drift into a metaphor for the chamber of the mind, Corbière's once-grand building is instead compared to an old lady, before having its physical existence undermined, when we are told that its walls are so full of holes as not to be walls at all. This furthers the play on presence and absence announced in the poem's title, and prepares the ground for the claim that the poet himself is only present as an 'erasure' (l. 80).

The theme of the poet as social outcast, whether pushed to the margins of society, or alone at the head of some intellectual aristocracy – both are suggested here by the altitude and hierarchy associated with a 'donjon' (< dominus) and the population of wild birds – are common motifs in nineteenth-century literature. Initially Corbière seems to be combining this with a play on Romantic notions of being at one with nature, but it soon becomes clear that this rural abode is no happy escape, and that the company of birds constitutes further torture. When we are eventually introduced to the poet figure he is a pitiful sight, a 'sauvage' who instead of having the 'aplomb' (l. 6) which the once-grand building could have lent him, has 'un plomb dans l'aile' (l. 16). The poet as bird is a metaphor commonly found in nineteenth-century poetry, as in Baudelaire's 'Albatros', where the poet draws on the bird's associations of loftiness and freedom at a time when society seemed increasingly hostile to the artist. Similarly in 'Le Cygne' Baudelaire fuses this metaphor with the theme of artistic creativity and inspiration to produce the image of failure of flight as artistic impotence, which is so familiar to the reader of nineteenth-century poetry. It is an image chosen by Mallarmé for imbrication in his notoriously complex poetic textures in 'Le Vierge, le vivace et le bel aujourd'hui' and 'Quand l'ombre menaça de la fatale loi'. Here Corbière exploits the association of failure of flight imagery with poetic impotence by playing on the expression 'du plomb dans l'aile', suggesting that this poet is not just living wild with the birds, in the sense of fulfilling the dream of a garret-ridden artist, but Corbière has pushed the metaphor so far that his poet-figure has been mistaken for a bird and shot. The introduction of the lead shot shatters the conceit, rendering the poet doubly alienated: having been forced to seek out the company of birds by the attitudes of society, he is now, thanks to the quick substitution of 'un plomb' for 'du plomb', made to stand out as different from the other birds, who peer down on him 'tombé là' (l. 17).

At first sight the choice of the Breton coast as backdrop in 'Le Poète contumace' complements the themes of nature and escape present in the poem so well that the setting 'sur la côte d'Armor' seems to function as a shorthand for these nineteenth-century poetic obsessions. To exploit Bretonness to the full a scene had to include not just nature, but also the sea, and so we are told three times of the setting here: once in the explicit 'sur la côte', once more in the literal Breton meaning of the name 'Armor', and again in the place of composition given at the end of the poem as Penmarc'h, which is a notoriously isolated coastal spot with mythological associations with the legend of Tristan and Yseult. Just as the familiar bird metaphor failed to provide lasting refuge for the poet, so the cliché of the Breton setting is destroyed when its connotations are undermined. Rather than exploit the Breton setting as an antithesis to Paris, where the poet is more at home, or at one with himself, this poet belongs no more on the Breton coast than he did in Paris. He is such a misfit that he is described here as a 'lépreux' (l. 24) or an 'Anglais' (l. 26), and later claims 'Je suis un étranger' (l. 95). So out of place does he seem, that, in a twist of logic that undermines any hierarchy set out in the opening cycle of 'Paris' poems, locals refer to him as 'Quelque Parisien/ De Paris ou d'ailleurs' (ll.29–30). In this neat subversion it emerges that his earlier designation as 'sauvage' has nothing to do with the wildness of the setting at Penmarc'h, 'Sur la côte d'Armor' (l. 1), nor his predilection for feathered friends, but rather 'sauvage' is made to mean 'strange', the adjective transformed in the same way as 'Parisian'.

This subversion is confirmed in further play on the clichés of Brittany and Bretonness, when a clutch of the most familiar clichés are assembled together:

Mes grands bois de sapin, les fleurs d'or des gênets,
Mes bruyères d'Armor ... – en tas sur les chenets.
Viens te gorger d'air pur [...] (ll. 101–103).

In this stanza Corbière initially seems to be living up to the expectations of a Breton poet engendered by the Romantic generation. This is the 'Breton' Corbière that Verlaine saw when he culled the images used in his 'Poète maudit' essay on Corbière from this poem. Verlaine lists a number of clichés: a backdrop of *bruyères*, *chênes* and coastline, a people at once *tendre* and *rude*, with their *croyances superstitieuses* (represented here by the reference to the *Ankou's* 'brouette de la mort' in 'satin de brouette' l. 162), in his attempt to characterize what he terms the 'Breton' Corbière, whom he sees as more compelling than the 'Parisian' one.[45] But through the medium of the rhyme scheme, Corbière throws these clichés on the fire with the 'fleurs d'or des gênets', condemned in the next line to be 'en tas sur les chenets', as if in answer to his admirer's portrait.

Verlaine seems to be trapped in the very duality that Corbière undermines in his cycle of 'Paris' poems. Similarly the duality of a 'Breton' Corbière and a 'Parisian' Corbière proposed by Verlaine is not borne out in 'Le Poète contumace', as this is no simple matter of a poet escaping from the stifling hierarchies of literary life in the capital to fill his lungs with the 'air pur' of Brittany. This poet belongs in neither. Just as in the poems forming the 'Paris' cycle the hierarchy is refused, and the dialogue blurred, here even in Brittany he is a 'lépreux', an 'Anglais', and an 'étranger'. The 'Breton' Corbière does exist, as he employs motifs, lexis and images deriving from a Breton experience, but he is not the 'enfant' ('enfant des bruyères et des chênes et des rivages que c'était') put forth by Verlaine. The opposition between what Corbière calls an 'enfant' and the sophistication of Parisian writers is undermined in the opening poems of *Les Amours jaunes*. The 'Breton' Corbière, to retain Verlaine's terms, is working on literary convention in the sophisticated and exhilarating way that Verlaine, and many other critics after him, right up to the present day, have shown that the Parisian Corbière does.

The 'Breton' Corbière certainly belongs in the parodic line of representations of Brittany. While he was not alone in undermining the clichés that make up the 'Brittany' that we know, the clue to his originality and enormous achievement is contained in the way in which 'Le Poète contumace' subverts clichés, that is through the medium of the rhyme scheme. A more violently disruptive engagement with the clichés that constitute 'Bretagne' is found in the detail of the text, in explosive word combinations. So unforgiving is his treatment

---

45   Verlaine refers to the 'Breton' version (as opposed to the 'Parisian' version) as '[le] Corbière que nous préférons' and '[le] Corbière plus superbe encore', *Les Poètes maudits*, pp.21, 22.

of the French language that Verlaine puts the emphasis on Corbière's non-Frenchness: 'quel Breton bretonnant de la bonne manière'.[46] This view was echoed in the decadent novel *A Rebours* (1884), in which Huysmans, similarly focusing on the disruptive verbal surfaces, has his character des Esseintes say of Corbière's poetry: 'c'était à peine français, l'auteur parlait nègre'.[47] There is little dispute that Corbière's originality as a French poet lies in his disruptive verbal textures. It is also clear that his uniquely important contribution to the Breton tradition has to do with his unconventional use of language. Whether this has anything to do with the Breton language, as Verlaine's choice of the word 'bretonnant' as an explanation for his strangeness suggests, or 'foreignness' more generally as Huysmans implies, is much less clear.

At first sight, much of the foreign feel to Corbière's poetry derives from the inclusion of real place names containing un-French consonants such as 'c'h' and 'k', and he also creates unfamiliar French by referring to culturally specific figures and motifs such as the 'brouette de la Mort', the vehicle of the native Breton incarnation of death (referred to in Aj 160, Aj 310), and the 'lavandière' whose nightly task it is to wash the linen of the dead. He also, to a limited degree, plays with literal translation from Breton, creating unfamiliar expressions in French, as in 'escabeaux de crapauds' (Aj 308) and 'Mois noir' (Aj 416, 340). Yet the lexical exoticism that peppers the collection, for instance the 'ankokrignets' (< Br. Ankoù krignet) and 'kakous' in 'La rapsode foraine et le Pardon de Sainte-Anne' (l. 165), in no measure accounts for the strangeness of the language in this poem. In any case there is just as much Latin sprinkled over *Les Amours jaunes*, or in the 'Gens de mer' section, and as much French dialect, as there is Breton proper. It is not only Breton lexis, nor even exotic lexis more generally, that is responsible for the non-French feel of Corbière's language. Rather it is provocative juxtapositions that allow him to explode words, forcing them to offer up their various and possibly unexpected meanings simultaneously, rather than be pinned down by the syntax to one meaning. This is clear in the word-play in

---

46   Paul Verlaine, *Les Poètes maudits*, p.22.
47   K.-J. Huysmans, *A Rebours* (Paris: Garnier-Flammarion, 1978), p.212.

the first line of 'Ça' (Aj 24–29), where the word 'essais' is opened up by its virtual repetition in 'essayé', and there is a similar play on 'passer' (Aj 34), and in the expression 'Une tête! – mais pas de tête' (Aj 52).

The same thing is happening to words, but much more powerfully so, in places where the syntax appears at first sight smoother. In 'Bâtard de Créole et Breton' (Aj 32), for instance, putting the word 'Créole' as an equivalence to 'Breton' forcefully removes 'Breton' from the folklore register to which it had been banished by the likes of Brizeux.

> Bâtard de Créole et Breton,
> Il vint aussi là – fourmilière,
> Bazar où rien n'est en pierre (Aj 32)

The pairing of 'Bâtard' and 'Breton', framing the opening line, and reinforced by sound patterning, equally forces the word 'Breton' into completely new company. On the one hand it is put in the company of 'bâtard', an insult, which subverts the notions of intactness and purity long associated with Brittany, and crystallized in Renan's 'La Poésie des races celtiques'. On the other hand, through sound-patterning rather than syntax, it is juxtaposed to 'bâtard's virtual echo – 'bazar' – with its Oriental connotations (< Persian 'souk'), but also its pejorative implication of lack of order and balance. Corbière is not presenting himself as a coherent poetic voice, and the mongrel idea he puts forth with the opening word 'bâtard' can be read as a characterization of the poem itself, and its texture, as both 'créole' and 'breton' are the names of languages, as well as adjectives of identity. The image created by the word 'fourmilière' for Paris first of all tells us that it has little substance, and the word itself takes us to one of its literary incarnations – in this case Baudelaire's 'fourmillante cité' in 'Les Sept vieillards' – rather than to a real place. So unreal is this Paris that it is described as a 'Bazar où rien n'est en pierre' (Aj 32), a negative definition that also allows one of the most enduring clichés of Brittany to resonate: that of its stones and associated timelessness.

Another of the Paris sonnets gives us an equally unexpected Brittany:

C'est la bohême, enfant: Renie
Ta lande et ton clocher à jour,
Les mornes de ta colonie
Et les *bamboulas* au tambour (Aj 40)

This poet's province is presented as both a version of Brittany, which is conjured up by such typical details as 'lande', and 'clocher', and at the same time a distant French colony. This is signalled by 'mornes de ta colonie' in the next line, transporting us to the little mountains of the Reunion Island or the Antilles, and then 'bamboulas', sweeping us up in an African dance. His merging of Brittany, Africa, and the Antilles suggests that anything that is not Paris is all the same anyway, either to him, or more likely to the levelling, homogenizing eye of the Parisian who sees no further than a certain degree of difference no matter which direction he looks in. Although we find colonializing discourse in French-language writing on Brittany long before Corbière, it is not until the twentieth century that comparisons between Brittany and overseas colonies galvanize Breton writers and thinkers into political commitment.

The first two poems in 'Armor', the section devoted to Brittany, exploit three of the most central clichés connected with Bretonness by forcing them together: these are nature, the coast and death. The rural idyll is a Romantic idea that Corbière targets quite explicitly elsewhere. 'Un riche en Bretagne' (Aj 312) directly parodies Georgic inspired poetry, and is especially scathing about the eighteenth-century translator into French of the *Georgics*, the abbé Delille (1770). This vogue had suited writers on Brittany particularly well, and had certainly marked the previous generation. Other writers, less sentimental than Brizeux, went beyond the Romantic notion of a harmonious merging of people with the nature surrounding them to the kind of animalisms found most famously in Balzac's comparison of chouan soldiers with goats. Corbière overturns this by parodying it in his angry poem 'La Pastorale de Conlie' (Aj 340–345), where his use of the verbe 'paître' makes soldiers into sheep (l. 11), confirming the comparison announced from the outset in 'comme des troupeaux' (l. 2). In the two opening poems of 'Armor', 'Paysage mauvais' and

'Nature morte', nature is put together with the themes of death and the coast.

Paysage mauvais

Sables de vieux os – le flot râle
Des glas: crevant bruit sur bruit...
– Palud pâle, où la lune avale
De gros vers, pour passer la nuit. (Aj 308)

First the promise of a 'paysage' is undermined by its quali-fication as 'mauvais', so that it no longer designates a pictorial genre beloved of the Romantics, but a sinister setting. This movement is repeated in the poem's opening words when the cliché of Brittany's attachment to the coast is shattered by the detail of the beach's composition 'de vieux os', bringing in the biggest cliché about Brittany: the association with death. The verb 'râler', with its conno-tations of death-bed agony, is used to adapt the more usual expression 'sonner le glas' into a chilling plural 'les glas'. Each wave of the incoming tide ('le flot') is a 'glas', bringing death not for one person, but more generally coming to engulf the pale land, wave after wave. The sea – *ar mor* in Breton – is a near homonym of death, 'mort', in French. The traditionally liminal site has already been won over by death as the beach is merged into the image of a church thanks to the 'glas' tolling. This beach is formed of the generations of lost sailors whose bones have made up the sand rather than fill the 'ossuaire' we might expect in a picture of a quintessential Breton church. The death-infused landscape is not the picturesque version of the 'culte des morts' cliché, but a more insidious force, creeping up from all di-rections, with the 'ossuaire' brutally reinvented as 'sables de vieux os'. Death seeps out from the title of the Brittany section, where the name 'Armor' has been chosen over the possible alternatives 'Bretagne' (never used by Corbière), or 'Armorique' (used in 'Saint Tupetu', Aj 316), as it allows the word 'mort' to sound. The rhyme 'Armor – mort' appealed to Corbière, and is used elsewhere in 'Le Naufrageur' (Aj 416–419). This rhyme's power to transform Brittany into 'mort' is surely why he opts for 'Armor' again in 'Cris d'aveugle' (Aj 336–339), where death seeps from it into the description 'Landes jaunes d'Armor' (l. 50), reminding us that yellow is a colour of mourning in Brittany,[48] and 'ciel défunt d'Armor' (l. 54), clashing with the 'fresh air' cliché of good health.

The drama in the second poem of 'Armor', 'Nature morte', is derived once again from the effect of words being forced together, against the grain of conventional usage.

Nature morte

Des coucous l'*Angelus* funèbre
A fait sursauter, à ténèbre,
Le coucou, pendule du vieux,

Et le chat-huant, sentinelle,
Dans sa carcasse à la chandelle
Qui flamboie à travers ses yeux.

– Écoute se taire la chouette...
– Un cri de bois: C'est *la brouette*
De la mort, le long du chemin...

Et, d'un vol joyeux, la corneille
Fait le tour du toit où l'on veille
Le défunt qui s'en va demain (Aj 310).

Continuing the pictorial titles, the conventional French title of 'dead nature' for what is known in English as a 'still life' is an excuse to introduce death in its native Breton form. Giving the poem's month of composition as 'avril' (as it was for 'Paysage mauvais'), the traditional month of awakening for both poetic and natural creativity, recalls the idea of the mild Breton spring, famous since Chateaubriand's passage describing the 'printemps en Bretagne'. The cliché of close-

---

48   This is well represented in literature. For instance Brizeux refers to a 'fille jaune', who is the bringer of death, in 'Le Chasse-Marée', *Les Bretons*, ed. by Taillandier, I, 161–62; and expressly in the poem 'Rosily': 'Enfin d'un ruban jaune (et dans tous nos villages/C'est la couleur encor du deuil et des veuvages)/Il noua son bouquet...', in *Histoires poétiques*, ed. by Taillandier, II, 321.

ness to nature takes a twist here as nature is shown to be replete with signs of death.

Just as the waves did in 'Paysage mauvais', wild cuckoos take over the role of the church in sounding the 'Angelus funèbre' for death's latest victim, who is presented as simply 'vieux', and 'défunt', and an owner of a cuckoo clock. The mythical, deathly version of the bird cry encroaches on domesticity through word play. Using this same bird makes it seem that the clock was calling him to death on the hour every hour, with the same monotonous predictability as the incoming tide, wave after wave. Then, worse even than all the deathly bird sounds, be they wild or items of domestic interior, is the cry of inanimate wood that they herald – the 'brouette', which allows the *Ankou* to gain entry into a still life by the back door. Rather than being a poem about nature or about death, this is about the particular Breton obsession with seeing death, and the supernatural, *in* nature itself. In this respect it is the same as Gauguin's painting of Jacob's struggle with the angel: 'La Vision après le sermon' (1888), which shows that the crowd of Breton peasant onlookers can *see* this spiritual struggle not just during the sermon inside the church, but afterwards, acted out in a match of traditional wrestling outside. Renan too had expressed this in his influential passage on 'le merveilleux' in 'La Poésie des races celtiques': 'Chez les Kymris, au contraire, le principe de la *merveille* est dans la nature elle-même, dans ses forces cachées, dans son inépuisable fécondité'.[49] Although it says the same thing as Renan, the shock of the formulation 'vieux os' is violent, and Corbière's image is brutal where Renan's was pretty. Corbière grabs hold of the clichés of Bretonness, strips them down to their linguistic bare bones, and then uses potent verbal configurations to make them destroy each other. This is especially effective in 'La Rapsode foraine et le pardon de Sainte-Anne' (Aj 320), which explores the unique blend of faith found in Brittany. It stands out as a most ambitious poem – simply his greatest according to T. S. Eliot[50] – and is one of those singled out by Verlaine.

---

49   Renan, 'La Poésie des races celtiques', in *Essais de morale et de critique* (Paris: Calmann-Lévy, 1928), pp.375–456 (415).

50   *Varieties of Metaphysical Poetry*, pp.218–9.

Brittany already in Corbière's day was famed for a natural and pure faith, blended with innocent superstition, of the type endearingly conveyed in 'Saint Tupetu' (Aj 316), which describes the Bretons' special relationship with this saint. This made an exception of Brittany in a France that, more generally, had lost her faith, a point that is conveyed elliptically in 'La Rapsode foraine et le pardon de Sainte-Anne' in the phrase: 'La France n'a plus de rois' (l. 159), following mention of the old belief that Kings had the power to heal with the touch of a finger. The blending of Christianity with older Celtic belief systems doubtless goes some way to explain Brittany's exceptional situation. For instance the superimposition of a Christian saint on a Celtic goddess Ana in some measure explains the Bretons' cult of Sainte Anne, which can in turn explain something of their love for their duchesse Anne (1477–1514). Breton faith, it is suggested in the coupling of 'foi' and 'lierre' (Saint Tupetu), is as natural as ivy. This unique blend is especially evident in the religious festivals known as 'pardons', that displayed a striking combination of the spiritual and the earthy, the religious and the pagan.[51]

Because of this peculiarity, the 'pardon' is a popular topic in the nineteenth century in both literature and the visual arts. Brizeux, for instance, devotes the first 'chant' in *Les Bretons* to a long description of a 'Pardon'.[52] His version is a pretext for a comprehensive portrait of Brittany, with a prologue paying much attention to the landscape, littered with *men-hîr*, dominated by the coast, and he also stresses the prestige of the ancient language. Corbière's poetic representation of the 'pardon' is different, and lacks the picturesque element that was often associated with these occasions, as he opts instead for a realistic, sometimes unpalatable, description. Along with this realism Corbière's poem conveys the mystery of the blend of otherworldliness and earthiness that characterizes the faith of Breton peasants. His portrayal is respected by Hélias, who said in *Le Cheval d'orgueil* that:

---

51   For the argument that the ludic, profane aspect of the *pardon* is inseparable from the religious dimension, see Philippe Lacombe, 'Corps, culture, religion: la dimension profane des pardons bretons', *Ethnologie française*, 30 (2000), 109–18.

52   *Œuvres complètes*, ed. by Taillandier, I, 103.

'le pardon, liesse et mystère, est bien encore ce que Tristan Corbière a décrit à la fin du siècle dernier'.[53]

In Corbière's version Sainte Anne is part of the Bretons' everyday life: 'bonne femme' (ll. 5, 95). She is represented in the poem by a rustic wooden sculpture so basic that she is described as 'taillée à coups de hache' (l. 25), and so approachable as to have become 'usée' (l. 29) to the point of decay 'En bois pourri' (l. 7). Anne is shown as one of them, engaging in familiar activities: 'Qui filais comme on fait chez nous' (l. 54). Her strength derives from her ordinariness. Corbière focuses on the trio of real people who form her family – Anne, Mary, Joseph – rather than the Trinity, as we are ironically reminded in the final line of the *cantique* quotation: 'Sans oublier la Trinité' (l. 115). Her role is greater than that intended and sanctioned by the Church, in that she is mixed in with superstitious symbols: 'Trèfle-quatre-feuille' (l. 50), and she is called on for protection against the curses bestowed by 'regards arides' (l. 63). Far from removing her from her pedestal, this ordinariness and relevance gives her a more powerful hold over people's lives. The balance is delicate, though, and the poem in fact explores a faith that is on the brink of collapse into meaningless superstition and commercialism.

Anne, or the Bretons' 'Mère', as she is also called, performs: 'sans que Dieu te voie' (l. 67), making her simultaneously sub-divine, and above God, the ambiguity of the phrase conveying her special status. Commercialism creeps into the picture of this timeless festival when the cost of the candle lit in her honour is included as an afterthought in parenthesis: 'Voici ton cierge:/ (C'est deux livres qu'il a coûté)' (ll. 113–14). The presence of commercialism becomes more sinister in the phrase 'propriétaires de plaies' (l. 131), and there is sarcasm in the suggestion that these pilgrims are made 'divine' by their suffering (l. 129), followed by the exaggerated idea that a halo of blood gives them sanctity (l. 130). This latter image is immediately shattered by the brutality of a 'moignon désossé' (boned stump) being shaken (l. 134), and the choice of the word 'cautère' (artificial wound) (l. 141), followed up in the shocking: 'Ces moignons-là sont des tenailles,/ Ces béquilles donnent des coups' (ll. 166–67). The earlier

53   Pierre-Jakez Hélias, *Le Cheval d'orgueil* (Paris: Plon, 1975), p.172.

claim: 'Les trous sont vrais' (l. 127) gains new urgency, and new doubt is injected into the idea of a halo of blood. The condemnation culminates in the bald statement 'le pasteur de Sainte-Anne est gras' (l. 195). The cliché of Breton spirituality, which had come to fruition in Renan, is shattered in this one statement that reverses the attitude towards the church found in Brizeux's *Marie*. We could not be much further away from his saccharine portrait of the 'vieux pâtre celtique'.

The faith cliché is undermined by Corbière, but it is just as clear that the Bretons themselves are not being condemned. Indeed the same bald statement redeems the pilgrims, suggesting that the authorities' vices far outdo those of the people. Corbière manages to say that their faith *is* the innocent variety familiar from the cliché, but at the same time that it is impure. It is not sentimental but natural, and organic, just as the Bretons are. Here he merges man and vegetation: 'Là, ce tronc d'homme où croît l'ulcère,/ Contre un tronc d'arbre où croît le gui' (ll. 137–38), with the syntactic echo underlining the comparison, followed by the more extreme: 'Un cadavre, vivant de lèpre,/ Fleurit' (ll. 155–56). The 'rapsode' herself seems to merge into the landscape, being alternately a part of the timeless stone of the 'calvaire' (l. 202) and a beast ('beugler' (to low), l. 201). The tempering of this with the description 'forme humaine' (l. 201) only casts more doubt on her humanity, as does her designation as 'ça' six times in quick succession (ll. 217–27). Such comparisons with nature have a heavy baggage in a Breton context, because of the way they have been put into the service of colonializing discourses. Corbière revisits them here in order to make a point obliquely about Breton faith, thus *using* the nature clichés to his own end.

Corbière forces words, no matter how overused and tired, to work for him, achieving fresh meanings through his close attention to their multiple associations, and to the power of provocative juxta-position. A straightforward play on the word 'perdus' (l. 89), allows a fusion of the sacred and the profane in the dual image of a drunkard searching for the way home ('le chemin de la maison', l. 92) and a faithful pilgrim searching for the way ('le clocher de l'église', l. 91). Corbière uses a similar, and more familiar play on the word 'choisis' (l. 164), to convey the idea of the reversal of fortunes of rich and poor. The potency of a word can be brought out by careful positioning, as in the case of 'chêne', which has a long history in the context of 'Bretagne'. 'Chêne' is one of the items listed by Verlaine, and traditionally it would have been used in a comparison to stress the strength of a man, as in Brizeux's poem about 'Les lutteurs',[54] or to stress spirituality, as in his 'Le Chant du Chêne'.[55] Brizeux goes as far as to make of oak a metaphor for male Bretonness, for instance in 'Le Chant du chêne' oak is the 'frère jumeau' of every Breton, and his 'colporteur' character in 'Journal rustique' fails to understand the 'vie errante' because of the way he is rooted to Brittany: 'Lui, dans le sol natal, dur chêne, enraciné'.[56] In Corbière's text his female character is literally a lump of wood, and a roughly cut, rotting one at that. The word 'chêne' itself, though, is reserved for the description of the spiritual side to Sainte Anne, who is presented here as a mother figure, with her heart of oak – 'cœur de chêne' – echoing the Breton idiom 'ur galon dener en ur bluskenn derv' (a tender heart in a shell of oak).

The most striking example of the potency of individual words is contained in this poem's opening stanza:

> Bénite est l'infertile plage
> Où, comme la mer, tout est nud.
> Sainte est la chapelle sauvage
> De Sainte-Anne-de-la-Palud...

The twin clichés of Brittany as a rural idyll and Bretons as a people of sentimentalized faith are undermined simultaneously through an audacious combinations of words. The whole drama of the poem is contained here, powerfully, in the disruptive verbal surface of the opening stanza. Two sacred words begin lines 1 and 3, and are all the more noticeable as the alternate lines begin with insignificant words 'Où' and 'De'. Each sacred word is then undermined by the end of its line: 'bénite' is forced into the company of 'infertile', which echoes its [e] and [i], and 'sainte' is even more radically undermined when coupled with 'sauvage'. This is not an innocent choice, for 'sauvage'

---

54 *Les Bretons, Œuvres complètes*, ed. by Taillandier, I, 151.
55 *La Fleur d'or, Histoires poétiques* (Paris: Alphonse Lemerre, 1884), p.15.
56 'Journal rustique', *Histoires poétiques, Œuvres complètes*, ed. by Taillandier, II, 174.

116

is a word which had enjoyed something of a golden age in the early part of the nineteenth century,[57] and is particularly potent in a Breton context. Certainly, from the shift in sensibility that culminated in Romanticism, 'sauvage' had a special resonance. If the first truly 'Romantic', or pre-Romantic usage of the word can be disputed, and may be traced back at least as far as Diderot in his *Entretiens sur 'Le Fils naturel'* (1757),[58] 'sauvage' is associated above all with Rousseau's *Rêveries du promeneur solitaire*:

> Les rives du lac de Bienne sont plus sauvages et romantiques que celle du lac de Genève, parce que les rochers et les bois y bordent l'eau de plus près; mais elles ne sont pas moins riantes. S'il y a moins de culture de champs et de vignes, moins de villes et de maisons, il y a aussi plus de verdure naturelle, plus de prairies, d'asiles ombragés de bocages, des contrastes plus fréquents et des accidents plus rapprochés.[59]

---

57   The chronological evidence furnished by the *Französisches Etymologisches Wörterbuch* (11,616b) is accompanied by cursory indications of the semantic range of *salvage* in medieval French and later (617b), with (in particular) the sense of 'qui vit en dehors des sociétés civilisées (de peuples, de gens') from 'ca. 1200', a gloss which transparently replicates that in Godefroy (Gdf 10,621b: 'En parlant des hommes, qui vit en dehors des sociétés civilisées'). A fuller picture with supporting quotations is supplied not only in Godefroy but also in the other dictionaries of Old French (Gdf 10,621b; Tobler-Lommatzsch 9,233–235; *Anglo-Norman Dictionary* 673b). Tobler-Lommatzsch in particular offers a range of well-documented meanings: 'rauh, unwirtlich (v. unbelebten Dingen)'; 'zumeist v. Personen: fremd, entfremdet, teilnahmlos, ungesellig, scheu, spröde'; 'roh, ungeschlacht'. Fom these, and from the supporting quotations, it it evident that the emergence of a 'Romantic' sense of the word is at least prefigured as early as the twelfth century, even if the semantic continuity up to and including Rousseau may be harder to establish. That the emergence of this sense arises within the history of French itself is indicated by the apparent absence of any such connotation in Latin, medieval or Classical (cf. *Oxford Latin Dictionary*; Jan Frederik Niermeyer; Charlton T. Lewis and Charles Short). I am indebted to David Trotter for his expert advice on the use of 'sauvage'.

58   See above for the relevant quotation.

59   Jean-Jacques Rousseau, 5th 'Promenade', *Les Rêveries du promeneur solitaire*, ed. by Samuel Silvestre de Sacy (Paris: Gallimard, 1972), p.93, first published posthumously 1782.

When equated with 'romantique', as here, 'sauvage' has positive connotations. However, it can also carry pejorative meaning, as when Balzac uses it of Brittany to refer to the backwardness of the province – in phrases like 'hommes à demi sauvages', 'la vie sauvage' – and to highlight his underlying comparison of Brittany with the uncivilized New World:

> les habitants de ces campagnes [sont] plus pauvres de combinaisons intellectuelles que ne le sont les Mohicans et les Peaux rouges de l'Amérique septentrionale, mais aussi rusés, aussi durs qu'eux. La place que la Bretagne occupe au centre de l'Europe la rend beaucoup plus curieuse à observer que ne l'est le Canada (*Chouans* 24).[60]

Any hint of admiration for the 'sauvage' here is minimal, but the sense is less fixed in an earlier usage in Jacques Cambry's *Voyage dans le Finistère* (1798). The closing sentence to this epic journey of observation and opinion brings about an astonishing combination: 'Rien n'était bizarre et sauvage comme un gentilhomme breton, qui n'avait pas quitté sa terre.'[61] This juxtaposition of 'gentilhomme' and 'sauvage' is only made possible by the presence of the qualifying adjective in 'gentilhomme breton'. In the environment of 'breton', then, 'sauvage' can be observed exchanging connotations of backwardness for those of nobility.[62] Sainte-Beuve comments on precisely this evolution:

---

60 This is complicated by the fact that the young Balzac is heavily influenced by Fenimore Cooper's novel on American 'savages': *The Last of the Mohicans*, as well as by Walter Scott's *Waverley*. For a discussion of the use of the word 'sauvage' in Balzac's *Les Chouans* see Jean Balcou, 'Les Bretons ce sont nos Indiens', p. 45.

61 Jacques Cambry, *Voyage dans le Finistère*, p.412.

62 For detailed discussion of the question of the 'noble savage' in this context, see Heather Williams, 'Writing to Paris: Poets, nobles and savages in nineteenth-century Brittany', *French Studies*, 57 (2003), 475–90.

> Et puis, ne l'oublions pas, on appelait autrefois sauvage et horrible, en fait de nature, ce qui, depuis qu'on a acquis le goût du pittoresque, est devenu simplement beau désert et site romantique,[63]

and himself makes the juxtaposition 'sauvage' and 'gentilhomme': 'cette beauté naturelle de l'esprit, conservée ou plutôt cultivée tout à coup par ce gentilhomme garde-bois au milieu de son existence si âpre et sauvage'.[64] Brizeux's calm use of this potentially explosive term in his preface to *Marie*, where he couples it with 'vert' to emphasize the land's fertility, freshness and unspoiltness, owes less to Balzac, and more to the Romantic admiration for those who live close to nature. It is used in Brizeux's stated aims for his collection:

> rien n'est frais comme les eaux du Castell-linn et du petit village de Stang-er-harô, ou de la montagne opposée; rien n'est vert et sauvage comme la vallée du Scorf (Preface to *Marie*, OAB, I, 1).

The potency of the term continues to be exploited after Corbière's day, as, for example, in Saint-Pol-Roux's poem 'Roscanvel' (1898), which perversely belittles the greatest of clichés about Brittany:

> Image d'un sou, couleur de biniou, village, minime village où les cloches ont l'air de dodiner au cou d'une immense chèvre de pierre, Roscanvel baigne ses pieds nus dans une mer menue dont la chair bleue se voit sous le frileux aller des voiles. [...] ô mon destin naïf à côté de ma fille mignonne et de mes fils mignons, emmi les chants de coq et le fenouil et la menthe sauvage.[65]

The belittling of the sea in 'mer *menue*' – which is reinforced semantically by the earlier 'village, *minime* village', and alliteratively by 'mignonne...mignons' – enhances the impact of restricting the most charged term of all 'sauvage' to the qualification of an innocent little herb rather than a wild scene: 'la menthe sauvage'. Restricting it to its sober botanical sense, Saint-Pol-Roux drains 'sauvage' of the force it would have carried within a description of a seascape or other

---

63   Sainte-Beuve, *Port-Royal* (Paris: Hachette, 1860), 5 vols, I, 39; first published 1840. For similar examples in George Sand see FRANTEXT.
64   Sainte-Beuve, *Port-Royal*, II, 233; first published 1842.
65   'Roscanvel', *La Rose et les épines du chemin*, (Paris: Gallimard, 1997), p.150.

natural spectacle, and thwarts its psychological potential. This is in contrast to another much later example – Jean-René Huguenin's novel *La Côte sauvage* (1960) – where the wildness of the title is internal and psychological, and is set in deliberate opposition to the sweetness of the setting he describes.[66] Huguenin's study of the mingling of landscape and psyche on the Breton coast completely overturns the *Rêveries* sense of 'sauvage' that had become common in descriptions of Brittany, but this time by re-channelling rather than denying its force.

At the close of the 'Rapsode foraine et le pardon de Sainte-Anne', the theme of the poet as alienated surfaces once again. Only at the end is the figure of the 'Poète' addressed directly, although we have already understood the 'rapsode' to be an alter ego. The poet is asked to show kindness to this poor desexualized, half-human outcast, and told that he will see in her a true smile and 'un vrai signe de croix' (l. 236). These last words ask the question implicit in the whole poem: whether the Bretons' faith is authentic, and indeed raise a question that is key to understanding Corbière's poetic voice: whether authenticity is possible. By mixing 'soutane' with 'pourri', and the violence of 'hache' with 'mère', he is able to say simultaneously what Renan says and what Balzac says. Thanks to his art of oppositional juxtaposition, Corbière manages to say something more profound than his predecessors, and his focus on its very limits produces a more profound portrait of faith. This is perhaps what makes of Corbière the first authentic voice of a Francophone Brittany.

---

66   Jean-René Huguenin, *La Côte sauvage* (Paris: Seuil, 1960). See also Ghyslaire Charles-Merrien, 'Jean-René Huguenin: un héros romantique des années 60', in *Ouest et romantismes*, pp.143–53.

Conclusion

Tristan Corbière exemplifies a subversive attitude towards literary convention. Whereas Brizeux and his generation had accepted the ready-made language of mainstream French poetry, albeit with the addition of lexical oddities for local colour, Corbière's irony cuts through the set expressions and tired conceits. By the time he is writing in the 1870s there is an established tradition of literature in French describing Brittany. Also by this time what we have called the 'representation of Brittany', or what critics have called 'le mythe breton' (Martin), or 'Bretagne représentation' (Bertho), has crystallized into a recognizable set of motifs. These include heightened spirituality, a cult of the dead, purity (both moral and racial), the picturesque, affinity with nature, gorse and broom. Although many of these conventional elements are to be found in Corbière's *Les Amours jaunes*, Corbière has not set himself up as 'poet of Brittany', neither an obedient one who gratefully re-packages the clichés, nor as a rebellious one whose project is to subvert the Romantic Brittany in order to deliberately expose it as a myth or invention.

When situating Corbière in our gallery of 'representations of Brittany', we must acknowledge that it is difficult, if not impossible, to untangle his anti-Romanticism from his quarrel with Romanticized pictures of Brittany. It even seems likely that Corbière was more interested in parodying Poetry with a capital 'P', that is figures like Hugo and Lamartine, than in specifically targeting writers on Brittany, such as Brizeux or La Villemarqué. In any case, it is not clear how much he knew about Breton culture. For instance, critics are not in agreement over whether Corbière knew the *Barzaz Breiz*,[67] though as Anne-Denes Martin has argued, the influence of the *Barzaz Breiz* was

---

67   We know it was introduced into literary education in the seminaries in Brittany, as there is an article praising this in the *Revue de l'Armorique* of 5 September 1846. Yves Le Gallo thinks that Corbière did not know it, but Christian Angelet suggests that he did; see his 'A propos de la Rapsode foraine: Corbière et Hersart de la Villemarqué', *La Nouvelle Tour de Feu*, nos 11, 12, 13, special issue 1985.

so pervasive that nothing that came after it could fail to be influenced by it.[68] Even if it is true, as is frequently argued, that a bourgeois francophone in Brittany would not normally have acknowledged any Breton heritage, it is all the more significant that Corbière should choose to borrow its mythology.

Ironically enough, Brizeux would *certainly* have described himself as the first authentic voice for Brittany. He emphasizes the fact that he writes from the privileged vantage point of an insider, so that his Brittany is genuine, and he goes further than simply describing himself as 'poet of Brittany' ('chantre de la Bretagne'), when he stresses that he is also the first: 'Bienheureux mon pays, Qu'avec amour le premier j'ai chanté'. Most accounts of the history of literature have left him out, however, and if he is remembered it is for his lack of authenticity, that is as a minor and somewhat derivative French Romantic poet with regionalizing tendencies, and not as a new or radical voice.

Corbière, on the other hand, was and is seen as authenticity itself, and despite superficial similarities he could hardly be more different from Brizeux. Both write shortish poems in French with Brittany as a backdrop or setting, but the radical difference lies in their respective relationships to Romanticism. Brizeux, writing in 1831, was clearly influenced by Romantic ideas and ideals, as seen in his use of the rural idyll, his valorization of the primitive, and his sentimentality. The relationship of Corbière's work to Romanticism is equally crucial but he parodies it, plays with its conventions, and subverts its language. Whereas Brizeux made his name by blending existing representations of Brittany with Romanticism, Corbière dared to couple 'sainte' with 'sauvage', and 'bénite' with 'infertile', 'mer' with 'nud', undermining the clichés as relentlessly as he subverts, say, Hugo and his sentimentality about sailors. He has been treated as an important episode in the history of this literature, and given that later writers on Brittany have been inspired by his audacity and his supposed, or imagined Bretonness, it does not matter whether he intended it or not.

Regardless of how 'Breton' Corbière really was, the emphasis on the 'foreignness' of his French suggests that verbal disruptiveness had

---

68   *Itinéraire poétique en Bretagne*, p.31.

come to be seen as a marker of authenticity. A glance back at the case of Brizeux, for instance on the issue of orthography, shows that real foreignness does not come from a peppering of one's text with foreign words. As we saw, the late nineteenth century had developed a taste for translations that drew attention to the non-Frenchness of the original material. The foreignness of Corbière's language has to do with what he does from the inside, with existing French syntax and lexis. Corbière's reception history gives an indication of the changing literary fashions in the French capital, and shows the beginning of a fertile period for linguistic inventiveness, when it came to be prized as a weapon against inauthentic portrayals and comfortable reading habits.

Chapter 3: Revolution in language

By the second half of the twentieth century, the relationship between the two main languages of Brittany had been reversed. Whereas in Brizeux's day most of his countrymen would have been unable to understand *Marie* and *Les Bretons* because he had chosen to write them in French, by now the majority of Bretons were unable to understand material written in Breton. Despite this turnaround, or indeed in large part because of it, Francophone Breton literature was just as much produced *in between* these two languages as it had been in the 1830s. A writer was theoretically still faced with a choice of writing either in the indigenous language of Brittany, or in the ever more dominant French language that had been imposed by the French state. What had changed beyond recognition was the nature of this choice. Writing in Breton now frequently meant writing in a second language, learnt from scratch, as many families had not handed the language down to the next generation. Writing in Breton also certainly meant a narrowing of one's potential readership,[1] although para-doxically the pioneering work of the *Gwalarn* movement in the first half of the twentieth century meant that there was now a tradition of modern literature written in Breton, with a small but extremely dedicated readership. What had in Brizeux's day been a relatively pragmatic choice between two linguistic media was now seen by many in the Breton movement as a radical political one, because by the time the 'revolutionary' poets of the 1960s and 1970s were writing, Brittany had awaked to its status as arguably postcolonial. Suppression of its language by the French state was seen as a key in this issue.

In this final chapter the political awakening is first outlined, with particular reference to the growth of the 'internal colonialism' movement, a nationwide movement in which Breton activists were

---

1   The Breton-language readership had never been large, but people could and did access Breton poetry such as Brizeux's through hearing poems sung.

key players. This politicization is inseparable from the cultural explosion, in particular from the work of the self-styled 'poets of decolonization', writing in the 1960s and 1970s. The 'awakening' of Brittany also has a crucial relationship with other decolonization movements, and the ways in which the Bretons draw inspiration from and proclaim solidarity with the postcolonial cultures of other areas colonized by France will be highlighted. I shall then survey selected literary works from the 1960s and 1970s. In order to assess how revolutionary this writing is I investigate the theories of poetic language propounded by the Breton 'poets of decolonization', and also the relationship between the work of these poets and past literature, particularly the work of the Romantic and post-Romantic writers who pioneered the French-language representation of Brittany. I argue that this relationship with the founding texts of Francophone Breton writing is crucial to an understanding of the nature of French-language writing in Brittany today. The final section will also suggest how postcolonial literary criticism, with its close attention to the detail of language – syntax and lexis – has been responsible for opening up this question.

Bretagne = colonie?

In the course of the twentieth century the Breton movement became thoroughly politicized. For its first century or so it had been essentially a cultural movement, deeply committed to the protection of the Breton language and culture, but stopping short of political engagement. All this changed with the new century and a new awareness of events on the world stage. The Breton movement had been internationalist in its outlook from the outset. In the nineteenth century, in the wake of the enthusiasm for Celtic philology, Brittany's attentions had naturally turned towards other Celtic regions, notably its Brythonic cousin Wales, whose rich medieval literary heritage made it a particularly attractive point of comparison. The 'Poésie des races celtiques' provides a famous example of such transnational

126

solidarity, as Renan here attempts to borrow for Brittany's benefit some of the glory of the Welsh tradition.

Literary and cultural ties between Wales and Brittany gave way to more political inter-Celtic co-operation in the twentieth century, with Ireland becoming the preferred point of comparison. While Wales still held special significance for politicized writers in the 1960s – witness the symptomatic fact that Paol Keineg specifies that his *Hommes liges des talus en transes*, dedicated to the Basque separatists Euzkadi ta Azkatasuna (ETA), was written in 1968 in Brest and Merthyr Tydfil[2] – Bretons had by now turned increasingly towards Ireland for inspiration. It was the experience of being in Ireland that prompted Yann Fouéré to lament the Bretons' lack of freedom within France,[3] it was from Dublin that Caouissin made his manifesto statement for the Front de Libération de la Bretagne (FLB) in 1968,[4] and it was to Dublin that Roparz Hémon was exiled. This internationalist outlook, in the course of the twentieth century, led to a scrutinizing of France's role on the world stage in what was an era of decolonization. This gave Bretons a new perspective on local problems such as the crisis in agriculture that plagued the French provinces, and led them, along with other regionalists in France (notably the Occitans), to campaign against the general economic underdevelopment of the regions of France, that was the result of the over-centralization of the French state.

Brittany, Occitania, and other regions of France were united in their opposition to the political and economic domination of the peripheral parts of the Hexagon by Paris. This state of affairs was also recognized beyond the ranks of the regionalist movement proper, and was provocatively termed 'séparisianisme' by Champaud in 1977, in a study that described the domination by Paris as 'le plus formidable

---

2   Paol Keineg, *Hommes liges des talus en transes, réédition augmentée de Le poème du pays qui a faim, et suivi de Vent de Harlem*, préface de Gwenc'hlan Le Scouëzec (Paris: P. J. Oswald, 1969).

3   Yann Fouéré, *En prison pour le FLB* (Paris: Nouvelles éditions latines, 1977), pp.32–3.

4   Statement made from Dublin, 28 December 1968, diffused by the Comité de la Bretagne Libre, and reprinted in Caerléon (pseudonym of R. Caouissin), *La Révolution bretonne permanente* (Paris: La Table Ronde, 1969), pp.289–94.

séparatisme économique, social et politique que la France ait jamais connu: le séparatisme parisien, ou "séparisianisme"'.[5] Such was the fervour by the 1970s that Richardot was able to claim that, 'La France que nous connaissons va exploser. Elle va tomber en miettes'.[6] When local problems were seen in the wider context of Parisian indifference towards the provinces on the one hand, and Parisian participation in decolonization on the other, solidarity between the French regions was finally cemented in the doctrine of 'internal colonialism', because as Champaud argued: 'le séparatisme parisien est un système de type colonial au sens strictement économique et social du terme'.[7] The actual term 'internal colonialism' was probably used for the first time in the winter of 1961–62 as a response to the strike of the Décazeville miners in Occitania. Like the demise of the Forges d'Hennebont metal-works in Brittany, Décazeville occupies a symbolic position in the history of interior colonialism, and is considered symptomatic of the behaviour of the French State by Robert Lafont, the most prolific theorist of the Occitan movement, in his key text *La Révolution régionaliste* of 1967. This study was the most cogent exposition of internal colonialism to date, and was soon joined in 1969 by a document in the same vein about Brittany. This was the manifesto of the FLB (Front de Libération de la Bretagne), which set out the ways in which Brittany too was in 'une situation coloniale type'.[8]

However, the Breton movement had long been pointing a finger at the French state's colonial record. In 1929 in *La Question bretonne dans son cadre européen* (1929) Maurice Duhamel attacked the so-called 'unity' of France as a myth, using its colonial record to expose France's darker side. A similar attitude fills the columns of *Breiz Atao*, mouthpiece of the Breton nationalist movement. From the 1930s its readers were urged not to take up the French Government's offer of farms in Algeria (November 1936), France's superior attitude and attacks on Ethiopia were condemned: 'Nous refusons de souscrire aux attaques répugnantes des Français de droite contre la prétendue

---

5   Claude Champaud, *Le Séparisianisme* (Rennes: Armor-Editeur, 1977), p.17.
6   Jean-Pierre Richardot, *La France en miettes* (Paris: Pierre Belfond, 1976).
7   Claude Champaud, *Le Séparisianisme*, p.59.
8   Caerléon, *La Révolution bretonne permanente*, pp.289–94 (289).

sauvagerie des Ethiopiens' (September 1935, February 1936), and the policies of Blum in North Africa were rejected (April 1937). These instances are no exceptions; the very first editorial of *Le Peuple breton*, written by Joseph Martray in 1947, is devoted to Algeria, and such an outlook then proves to be a guiding principle of this publication. By the time Yann Poupinot labelled Brittany 'une colonie qui s'ignore' in his study of economic underdevelopment in Brittany and Algeria,[9] the comparison between the two had become almost routine. However, the Algerian war was undoubtedly responsible for a sea change within the Breton movement. The Union Démocratique Bretonne (UDB) actually presents its mission statement, entitled *Bretagne = colonie* (1972), as largely a response to the war on the part of young Bretons:

> L'UDB a été fondée en 1964 par un groupe de jeunes qui avaient pris conscience, à la lumière de la guerre d'Algérie et des premières manifestations populaires, du malaise breton, de la situation coloniale de la Bretagne au sein de l'Etat français. [...] Luttant pour réclamer une solution démocratique en Algérie, ils ont été conduits à réfléchir en même temps à la situation concrète du peuple breton et, par voie de comparaison, à découvrir le caractère colonial de cette situation (mais sans identification simpliste).[10]

This is echoed by Morvan Lebesque in his celebrated essay *Comment peut-on être breton?*, where he claims that it is essentially *since the Algerian war* that he has hated France.[11] This reaction was not confined to Brittany; in the Occitan movement the term 'algérisation' was coined as a precise way of conveying the extent of the underdevelopment suffered by the French regions.[12] The Breton movement, and more generally the regional question in France, had been radically changed, inspired by other countries fighting free from their colonial masters: 'L'ère de la décolonisation intérieure d'Etats capitalistes est à

---

9   Yann Poupinot, *Les Bretons à l'heure de l'Europe* (Paris: Nouvelles Éditions Latines, 1961), p.70.
10   *Bretagne = colonie* (Rennes: UDB, 1972), pp.105–6.
11   Morvan Lebesque, *Comment peut-on être breton?*, vii.
12   Robert Lafont, *La Revendication occitane* (Paris: Flammarion 1974), p.270.

réaliser, maintenant que la décolonisation politique du Tiers-Monde est avancée',[13] claimed the UDB.

If the economic arguments for the postcolonial status of some of France's regions were substantial, what really cemented the solidarity between different types of 'colony' was the shared experience of State education: 'l'école est la même pour tous: Bretons, Africains, Arabes hier'.[14] Educational and linguistic policy in the French regions had been every bit as oppressive as that experienced in France's overseas colonies. The way the French education system inculcated a centralizing, biased account of history amounted to more than selectivity with the truth. For Bretons of the 'revolutionary' generation it constituted a lie, and thus the major part of *Comment peut-on être breton?* is devoted to demonstrating how France has provided Bretons with a pseudo-history, while just as deliberately robbing them of their mother tongue.

Suppression of language is one of the main instruments of colonialism, and from the Revolution of 1789 in particular, France's regional languages were notoriously persecuted. Initially they were tainted by association with counter-revolution, and then a century later, the education reforms of the early 1880s were parallel in strategy to the assimilationist educational policy pursued in French territories abroad. Well into the twentieth century, children who were heard speaking a language other than French in school would be punished, and forced to wear what was called the 'symbole' in Brittany, to signify their failure to modernize and assimilate. This sense of cultural affinity with other colonized peoples accounts for the fact that work on Arabic language and culture appeared so regularly in Brittany, for instance poems of combat, directly comparing Breton and Algerian problems, were translated into Breton in the journal *Al Liamm*,[15] and throughout the 1960s *Al Liamm* typically gave attention to comparisons of the status of Breton and Arabic on the radio (1962), to the

---

13   *Bretagne = colonie*, p.110.
14   Marie Rouanet, ed., *Occitanie 1970: Les poètes de la décolonisation/Occitania 1970: los poètas de la descolonizacion: anthologie bilingue* (Paris: Oswald, 1971), p.9.
15   See Yann-Ber Piriou, 'Barzhed er Gorventenn', *Al Liamm*, 88, pp.339–47.

place of Arabic in the education system (1964), to 'Arabisation' in Algeria (1966), and to cultural decolonization in Algeria (1967). *Pobl vreizh/Le Peuple breton* also published much similar material in the 1970s.

The symbolic importance of a shared, standardized language as a prerequisite for the creation of a feeling of group identity is perhaps best illustrated by the case of French itself.[16] The fact that the phrase: 'le français est la langue de la République' was added to the Constitution in 1992, on the ratification of the Maastricht treaty, shows a desire to protect French from the perceived threat of English, but it also suggests the inseparability of the notion of Frenchness from the French language. In practice the addition of this phrase constitutes a renewed threat to regional languages, and to France's own cultural diversity.

This new political awareness infused the work of the so-called poets of decolonization, who included Paol Keineg, Kristian Keginer, and Yann-Ber Piriou. These were poets who saw themselves as activists as much as artists, and whose purpose it was to engage people in the political process. Forewords to collections of poetry from this time are infused with the language of political struggle, or, in some cases, form calls to arms. In his preface to Paol Keineg's *Chroniques et croquis des villages verrouillés*, published by Oswald, Yves Rouquette explains:

> Pour présenter *Hommes liges des talus en transes*, Oswald avait fait appel non pas à un poète, mais à un militant politique breton: Le Scouëzec. Je veux croire qu'aujourd'hui, avec moi, c'est moins à l'écrivain qu'au militant occitaniste qu'il a recours. Il fallait en effet un militant politique [...].[17]

Yann-Ber Piriou's preface in his edited collection *Défense de cracher par terre et de parler breton: poèmes de combat*, reads like a political

---

16   For a discussion of this, in the context of internal colonization, see Peter McPhee, 'A Case of Internal Colonization: The *Francisation* of Northern Catalonia', *Review*, 3:3 (1980), 399–428 (406).

17   Yves Rouquette, preface to Paol Keineg, *Chroniques et croquis des villages verrouillés comprenant, en édition bilingue, Barzhonegou-trakt (poèmes-tracts)*, preface by Yves Rouquette (Honfleur: P.J. Oswald, 1971), pp.7–8.

tract, giving a characteristically extreme and flowery summary of oppression at the hands of the French. Musicians, singers, and poets alike saw it as their responsibility to express support for strikers, impoverished farmers and imprisoned militants, and so strikes and protests provided opportunities for songs to be sung and poems to be written, with the whole event rounded off by a *fest-noz* (evening of traditional Breton dancing). Political events frequently provided impetus for literary activity; for instance Xavier Grall wrote *Keltika Blues* on FLB arrests, and he and Anjela Duval went as far as to write letters and articles in support of FLB and Armée Révolutionnaire Bretonne prisoners.[18]

This intimate connection between the cultural and the political was far from being unique to Brittany. It is worth rememberting that the word 'négritude' first appeared in Césaire's *Cahier d'un retour au pays natal*, and not in a political treatise. Indeed Francophone theorists frequently provide inspiration for the Breton movement, and their work is also used for backup, as in the UDB booklet, which made explicit reference to Albert Memmi's 'Portrait du colonisateur et du colonisé' in explaining how Brittany's case fulfilled the criteria of cultural colonialism, and cited Sekou Touré as an authority for the definition 'colonisé'. The Bretons' poetry is full of references to key figures such as Malcolm X and Aimé Césaire, along with more general statements of solidarity with groups such as the Basque separatists ETA 'victimes de la répression française et espagnole' (dedication of Keineg's 'Hommes liges des talus en transes'), and other colonies, as in the following example:

> c'est un de nos villages qui brûle
> quand un de nos frères saccage un village vietnamien
> c'est nous tous qu'il assassine
> quand il fracasse le crâne d'un enfant algérien.[19]

---

18   The close ties between political activism and poetry in Brittany at this time are explored in *Nos années Breizh, La Bretagne des années 70*, ed. by Yves Quentel and Daniel Yonnetf (Rennes: Apogée, 1998).

19   Paol Keineg, *Hommes liges des talus en transes*, p.52.

In describing the new generation of poets in Brittany Piriou draws comparisons with Algerians who have lost their mother tongue, as well as with Basques, and the collection *Défense de cracher par terre et de parler breton* is dedicated: 'aux Africains et aux Antillais qui savent ce qu'"être colonisé" veut dire; aux Français; aux Occitans, aux Catalans; aux Basques de l'Hexagone' (p.36).

Breton literature could never be the same again. It now looked outwards and onwards, rather than backwards to an idealized Celtic past, as so much nineteenth-century work had done. This same political awakening also profoundly affected Bretons' attitude towards the past and its literary production, as the situation in nineteenth-century Brittany was now recognized, in retrospect, as a colonial one. After the Revolution, the task of redefining the new, modern France had naturally involved a certain focus on its opposite, that is on what France was not. In this way, the primitive cultures found in the New World and in France's overseas colonies generated much interest, becoming a point of comparison for Brittany, as it was perceived as primitive and backward compared to the rest of France. Indeed the gulf of cultural difference that separated nineteenth-century Brittany from the rest of the *République une et indivisible* was felt by some to be so vast as to warrant the use of the language of colonialism:

> La Basse-Bretagne, je ne cesserai de le dire, est une contrée à part, qui n'est plus la France. Exceptez-en les villes, le reste devrait être soumis à une sorte de régime colonial. Je n'avance rien d'éxagéré,

wrote Auguste Romieu, the 'sous-préfet' of Quimperlé (Finistère), for the *Revue de Paris* in 1831.[20] Balzac's language in his novel *Les Chouans*, written around the same time, may be less explicit, but it is no less 'colonizing' in the frequent comparisons of Bretons to primitive native Americans.

Whether or not we agree that the situation in Brittany can be legitimately, or even usefully compared to a colonial one, we see that Balzac certainly thought so, and that administrators in the nineteenth century were also happy to do so. What is even clearer is that the

---

20 From an article on the 'Chouans', the last in a series of four by Auguste Romieu, in the *Revue de Paris*, 30 (1831), 145–54 (153).

statement 'Bretagne = colonie' became, in the 1960s and 1970s especially, much more than the title of a polemical booklet by the UDB, and more even than a political slogan. It was built into a coherent doctrine that inspired a generation to political involvement, while also transforming the face of literature in Brittany.

Postcolonial literature

At this time of acute political awareness, the nineteenth-century origins of the Breton cultural revival were rejected as colonializing, and the literature of Breton-born writers such as Brizeux, who had chosen to write in French, and 'to Paris', was reviled, though La Villemarqué's collection of poems, the *Barzaz Breiz*, was a notable exception, and is even argued to have caused the political movement. Lebesque, for instance, in the context of a potted history of the literature of Brittany, cites passages on oppression from the *Barzaz Breiz*, along with the comment: 'Où sommes-nous donc? En Bretagne, en Algérie, au Kurdistan ou au Vietnam?'[21] While it is certain that poets and self-styled revolutionaries dipped into the nineteenth century for inspiration in this way, there is no real continuity between a movement that was the product of *literary* Romanticism, and the later activity that resulted from a political *prise de conscience*. As the Breton historian Guiomar puts it:

> Bref le bretonisme [that is the nineteenth-century version] n'est qu'une construction d'intellectuels à visée culturelle; si ultérieurement des mouvements politiques ont cru y trouver un appui, ce serait désormais une contre-vérité

---

21   *Comment peut-on être breton?*, p.14. See also Donatien Laurent, *Aux Sources du 'Barzaz Breiz'* (Douarnenez: Ar Men, 1989), p.11. See also Jean-Yves Guiomar, 'Le Barzaz-Breiz de Théodore Hersart de La Villemarqué', in *Les Lieux de Mémoire*, ed. by Pierre Nora, 3 vols (Paris: Gallimard, 1992), II, 527–65; 'On ne peut dire que le mouvement breton est né du seul *Barzaz-Breiz*, mais sans doute peut-on dire que, sans cet ouvrage, il n'existerait pas', (p.554).

que d'en faire le maillon dix-neuviémiste de la chaine ininterrompue d'un nationalisme breton continu.[22]

The founding of Gwalarn (Breton-language journal) in 1925 by Roparz Hemon marked the first systematic break with the Brittany invented by nineteenth-century enthusiasts. Gwalarn's explicit aim was to save the language, and its radical method was to produce literature in Breton that broke with the traditional subject matter that readers had come to expect of 'Breton' writers in either language. In other words it looked outwards to the wider world by treating universal themes. Such a turnaround only happened in a systematic way in the 1960s in the case of French-language writing in Brittany. As a consequence of this switch, anything Romantic or picturesque is rejected in the work of the poets of decolonization. Their stormy relationship with the poetry of perfect cadences and regular rhythms is evident on every page. As the Occitan poet Yves Rouquette put it:

Fuir tout pittoresque
Nous ne sommes pas
Des poètes paysans
Nous n'avons pas de sabots à poser à la porte d'aucune ferme
Et les formules nous les avons oubliées.[23]

The Brittany described by Paol Keineg in the poem 'Il est défendu de cracher par terre et de parler Breton' is deliberately unfamiliar to the student of Romantic literature:

---

22 *Le Bretonisme*, p.14. Guiomar's is one of the standard texts on the early roots of the Breton movement. Histories of its twentieth-century episode are notoriously biased and many have been criticized as unreliable. However, Alain Déniel, *Le Mouvement breton 1919–1945* (Paris: Maspero, 1976) is generally considered an accurate account, and on the hotly-debated episode during the Second World War, see Kristian Hamon, *Les nationalistes bretons sous l'occupation* (Relecq-Kerhuon: An Here, 2001), and Gwenno Sven-Myer, *Digwyddiadau 1940–1944 a'r Llydaweg*, unpublished doctoral thesis, University of Wales Aberystwyth (2003).

23 Yves Rouquette, 'Fidèles', *Rouergue, si, précédé de Ode à saint Aphrodise et suivi de Messe pour les cochons*, édition bilingue (Paris: Oswald, 1972), p.93.

Lèvres et yeux gommés
os de la face éclatés
gisements de sang froid dans les veines
racines des doigts tranchées
aubépine fanée de notre haleine.[24]

The image created here is neither Celtic nor seafaring, it is perhaps savage, but not noble. The state of humanity in this poetry is a sorry one, and the only hint of the usually grand and inspiring Breton nature – hawthorn – is in its death throes ('fanée').

Instead of the fertile, pretty natural imagery we have grown to expect in poetry on Brittany, we are transported to a landscape that is wounded: 'terre de cicatrices humides', and decaying, a scene containing 'oiseaux lents et pourris', 'moisissures', and 'pus'.[25] Whole villages are 'verrouillés' (Keineg), and presented as bleak dormitories, which the faceless workers are forced to leave at the crack of dawn to travel to the tyranny of the modern factory (Sten Kidna).[26] The Bretons who people this landscape are faceless: 'Vous n'avez plus de visage/ vous n'avez plus de lèvres/ vous n'avez plus de bouche'.[27] Their fate is compared to that of the negro by Per Denez,[28] and also by Yves Rouquette in his preface to Keineg's work: 'Nous voici nègres',[29] and elsewhere to other victims of France's domination such as the 'Arab, va breur karet' and 'L'Enfant algérien'.[30].

The charming rural idyll had been one of the biggest clichés of Brittany. As the discussion of Brizeux showed, the inclusion of images of a simple, traditional way of life, and quaint exoticism of costume was virtually a condition of entry into mainstream literature. The 1970s poets were acutely aware that the only literary Brittany tolerated by Paris was the one that followed a recognized formula,

---

24   Paol Keineg, 'Poèmes-tracts', in *Chroniques et croquis*, pp.95–7 (95).
25   Paol Keineg, 'Exploitation', and 'Dans la plaie pâle de l'aurore', *Chroniques et croquis*, pp.P105, 48.
26   Sten Kidna, 'Bemdeiz da c'houlou-deiz', in *Du a Gwyn: Cerddi Cyfoes o Lydaw*, p.92
27   Paol Keineg, 'Rennes Citroën', *Chroniques et croquis*, p.91.
28   Per Denez, 'Negro Song', in *Du a Gwyn*, p.20.
29   Yves Rouquette, *Chroniques*, p.11.
30   Yann-Ber Piriou, *Défense de cracher par terre et de parler breton*, pp.70, 151.

with any cultural difference confined to the level of the picturesque. As Yann-Ber Piriou puts it:

> Bref, les Bretons ne sauraient prétendre à l'existence littéraire qu'à condition de respecter certains impératives folkloriques, aux ingrédients et dosages bien déterminés. On prend un calvaire, deux clochers à jour, trois coiffes, quelques notes de biniou; on agrémente d'un bouquet d'ajonc d'or, d'une touffe de bruyère, d'un brin de genêt; on brasse du vent, de la pluie et de la brume; on marie le cidre doux aux crêpes dentelle. Les korrigans de la lande interviennent alors qui assurent la transfiguration mystique du décor en y associant une duchesse, deux chouans, un pêcheur d'Islande, quelques cols bleus, un couple de biniches, un trio de bonnes sœurs, un recteur de paroisse, une demi-douzaine d'anciens combattants et un quarteron de ministres inconditionnellement dévoués à la cause de la France éternelle.[31]

The response to the nature cliché in the work of modern poets is radical. The Bretons here are neither at one with their landscape nor merging into it, as they would have been in the nineteenth century, but are alternately imprisoned by it or banished from it (Anjela Duval).[32] Whole villages have been abandoned altogether (Hélias),[33] as the inhabitants have left on the 'petit train colonial' (Keineg).[34] Whereas Brizeux's Marie's life of simple poverty was to be admired, and even envied, here the sad fate of the 'ouvrière' is contrasted with that of the factory boss's wife (Keineg).[35]

These poets fought against this construction of Brittany because more than an aesthetic issue was at stake. The Parisian preference for a comfortingly familiar, if quaint, version of Brittany, which focused on all the unthreatening differences that we would now dismiss as 'folklore', came to be understood not just as patronizing, or even inaccurate, but as indicative of a colonial attitude. As Lafont argues, the promotion of 'folklore' is explicitly linked to a colonialist attitude at the centre:

---

31 Yann-Ber Piriou, *Défense de cracher par terre et de parler breton*, pp.5–6.
32 'Divroañ', in *Du a Gwyn*, p.28.
33 Pierre-Jakez Hélias, 'An Dilez', in *Du a Gwyn*, p.60.
34 Paol Keineg, 'Dépopulation', *Chroniques et croquis*, p.41.
35 Paol Keineg, 'Transocean, Brest', in *Chroniques et croquis*, p.101.

Nous savons que les pouvoirs colonisateurs ont favorisé le folklore des peuples soumis. Ce folklore ne peut être utilisé positivement par ces peuples qu'une fois abolie la dépendance économique et reconstituée la véritable dignité culturelle. Pour l'instant il est à ranger parmi les phénomènes de déculturation que la colonisation entraîne avec elle.[36]

So, rejecting nineteenth-century representations was more than a matter of tinkering with the clichés of the past, it was a real political issue. Politicized Bretons therefore *had* to reject Brizeux, just as Occitans had to repudiate Mistral and the Félibriges, for having grounded Provençal identity in an idyllic rural past.[37] As William Calin's study of Scots, Breton and Occitan literatures has shown, minority literatures in the twentieth century are united by a need to reject the version of their region that was created by Romanticism.[38] This also explains the ferocity of the debate that surrounds the work of Pierre-Jakez Hélias, whose autobiography *Le Cheval d'orgueil* (1975) was seen by Breton nationalists as a betrayal because it glorified folklore at a time when the damage already done by this attitude had become clear. This work also reinforced the cliché of the Bretons as incurable nostalgics.

Nostalgia is another of the biggest clichés about Brittany, and one of the most reviled because of its political significance. It is also one of the most inescapable ones, because as we saw, the French-language literature of Brittany began in an atmosphere of nostalgia because it was born with Romanticism, and it is difficult to disengage the two. Indeed it could be argued that Brittany would not even have

---

36   *La Revolution régionaliste*, pp.208–9. On this point see also Peter McPhee, 'A Case of Internal Colonization'; and Nathalie Dugalès, 'La Représentation de la Bretagne et des Bretons dans la presse française: étude comparée des journaux *Le Monde, Libération, Le Figaro*', in *Et la Bretagne?: Héritage, Identité, Projets*, ed. by Nathalie Dugalès, Ronan Le Coadic and Fabrice Patez (Rennes: Presses universitaires de Rennes, 2004), pp.97–116. This process of 'folklorisation' has been identified and discussed with specific reference to Béarnaise in Pierre Bourdieu and Luc Boltanski, 'Le fétichisme de la langue', *Actes de la Recherche en Sciences Sociales*, 4 (1975), 2–32.
37   See Lafont's *Mistral ou l'illusion* (Paris: Plon, 1954), and elsewhere: 'Le discours félibréen finit en représentation touristique', Lafont, *Clefs pour l'Occitanie* (Paris: Seghers, 1971), p.138.
38   *Minority Literatures and Modernism.*

become a popular subject matter for literature if the mood of the day had not already been one of nostalgia for some lost, pure, innocent, age. Brittany did more than just display the fashionable characteristics, as Breton peasants were perceived to be not just nostalgic, but *more* nostalgic than any other people. Typically, La Villemarqué tells of a Breton conscript who dies near Bordeaux of 'mal du pays' in a poem of the same name, and his editorial note to this poem sums up the cliché conveniently: 'Loin de leur patrie [...] les Bretons n'existent qu'à moitié. Souvent ils meurent du regret de ne plus la voir'.[39] This image of the Bretons is confirmed in Corbière-père's seafaring novel *Le Négrier*:

> Il y avait quelquefois des jours de fête pour les prisonniers. Chaque province célébrait, à une époque marquée de l'année, un anniversaire cher au pays où l'on était né. Les Bretons se distinguaient surout par l'espèce de culte qu'ils avaient voué à la patrie absente.[40]

Examples from Brizeux abound, as he makes nostalgia for his homeland central to his poetic project, as in: 'Souvenirs du pays, avec quelle douceur,/ Hélas! Vous murmurez dans le fond de mon cœur' ('Le Retour', *Marie*, *OAB*, I, 107), and: 'En tous lieux un départ est chose triste à voir;/ Mais dans notre Bretagne, oh! c'est désespoir!'.[41] By the end of the nineteenth century the Breton exiled in Paris had become a clichéd figure, heavily exploited in literature from the popular songs of Botrel to the short stories of Gustave Geoffroy, such as his 'La Gare' (that is Montparnasse), which tells of the fate of a Breton woman, Jeannik, who goes to serve in Paris.[42] Hélias's case shows the problem of nostalgic folklore erupting in the heady atmosphere of the 1970s. To his critics he was no better than a traitor, and this is still an issue today, as we see in the columns of the journal *Hopala!* in a caustic review of the surprise publishing hit by

---

39   La Villemarqué, *Barzhaz Breizh: Trésor de la littérature orale de la Bretagne* (Spézet: Coop Breizh, 1997), p.455.
40   Edouard Corbière, *Le Négrier* (Saint-Malo: Éditions L'Ancre de Marine, 1990), p.136.
41   'Le Marché de Kemper, *Les Bretons*, ed. by Taillandier, I, 239.
42   See Gustave Geffroy, *Nouveaux contes du pays d'Ouest* (Paris: Georges Crès, 1920), pp.169–77.

Déguignet – *Mémoires d'un paysan Bas-Breton* – which is full of anti-nostalgia.[43]

Hélias is perhaps the most famous 'regional' writer in France in recent times, but it is difficult to separate his major French-language work *Le cheval d'orgueil: mémoires d'un Breton du Pays bigouden* from the fierce debate provoked when it was first published in 1975,[44] most notably the book-length critique, or reply, by Xavier Grall: *Le Cheval couché* (1977). Hélias was found guilty by Grall and others of dwelling on the past, and of perpetuating a number of damaging myths about Brittany. Death and nature figure prominently, as we might expect, but poverty is arguably the most important theme in the *Cheval*, as the fact that Hélias's grandfather was so poor that he could only afford a 'horse of pride' rather than a real horse, is a central premise. A certain glorification of poverty is implicit in the book's nostalgia, as when the narrator regrets the passing of old farming methods, lamenting the replacement of the 'battage à quatre chevaux' with the combine harvester (*Cheval* 344). This extends into admiration for the suffering of poor people who went without food, and without modern devices such as the washing machine.

Stoicism and living in harmony with nature were both consequences of poverty that impressed Hélias and exasperated his critics. For Hélias the closeness to nature provided evidence of a superior wisdom. Of his grandfather he says:

> Mais jamais aucun philosophe ne m'a impressionné autant que lui. Quand je suis trop tenté d'admirer quelqu'un, je revois le visage d'Alain Le Goff et je m'en tiens à la juste mesure. Ne me parlez pas de héros, je vous prie (*Cheval* 28),

and later:

---

43 Jean-Yves Le Disez, *Hopala!* [actually entitled *Noir/Blanc* at this time], 1 (1999), 85–7.

44 Hélias's book had previously been published in the form of some 150 separate episodes, written in Breton, in various papers. Hereafter abbreviated to *Cheval*, with page references given in the text to *Le Cheval d'orgueil: mémoires d'un Breton du Pays bigouden* (Paris: Plon, 1975).

Alain Le Goff déclare que la guérison de tous les maux de corps se trouve autour de nous, à notre portée dans des herbes qui portent précisément en breton le nom du mal qu'elles guérissent ou celui du saint qui en protège (*Cheval* 124).

However, to his critics, this last comment primitivizes the Breton people, making them the twentieth-century equivalents of Romanticism's noble savages. Equally damaging, in their view, is the way that his comment primitivizes the Breton language. His attitude towards the language is the issue that most enraged Hélias's critics, as in his book Breton seems little more than something to be nostalgic about, and the story of its demise is told with resigned sadness rather than anger. Peasant attitudes towards French are shown to range from innocent curiosity (the narrator's mother, *Cheval* 54), to active promotion as a tool crucial for self-advancement. The grandfather tells young Pierre he would be better off learning French than the ancient craft of making wooden clogs: 'Mais il vaut mieux apprendre à lire, à écrire et à parler en français' (*Cheval* 100). Regardless of whether Hélias's portrait was actually honest, it was an immensely frustrating one for nationalists, as for them telling the story of language loss in Brittany in this selective way was tantamount to betrayal.

Indeed, in his other works, where he situates himself more explicitly in the fight for the preservation and revival of the Breton language, it becomes clear that Hélias does not agree with the aim of standardizing the language and its orthography. This was a key issue within the Breton movement, but Hélias did not see its relevance, arguing instead that people were attached to Breton precisely because it was so specific to their own private sphere, and their own neighbourhood and context, rather than to public life (*Cheval* 529). Nor did he agree with Gwalarnist literary ideals, as he was sceptical of the value or relevance of what he described as the 'tentation intellectuelle', that is: 'créer une littérature sans grand rapport avec le vieux fonds oral [...] essayer de créer une langue unifiée' (*Cheval* 538). As far as his critics are concerned, his real crime lies in his attitude towards the future, and his failure to rally the troops. It is a comment such as this that makes him hated by present-day language campaigners: 'J'ajoute ceci, qui n'est pas négligeable: notre civilisation bretonne est notre vie privée à l'intérieur de la civilisation générale de la France, qui commande notre vie publique.[45] His treachery was confirmed by the fact that his book was published not as literature, but as part of a series by the publisher 'Plon', called 'terre humaine', which specialized in testaments of civilizations heading for extinction.[46] As Grall put it, Hélias was an 'être tombal' (deathly being), and he continues: 'J'ai la rage de constater que toutes ces enquêtes savantes, sociologiques et ethnologiques, tendent à inventorier les agonies et à faire de ce pays vivant une sépulture'.[47]

Presumably none of this would have mattered terribly had the book not been such an astonishing success, selling three million copies and being translated into numerous languages. Thus the book's popularity suggests that Hélias had successfully written to the expectations of the French-reading public, in a manner not so different from Brizeux. This is confirmed, for Grall, in its inclusion in an episode of Bernard Pivot's cultural TV show 'Apostrophes'. Grall argues that the fact that Hélias had been invited along with Le Roy Ladurie, author of *Montaillou, village occitan*, rather than with other Bretons, reveals a centralizing attitude, proving that cultural difference within France is only tolerated if restricted to the level of folklore, or the picturesque: 'Et c'est à peine s'il y fut question de la Bretagne. On parla, d'ailleurs fort bien, des civilisations rurales de l'Hexagone. Pouldreuzic et Montaillou, c'était kif-kif, c'était pareil![48] Like Brizeux, Hélias is a controversial figure, whose French-language work is often reviled, despite, or perhaps precisely because of, the fact that he brought Francophone Breton writing into the French mainstream, however briefly.

The equally impassioned debate surrounding the cartoon character Bécassine goes a step beyond the rejection of clichés about

---

45   Pierre-Jakez Hélias, 'Lettre aux étudiants bretons sur les perspectives d'une culture bretonne' [1966], in *Lettres de Bretagne* (Paris: Galilée, 1978), pp.51–78 (55).

46   On the book's beginnings, see the article by comissioning editor and founder of 'Terre humaine', Jean Malaurie, 'Histoire de la naissance du *Cheval d'orgueil* et révélation d'un écrivain', in *Hélias et les siens/Hélias hag e dud*, KREIZ 15, ed. by Jean-Luc Le Cam (Brest: CRBC, 2001), pp.219–24.

47   Xavier Grall, *Le Monde dimanche*, jan 1976.

48   Xavier Grall, *Le Cheval couché*, p.50.

Brittany, as Bécassine was the object of a gradual but deliberate act of complete reclaiming. Born in 1905 in the magazine *La Semaine de Suzette*, her story was then published as separate books from 1913 onwards, and is still popular with French children today. Bécassine is a simple girl from deepest Brittany, who speaks poor French, has no mouth, and is most famous for her inability to understand anything much about what is going on around her. She follows a trajectory typical of young Breton girls, serving first with Monsieur et Madame de Grand-Air in a Breton château, and then going to Paris as a nursemaid. She is more than just typical of Bretonness, she is made to incarnate Brittany in a key episode in *L'Enfance de Bécassine*, where the Union of France and Brittany is acted out in a village pageant. Bécassine is chosen to represent Brittany because she is appropriately smaller in size than the girl representing France. This difference in size comes in handy when little Bécassine/Brittany tries to break free and do her own thing: 'la Bretagne se révolte! La France la maintient vigoureusement'.[49] The other characters in the books wear typical Breton costumes and clogs, play the 'biniou', dance in traditional fashion, and their landscape is strewn with standing stones.

The fact that 'bécassine' is today an insult meaning 'silly little girl' in colloquial French, leaves us in no doubt that this clichéd image of Bretonness is potentially damaging, and a backlash against it was hardly surprising. This began in 1936 with a play called *'Bécassine' vue par les Bretons*, in which fifteen-year-old Mona, the eldest of three children, has to leave for Paris to help her grandmother. She goes into service, and is ridiculed by Nicole, the daughter of the house, and called a 'bécassine', but Mona stands up to them, and so the cover illustration shows a 'Bécassine' being trampled by a proud, serious young woman in Breton costume. The play was created by the

---

49   Caumery [pseudonym of Maurice Languereau] and Joseph P. Pinchon, *L'Enfance de Bécassine* (Paris: Gautier-Languereau, 1913), p.9. The choice of Bécassine for this role had followed some interesting discussion: 'Ce n'est pas mal, dit M. de Grand-Air, mais la Bretagne est aussi grande que la France. Ça n'est pas vraisemblable. Il faut une enfant plus petite pour la Bretagne', ibid., p.8.

girls of the Chorale Notre-Dame de Lambader in Plouvorn, and then edited and translated. The editors hail it as:

> Une réponse magnifique à ceux qui ont tenté de ridiculariser les Bretonnes en les représentant sous les traits d'une marionnette frisant la bêtise, l'ignorance, et affublée d'un accoutrement ridicule, tournant en dérision le costume breton féminin. [50]

Not long after the play, the 1939 film of Bécassine by Caron caused such protest that it was not shown on the big screen in Brittany until as late as the Douarnenez film festival of 1989. Plans to show it on television in 1995 for Bécassine's ninetieth birthday caused further protest, as did the design of a postage stamp to celebrate her centenary in 2005.[51] Also in 1939, in the Musée Grévin waxworks in Paris, Bécassine was symbolically murdered by three student members of Breiz Atao: Jadé, Mahé and Guérin. Their attack on her, which included stealing her nose, caused them to be apprehended by the police, but they were soon released.

During the political awakening of the 1960s and 1970s Bécassine was seized on because she was such a recognizable symbol of Breton servitude. She appears, for instance, in the first issue of *Bretagne révolutionnaire*, with the comment: 'Aujourd'hui elle a retrouvé sa bouche [...] maintenant elle dit merde à la marquise, en attendant de lui servir des grenades en guise d'artichauts'.[52] By the 1970s she had been adopted as a militant symbol by other regions of France too. In *Lutte occitane*, a cartoon strip (reproduced from *Le Trognon*, a Rennes

---

50   Léone Calvez and Herri Caouissin, *'Bécassine' vue par les Bretons*, comédie dramatique en 4 actes (Pleyber-Christ: Ronan, 1937), créée le 26 décembre 1936 à Plouvorn, par les jeunes filles de la Chorale de Notre-Dame de Lambader. The preface adds, on the question of language: 'Nous avons tenu à publier une traduction française intégrale de la pièce pour qu'elle puisse être également représentée dans les localités de Bretagne où la langue bretonne n'est malheureusement ni connue, ni parlée. Mais, dans les localités bretonnantes, dans les villes mêmes où l'on parle le breton, nous insistons pour que la pièce soit donnée avec le dialogue bilingue'.

51   For an account of this, see Jacqueline Gibson, 'Bécassine, C'hoazh hag Adarre', *Breizh* [formerly *Keleier Breizh*], 40 (2005), 21.

52   *Bretagne révolutionnaire*, 1 (1 avril, 1969), p.1.

journal), shows Bécassine shedding her traditional costume, and donning first the Citroën dungarees, and then arming herself. The accompanying text explains:

> le dessinateur l'a faite sans bouche car Bécassine c'est l'esclave muette qui ne dit que trois mots bretons. [...] Aujourd'hui commencent les 'nouvelles aventures de Bécassine': La Bretagne se révolte et en se révoltant de façon aussi générale elle pulvérise les images du passé.[53]

Bécassine is also drawn on by Richardot in his work on the politico-economic consequences of over centralization in France, and he examines the way in which her negative energy has been re-harnessed in a postcolonial context:

> Qui aurait pensé, en dehors de la Bretagne, que cette brave Bécassine était mal vue par son pays d'origine? Elle est à la Bretagne ce que le 'Nègre Banania' était jadis à l'Afrique. Les nationalistes africains, Senghor en tête, avaient tellement protesté contre lui que la grande marque de petit déjeuner avait dû changer la présentation de ses produits.
>
> Mais un changement vient d'intervenir: récemment, Bécassine a rendu son tablier à la Marquise de Grand-Air. Elle a acheté une mitraillette et s'est remise à parler breton: 'Ha Malloz-Ru Dar C'hallaoued!', dit-elle en brandissant sa mitraillette. Cela signifie dans la langue réssuscitée: 'Malédiction, rouge aux Français'. Bécassine est déchaînée.[54]

The figure of Bécassine was re-invented in numerous other ways, such as in a play by Keineg: *Nevez-amzer ar Bonedoù Ruz* (1972), in which she rallies the troops, and in anti-Bécassine posters by L'Unaviez Oberiou Breiz, which were designed by Xavier de Langlais. Bécassine even figures in the heated debate around Françoise Morvan's recent book *Le Monde comme si*. Reviewing the book in *Hopala!* Prémel condemns the author by saying that she combines the worst aspects of both Bécassine herself and Mme de Grand-Air, a comparison that was invited by the fact that Morvan herself uses Bécassine as an

---

53 *Lutte occitane: organe d'information et de combat de 'lucha occitana', rédigé par des équipes militantes*, 5 (Novembre 1972), p.16.

54 Jean-Pierre Richardot, *La France en miettes*, p.146.

intertext.[55] It is clear that she has been completely reclaimed, and cannot today be taken at face value.

Revolutionary poetry

The same 'revolution' or movement of 'reclamation' is seen in the way in which hybridity is embraced in postcolonial literature. The linguistic hybridity of Brittany is the result of cultural genocide:

> Dans la société colonisée, le bilinguisme lui-même, ailleurs source de richesses culturelles n'est qu'une phase de la guerre d'usure que la langue du pouvoir colonisateur livre à celle du colonisé, progressivement écrasée, étouffée, éliminée. Munis de leur seule langue, les colonisés sont des étrangers dans leur propre pays.[56]

Embracing this hybridity can thus be seen as the ultimate act of reclamation. The importance of the French language for France's sense of identity is beyond doubt, and it is clear that the symbolic value of a language is more acutely felt in a colonial context. Given that colonial-style repression is the explanation and justification for why these modern poets write in French rather than in Breton, this political issue is inseparable from French-language Breton literature, whether the author likes it or not. This political aspect was stressed in the journal *Bretagnes*, which represents the first concerted attempt to define Francophone Breton literature. In their first editorial (1975) Keineg and Keginer claim that: '*Bretagnes* existe pour rompre la colonisation de la littérature', and in the second the connection between questions literary and political becomes even clearer: '*Bretagnes* se doit de gagner sa place dans l'entreprise de décolonisation de notre peuple'. The journal was relatively short-lived, but this debate raged on elsewhere, and material from the columns of journals such as *Le Peuple Breton*, together with prefaces and 'arts

---

55 Gérard Prémel, *Hopala!* 14 (2003), 77.
56 *Bretagne = colonie*, p.33.

146

poétiques' from the period, form a coherent theory of 'revolutionary poetry'.

Keginer explains in a short essay, 'Point de départ: une poésie révolutionnaire bretonne existe', how Breton literature of French expression is necessarily revolutionary, and that this has nothing to do with the subject-matter itself. Rather it is the nature of the relationship between the two languages that makes the literature inescapably political:

> On conçoit qu'il puisse y avoir une poésie de langue bretonne. Phénomène plus étrange: comment se fait-il qu'il existe une poésie bretonne de langue française? Il ne suffit pas pour cela qu'il y ait en Bretagne des poètes s'exprimant en français. Il faut encore que ces poètes aient conscience de *parler breton*, même dans une langue étrangère imposée ou non comme, par exemple, le français; pour cela, une *saisie* politique de l'existence d'un peuple breton est nécessaire, tout comme, dans la même situation, le poète noir qui écrit en français doit *saisir* qu'il est Noir pour cesser d'écrire dans la langue française, et parler enfin dans la *langue noire*, même si c'est avec des mots français. Ce changement est véritablement une révolution. Il s'accompagne forcément, et c'est la même démarche, d'une analyse radicale da la situation coloniale du pays, l'un et l'autre ne naissant que l'un par l'autre, pour finir par ne faire qu'une seule attitude combattante. On comprend donc qu'il est inutile d'ajouter le mot *révolutionnaire* à l'expression *poésie bretonne de langue français* qui signifie, par le caractère subversif de sa seule existence: poésie révolutionnaire'.[57]

Francophone Breton writing was therefore inescapably political in the same way that black writing was, and for the same reason, as Keginer points out here. In similar vein in 1948 Sartre had sought to explain: 'pourquoi la poésie noire de langue française est, de nos jours, la seule grande poésie révolutionnaire', in *Orphée noir*, reprinted as a preface to Senghor's *Anthologie de la nouvelle poésie nègre et malgache de langue française*.[58] These Breton poets felt that they had more in

---

57 Kristian Keginer, *Un dépaysement, précédé d'une Mise au point et suivi d'un Point de départ (Une poésie révolutionnaire bretonne existe)*, préface de Paol Keineg (Paris: Oswald, 1972), pp.69–72 (p.69).
58 Sédar L. Senghor, *Anthologie de la nouvelle poésie nègre et malgache de langue française*, précédée de *Orphée noir* par Jean Paul Sartre (Paris: Presses universitaires de France, 1972), first published 1948, xii.

common with writers from overseas countries that had been colonized by France than with mainstream Parisian writers, and they draw inspiration from this earlier writing. However the restrained descriptions of the state of biculturality found in Senghor's anthology, such as the expression of a desire to: 'apprivoiser, avec des mots de France,/ Ce cœur qui m'est venu du Sénégal',[59] does nothing to prepare us for the violent language found in Breton work of the 1970s. Even when directly describing oppression, Sartre uses polite, quiet language in comparison to Keginer:

> Le héraut de l'âme noire a passé par les écoles blanches, selon la loi d'airain qui refuse à l'opprimé toutes les armes qu'il n'aura pas volées lui-même à l'oppresseur; c'est au choc de la culture blanche que sa négritude est passée de l'existence immédiate à l'état réfléchi (*Anthologie de la nouvelle poésie*, p.xv).

Keginer writes with a violence reminiscent of, but also surpassing, the rhetoric of the Revolution, most notoriously used by the Abbé Grégoire in his report on France's regional languages:

> Le peuple breton est bilingue, mais sa poésie est une, puisque sa source est unique. Lorsque les mots bretons la révèlent, même si elle crie de douleur et de révolte, elle est fondamentalement sereine, et souveraine: elle parle sa vraie langue. Mais les mots français la retournent comme un gant, lui jettent la tête en bas. La poésie bretonne de langue française – c'est par cette *contra-diction* qu'elle est politiquement révolutionnaire – entretient avec la langue française des rapports incestueux et meurtiers: née de cette langue étrangère, quoique sa source soit ailleurs, elle s'y marie afin de la mieux détruire, et pourtant son exigence propre la lui fait aimer et servir.[60]

This work came into its own in the 1990s, when the definitional and theoretical questions were taken up and refined by postcolonial critics, notably at the Centre d'Études des Littératures et Civilisations Francophones at the University of Rennes, with Pascal Rannou, Marc Gontard and Thierry Glon among the most prolific contributors to the debate. Much important work has been disseminated in the centre's journal *Plurial*. The idea of 'métissage', or hybridity, is key to the pioneering analyses of Francophone Breton works that have appeared

---

59   Léon Laleau, *Anthologie de la nouvelle poésie*, p.108.
60   Keginer, Kristian, *Un dépaysement*, p.69.

in *Plurial* and also in book-length studies by its editors, in particular work concentrating on Corbière, Hélias and the poetry of the 1960s and 1970s. In an important issue of *Plurial* entitled *Écrire la Bretagne*, Bernard Hue argues that modern Francophone Breton litera-ture shows us the change that has come about in Brittany and in Breton identity, concluding that: 'bretonnité = altérité'.[61] Another issue, comparing Brittany, the Maghreb, and Québec, takes its conceptual frame from Tahar Ben Jelloun, presenting the idea of 'métissage' as a positive, forward-looking value: 'l'avenir est au métissage'.[62] Marc Gontard takes as guide the statement by Jean-Loup Amselle: 'qu'il n'y a pas de culture en dehors de l'interculturalité'.[63]

On the simplest level hybridity can be the result of cross-fertilization. For instance Gontard calls Grall's form 'la sône' a 'forme métisse', as it is the result of a meeting between French poetry and the native Breton poetic form know as the 'son'.[64] The main focus of the critical energy is on the language, and the relation between the two languages of Brittany, as manifested in the detail of the French. Again, language can be 'hybrid' on a superficial level; for instance Gontard claims that the Breton language is present in Grall's *Les Vents m'ont dit*, despite Grall talking of a sense of loss dominating his feelings for the language:

> Même pour l'écrivain non-celtisant, la langue n'est donc pas morte et fonc-tionne comme palimpseste, marquant pas ses 'ker', ses 'tre', ses 'pen', ses 'arc'h', une identité sonore par rapport au français dans lequel résonne la langue oubliée.[65]

Pascal Rannou's work on the language of Hélias's *Cheval* has sought to show that the inclusion of Breton words in the main French text can go beyond the level of lexical exoticism, and his focus on more subtle,

---

61 Bernard Hue, 'Le temps des évidences', *Écrire la Bretagne 1960–1995*, ed. by Bernard Hue and Marc Gontard, *Plurial* 5 (Rennes: Presses universitaires de Rennes, 1995), 11–13 (12).
62 Bernard Hue, 'Du mythe à la réalité', *Métissage du texte: Bretagne, Maghreb, Québec*, ed. by Bernard Hue, *Plurial* 4 (1994), 5–6 (5).
63 Marc Gontard, 'Effets de métissage dans la littérature bretonne', 27–39.
64 Ibid., p.35.
65 Ibid., p.37.

textual evidence of Hélias being 'caught between' cultures gets beyond the polarization in the press into blanket praise for this great man, and extreme condemnation by the likes of Grall. Rannou uses Hélias as a test-case in his larger project of defining Francophone Breton literature. His reading is not only the first to be based on the detail of Hélias's language, but it is also one of the first to explore the connection between close textual analysis and the defining of Francophone Breton literature, in proposing:

> une interrogation sur la notion de littérature bretonne francophone et la possibilité qu'elle puisse véhiculer une 'bretonnité' lisible non seulement dans les thèmes abordés mais aussi dans la saveur même de la langue.[66]

The key to characterizing this French lies in asking what sort of translation is taking place in this text. The way in which Hélias translates literally from the Breton is condemned by Grall as a 'tentative de folklorisation', because, for example, translating 'ifern yen' as 'enfer froid', when 'enfer cruel' would be more appropriate, or using 'mignon' to translate the Breton word for friend, when it would be more accurate to translate it as 'ami', makes Breton life seem quaint and curious. Grall goes as far as to argue that this makes Hélias's text 'colonializing':

> la conséquence d'une tentative de folklorisation, de dépècement colonial de la langue bretonne, et de gommage de celle-ci pour la plus 'grande gloire' du français – langue dans laquelle fut conçu Le Cheval d'orgueil.[67]

Rannou also argues that Hélias's manipulation of French is more than ludic, and that the author is playing not just with the two languages, but with the competence of his readers in each language, thereby setting up a barrier, or making 'insiders' and 'outsiders'. He concludes

---

66 *Inventaire d'un héritage: essai sur l'œuvre littéraire de Pierre-Jakez Hélias* (Relecq-Kerhuon: An Here, 1997), p.14. He concludes that: 'Criblés d'emprunts et de calques, ce texte s'inscrit dans le droit fil d'une littérature métissée', p.101.

67 *Le Cheval couché*, p 99.

that: 'ce texte s'inscrit dans le droit fil d'une littérature métissée'.[68] So Hélias is criticized here not only, or not so much, for his choice of one language over the other, but for what he does with the French langauge at the micro-level of the text. Instead of providing a smooth, 'neutral', translation, he produces slightly odd-sounding French, in a careful attempt to offer the French reader a safe degree of alienation, or the charm of exoticism.

Conclusion

While the nineteenth century saw representations of Brittany switch from overwhelmingly negative to mainly positive images, the twentieth century brought complete revolution. Now Brittany could be portrayed as wretched and exploited by Bretons themselves, fuelled by anger and inspired by political commitment. Also, from the nineteenth to the twentieth century there has been a transformation in the cultural make-up of Brittany, as well as in attitudes towards Bretonness. The changes to its make-up are clear in statistics on language usage, but the attitude change is best seen in the domain of literature. Folkloric representations of Brittany are now highly controversial and cannot be taken at face value. Influential movements within both Breton-language and French-language literatures eschewed traditional Breton material, as it was considered fit only for the museum. Instead writers attempted to look outwards beyond Brittany, and, more importantly, beyond France, with the result that literature could no longer espouse traditional or clichéd imagery in an unthinking way without causing controversy, as the case of Hélias demonstrates. Gone were the scenes of sublime natural grandeur, the pure people, the untainted landscapes and liminal coastlines, all harking back to a world of Celtic warriors,

---

68   *Inventaire d'un héritage*, p.101. His full argument reads: 'Le métissage textuel du *Cheval* n'a pas qu'une origine ludique. C'est une manière de psychodrame lingistique où l'auteur jongle avec ses langues et distingue ses lecteurs selon leur degré de compétence, qui en fait des élus ou des exclus', p.106.

as literature now spoke of factory workers and deserted villages. The two extremes of rural idyll and factory floor are far from being unconnected fields of reference. The most radical modern literature engaged deliberately with the clichés, with writers exploiting the nature cliché or the 'culte des morts' cliché, or explicitly re-clothing an individual cliché, as in the case of the despised caricature Bécassine.

The strongest evidence of a revolution in attitudes and in the Bretons' self-image is seen in the most subtle place, that is in the semantic evolution or revolution of individual words. An explicit example would be Xavier Grall playfully, but powerfully, glossing Finistère (< Finis + terre) as 'le début du monde', making of Brittany's westernmost tip the beginning rather than the end of the earth, with the reversal speaking volumes of the rebellion, resistance, defiance and 'rage' (his own word) that permeate his writing.[69] With similar newfound confidence and energy, even words such as 'sauvage' and 'barbare' can be used anew, and so the poet Glanndour is able to describe himself with pride as a 'sauvage': 'Je suis un sauvage, fils d'une race indocile et indomptée'.[70] The same reversal can be observed in the case of the word 'barbare'. The use made by Le Quintrec of a quotation from Brizeux in his preface to an anthology of Breton poetry demonstrates the semantic distance that the word has travelled. Where Brizeux describes his return from civilized Italy to his native province thus: 'Des villes d'Italie [...] J'arrivai [...] je redevins barbare', Le Quintrec retorts: 'Que ne le redevint-il pour de bon? Il serait aujourd'hui un poète du premier banc et non ce petit romantique presque oublié'.[71]

The word 'barde' shows most clearly how ideas can come full circle. In the nineteenth century its meaning was far from fixed, as we saw in chapter 1, where we charted the development of the word

---

69   Xavier Grall, *La Fête de nuit* (Saint-Brieuc: Éditions Kelenn, 1972), p.36. There is also a similar play on 'Penn-ar-bed' (the Breton name for Finistère), translated literally as 'tête de l'univers' in *Le Cheval couché*, p.73.

70   Maodez Glanndour, *Kregin-Mor* (Brest: Al Liamm, 1987), p.11.

71   Charles Le Quintrec, *Les Grandes heures littéraires de la Bretagne* (Rennes: Ouest France, 1978), p.52. The quotation is from Auguste Brizeux, 'Les Quêteurs', *Les Bretons*, in *Œuvres complètes*, ed. by Taillandier, I, 112–13.

'barde' from being little more than a convenient rhyme for 'bombarde' in a Celtic setting ('Le Retour', *Marie*, OAB, I, 7), to new heights when juxtaposed with 'arabe'. What is clear is that it was understood as having a set of connotations that were separate from those of the word 'poète'. In the twentieth century, though, Le Scouëzec can present Keineg as the voice of his people by claiming that he is less a poet than a 'barde', going on to link him with ancient Welsh bards such as Llywarch Hen.[72] In his 'Point de départ', Keginer links up modern 'revolutionary' poets Keineg and Gwernig with Welsh bards Taliesin and Myrddin, showing that the label 'barde' had been definitively reclaimed from the realms of folklore.[73] For Gontard, what makes Keineg the poet of decolonisation par excellence is that his first collection *Le Poème du pays qui a faim* (1966):

> est, sous forme de récit *bardique*, un cri contre l'aliénation séculaire de le Bretagne et contre la politique coloniale dont elle est victime, révélée métaphoriquement par la guerre d'Algérie (my emphasis).[74]

The fact that the language balance in Brittany is now statistically the opposite of what it was in the nineteenth century has given new potency to the choice of language used by a given writer. The theory of revolutionary poetry discussed in this chapter is a direct result of the political impact of language loss on a people. However undeniable the creativity and energy that is displayed in the work of the poets of decolonization, an energy that is inseparable from a real political awakening, it is debatable whether these modern poets are as revolutionary as their nineteenth-century forebear Corbière. For the poets discussed in this chapter, Corbière is more of a Breton poet than Brizeux can ever be. Although he has no direct legacy, his textual disruptiveness has provided inspiration irrespective of *why* he was disruptive. Despite his having no pro-Breton or pro-Celtic agenda, critics agree that Corbière is both the first and the best 'authentic voice' in French for Brittany. Attention to the detail of literary

---

72   Gwenc'hlan Le Scouëzec, preface to Paol Keineg, *Hommes liges des talus en transes*, p.10.

73   Kristian Keginer, *Un dépaysement*, p.71.

74   Marc Gontard, 'Pour une littérature bretonne de langue française', p.26.

language, as advocated by critics writing in *Plurial*, has opened up earlier Francophone Breton literature as 'postcolonial'. The work of the 1970s writers, in setting out the theory of revolutionary poetry, is both what allows us to look back as far as the 1830s through a new lens, and also what has prepared the way for the embracing of a postcolonial framework in the 1990s.

Conclusion: Between languages

We can now return to the fundamental question that has guided my discussion: what makes a Francophone Breton writer? or what characterizes this writing that is both a missing chapter from the story of French literature, and that is dismissed, if not denied, by many Breton militants? We have seen that different writers and different eras have had opposing understandings of what might make authentic Breton literature of French expression.

For Auguste Brizeux it meant fulfilling the requirements of the day. With his emphasis on birth and language competence, as well as suitable subject-matter, and even appropriate attire, he exemplifies the idea that the personality behind the writing is key. He invents for himself the role of 'chantre de le Bretagne', and is arguably the first to make a deliberate and sustained attempt to represent Brittany in the French language. His poems are not the first French-language descriptions of Brittany, but he is the first to define himself in terms of this project. He writes almost exclusively about Brittany, and with his début collection *Marie*, he is the first Breton to be successful in mainstream French culture, that is to be championed by Paris critics. He owes his success and fame to his exploitation of the traditional associations of Brittany, but while acting out a role may have brought him success in his day, he was soon attracting attention for his *lack* of authenticity. Perhaps Brizeux went from 'selling' Bretonness to selling out, a view that is expressed in the *Histoire littéraire et culturelle de la Bretagne*:

> Ensuite il a suffi au poète de marteler quelques alexandrins assez patriotiques pour enflammer les cœurs. Son amour pour son pays [...] était si réel qu'il suppléait à son manque de génie (p.97).

Although he is more often remembered now as an example of how *not* to be an authentic Francophone Breton writer, the 1830s nevertheless mark a turning point in the history of Brittany, in that this is when

Bretons themselves began writing about Brittany in what was for most an alien tongue: French. Brizeux's importance in this crucial development must not be underestimated, and authentic or not, he can be considered the father of this literature produced between languages.

Investigating the precise way in which writing is caught between two languages leads us to a more sophisticated answer to the same question. To Brizeux his biculturality was an uncomplicated fact, as he viewed the choice between two languages as little more than a pragmatic matter, and his view of translation was unproblematized. Thus the way in which he was 'caught' between languages, and between cultures, was relatively straightforward. In the 1970s, in contrast, the poets of decolonization were 'caught' extremely self-consciously. The fact that these writers had lost, or had been deprived of, the language that would have given their work automatic legitimacy as 'Breton' is key to their theory of poetic language. It is also the justification both for their positioning themselves alongside other 'colonized' cultures inside or outside the Hexagon, and for the adoption of a postcolonial framework by literary critics. However, the case of Tristan Corbière teaches us just as much about authenticity as either of these extremes; or rather, his reception history from the 1880s to the 1990s provides a valuable insight into different understandings of Breton voices in the French language. Though his reception tells us more about a vogue for 'foreignness' as a marker of great literary achievement than it does about Brittany per se, it is Corbière, rather than Brizeux, or any of the twentieth-century poets, who is hailed today as the first authentic voice of a Francophone Brittany.

The discussion in the three successive chapters has shown that different Francophone representations of Brittany from 1789 to the present have very different relationships with the French language, and that this relationship is by no means determined by whether a writer is Breton-born, bilingual, or an 'insider' on the one hand, or a visitor from Paris on the other; nor does it follow a strictly chronological development. 'Authenticity' has to do with the author's treatment of the French language. It seems that in order to get to the 'true' Brittany a writer must do something to the French language:

destroy it, subvert it, or perhaps simply work with it in the intense way that the greatest poets always work with language.

Traditionally, at its beginnings in the wake of Romanticism, Francophone Breton literature was expected to be 'poetic' in the sense summed up by the phrase 'Bretagne est poésie'. Though this was borrowed from Marie de France, the idea of Brittany's 'poeticness' took off in the nineteenth century, and was used by Tiercelin as the motto for his journal *L'Hermine* in the 1890s. At around the same time, Arthur La Borderie was describing Brittany as an 'être poétique', and claiming, in a more elaborate characterization of the province, that: 'la Bretagne n'est pas seulement une langue, un caractère, un peuple, une histoire; la Bretagne en outre est une poésie, une poésie dans le passé et dans le présent'.[1] By the early twentieth century such pronouncements on Brittany's innate poeticness border on the comical, as in the following pronouncement by Anatole Le Braz:

> Car enfin la Bretagne n'est pas seulement une Hespérie française, enfantée par décret divin pour être une terre de poésie: elle est en soi une poésie, la plus riche, la plus jaillissante, la plus intarissable des poésies [...]Il [le Breton] ne naît pas seulement poète: l'aiguillon poétique est en lui comme une fatalité héréditaire, comme une sorte de mal royal.[2]

Increasingly, however, Brittany was expected to be poetic in the sense in which 'poetic' has been understood at least since the time of the 'poètes maudits', and also by the 'négritude' and decolonization movements, that is in the radical sense of subversive of language.

Our understanding of Brittany is enhanced by considering it as a postcolonial culture. As I have argued, it warrants this by virtue of its treatment at the hands of France. By the second half of the twentieth century it becomes essential to consider the postcolonial context because of the movement of solidarity with other 'colonized' cultures

---

1   Arthur de la Borderie, *La Bretagne et son histoire* (Rennes: Plihon, 1891). This is the published version of his inaugural lecture, of 4 December 1890, cited in Guiomar, *Le Bretonisme*.

2   Anatole Le Braz, preface to Camille Le Mercier d'Erm, *Les Bardes et poètes nationaux de la Bretagne armoricaine* (Rennes: Plihon et Hommay, 1918), pp.xiv–xv.

that dominated the political picture by the 1960s and 1970s. In any case, postcolonial literary criticism has now taken root in Brittany, and exciting re-readings of works both canonical and forgotten are being produced. Brittany's precise place in postcolonial studies, as well as French Studies, remains unclear none the less, if not controversial.

In the case of Anglophone Celts, the debate has moved further, and the postcolonial framework has been refined. As we saw in the introduction, the Celtic peripheries of Britain were, until comparatively recently, thought irrelevant to postcolonial criticism, as summed up in *The Empire Writes Back*'s criticism of Ireland, Wales and Scotland for what is termed 'complicity' (see above). What these editors condemn as 'complicity', though, can make for more subtle models of cultural interpenetration, such as that of the 'willing conspiracy', advanced by Patrick Sims-Williams:

> The Celts themselves have often been ready to see their own reflection in the Celtic racial myths offered them, and to dance to their tunes. Indeed, I would go further and maintain that such Celtic racial myths are to a considerable extent the product of willing conspiracies between non-Celts and Celts, particularly Celts living in exile and interpreting their people to a foreign audience, with varying degrees of sincerity; a list of such Celtic 'conspirators' might include Geoffrey of Monmouth, Gerald of Wales, James Macpherson, Iolo Morganwg, Hersart de La Villemarqué, Ernest Renan, Alexander Carmichael, and even David Lloyd George playing up to the role of 'Welsh wizard' in English politics. [...] In other words, racial stereotypes of the Celts are not solely invented and maintained by non-Celts in an imperialist context, important though this context has often been'.[3]

A similar argument is made by M. Wynn Thomas, who uses Bhabha's idea of hybridity in his bold re-reading of the two literatures of Wales. He uses the example of Dylan Thomas being referred to as a 'hyphenated' Welshman ('Anglo-Welsh'), as illustration:

> But the term 'hyphenated' is as much of a hindrance as a help, since it implies a fundamental distinction between true (Welsh) Welshness and mongrel (Anglo-

---

3   Patrick Sims-Williams, 'The Visionary Celt', p.77.

158

Welsh) Welshness. Much more useful in the Welsh context is the term 'hybrid', in Bhabha's sense of the word.[4]

The length of a given 'colonial' situation, while making definition of the region as 'colonized' controversial, and even disqualifying it for some, can add to the complexity, challenge assumptions, and make it an important addition to the portfolio of case studies.[5] For instance, some more recent work on other Celtic literatures has critiqued the way much postcolonial criticism is predicated on a homogenized 'West'.[6] The material presented in my discussion, while constituting the first sustained analysis of the representation of Brittany in French-language literature, provides an original case study for scholars of postcolonial theory. If, on the one hand, it demonstrates the importance of a postcolonial framework for understanding Francophone Brittany, my study also suggests what Brittany has to offer to postcolonial criticism, as well as to French Studies.

As far as nineteenth-century studies are concerned, adding Brittany to the picture gives us a more nuanced understanding of the building of the nineteenth-century French canon. Despite the fact that the major figures of nineteenth-century French literature have nearly all written about Brittany, if not travelled there to document their fiction (this includes Balzac, Hugo, Stendhal, Flaubert, Merimée, and Michelet, not to mention the native Bretons Chateaubriand, Renan, and Lamennais),[7] Brittany remains absent from our histories of French

---

4   M. Wynn Thomas, *Corresponding Cultures: The two literatures of Wales* (Cardiff: University of Wales Press, 1999), p.49. See also his *Internal Difference,* and, ed., *DiFfinio Dwy Lenyddiaeth Cymru* (Cardiff: University of Wales Press, 1995).

5   This assumption is behind a recent survey of Welsh-language literature from the tenth-century poem *Armes Prydein,* to the twentieth century, by R. M. Jones, *Ysbryd y Cwlwm: Delwedd y Genedl yn ein Llenyddiaeth* (Cardiff: University of Wales Press, 1998).

6   See, for instance, Daniel Williams, 'Pan-Celticism and the Limits of Post-Colonialism: W. B. Yeats, Ernest Rhys, and Williams Sharp in the 1890's', in *Nations and Relations: Writing Across the British Isles,* ed. by Tony Brown and Russell Stephens (Cardiff: New Welsh Review, 2000), pp.1–29.

7   For a synthesis see Eugène Bérest, 'Les voyageurs français en Bretagne', in *Histoire littéraire et culturelle,* II, 177.

literature. Examining and comparing what these writers do with Brittany offers new insights into Romanticism and post-Romanticism, and provides different perspectives on France. The case of Brizeux's *Marie* illustrates how 'otherness' could be packaged to please the French, or specifically the Parisians, at this time. Showing how the Breton author had to walk a tightrope, showing desirable 'local colour' of the type that would stimulate but also soothe Parisians, it exposes the limitations of the nineteenth century's interest in cultural difference. The inevitability of what I have termed 'writing to Paris' suggests that Romanticism is fundamentally inward looking, no matter how much it claims to be interested in discovering 'the other', or the new. Brizeux's case shows how cultural difference could be hijacked as part of the basically centralizing project of regionalism, which was to invent a cosmetically diverse 'patrie' composed of contentedly inferior 'petites patries'. Also, any attempt by historians of literature to redress the balance is complicated by the paradox that the very people behind the centrifugal forces of regionalism are those who also seek the sanction of the centre, of the Parisian, mainstream-French critics. The centripetal force in Brizeux is just as present as it is in the cry of the young Mallarmé exiled to 'ce misérable Tournon': 'J'ai besoin d'hommes, de Parisiennes amies, de tableaux, de musique',[8] which means that Brizeux's 'regionalizing' pieces are – intellectually – written to Paris. Might we go as far as to say that Brizeux is actually taking part in the construction of 'Frenchness', or that 'Bretagne' was created by Paris, with the help of some Bretons who essentially became Parisians in order to take part in the creation process?[9]

This study also allows us new ways of understanding Frenchness. For regionalists, France is not only composed of a mosaic of internal differences, but the way in which these differences have been, and to a degree are still, regarded by the State, renders France undemocratic.

---

8   Letter to Cazalis, from Tournon, July 1864, *Œuvres complètes I*, ed. by Bertrand Marchal (Paris: Gallimard, 1998), p.660.

9   This would be mirrored in the case of Ireland, as shown by David Cairns and Shaun Richards, *Writing Ireland: Colonialism, Nationalism and Culture* (Manchester: Manchester University Press, 1998), p.8, and Declan Kiberd, *Inventing Ireland*, p.83.

Although present all along in 'regionalist' thought, as shown in an early instance from a seminal study of Alsace:

> Ainsi, par suite de leur conception abstraite de l'homme, et de leur incapacité à saisir le réel, les Français en viennent à pratiquer une politique en opposition absolue avec les principes élémentaires de la démocratie.// Ce vice de la pensée démocratique française, qui se manifeste également dans notre politique africaine et coloniale,[10]

the undemocratic nature of France has recently come to the fore in the context of increased European integration. France's double standards, in refusing for itself the cultural heterogeneity that it actively promotes in other areas such as Québec and Belgium,[11] have led regionalist writers to reclaim the rhetoric of democracy. The issue has been clearly set out recently in an ingenious piece by Jean-Yves Le Disez: 'Mes filles expliquées à la République', which consists of a dialogue between himself and 'la République', accusing 'her' of making it difficult for him to explain and justify her to his own Breton-speaking daughters. He pays particular attention to the European charter for minority languages, and draws a comparison between the Bretons of the nineteenth century and today's Beurs, and with the situation in the 'banlieues':

> la question de la langue bretonne et le malaise des banlieues sont liés, [...] les périphéries, toutes les périphéries, contestent le monolithisme du centre [...]. Tu fais l'innocente mais tu sais fort bien que le seul article de cette convention sur les droits de l'enfant que tu n'as pas signé concerne précisément le droit de chaque enfant appartenant à une minorité linguistique d'employer la langue minoritaire avec les autres members du groupe.[12]

---

10 Frédéric Hoffet, *Psychanalyse de l'Alsace*, avant-propos de Germain Muller (Colmar: Éditions Alsatia, 1973), p.187, first publ. 1951.

11 As Jean-Pierre Simon puts it: 'Le nationalisme français admet d'ailleurs parfaitement pour les autres ce qu'il refuse pour la France', *La Bretonnité*, p.154.

12 Jean-Yves Le Disez, *Noir/Blanc* [i.e. *Hopala!*], 1 (1999), 14–24 (22). As the title indicates, the piece is intended partly as a response to Régis Débray, *La République expliquée à ma fille* (Paris: Seuil, 1998).

161

He goes on to accuse France of having double standards, claiming that all he wants is for 'liberté, égalité, fraternité' to be applied to his own daughters.

The theme of 'republican values' has taken off in this journal, as a later contribution by Félix Castan explains:

C'est le concept de République qui est en cause [...]. Une politique d'exclusion des cultures et des langues, dans l'intérêt d'une seule, traduit une conception incompatible avec l'idéal républicain de cohabitation des disparités. [13]

'Colonial' comparisons have given way in the Breton debate to discussions of 'French democracy'. According to today's regionalists, they are fighting for more than their own rights as minorities, as France needs to be saved from itself: 'Ce ne sont pas seulement des minorités qu'il faut sauver: c'est d'abord la France qu'il faut guérir. La guérir d'un délire de pureté linguistique et culturelle'.[14] To them, France's intolerance of its own internal diversity only tells us of its fear of the perceived cultural and economic threat from the 'Anglo-Saxon' world, and fear of its own decline on the world stage.[15]

The literature produced against this backdrop can fall 'between' cultures and languages in different ways. Either it apologizes for not being in Breton, or this apology is implicit in the use of parallel text, or it relies on the Breton language for its *raison d'être*, as in the *Barzaz Breiz* (which are after all 'translations'), or even in Brizeux, with his emphasis on the language as research tool. Literature that uses lexical exoticism to achieve a 'poetic' value is also reliant on Breton, just like work that explicitly theorizes the loss of Breton, or attempts to reclaim the energy generated by rage at the loss. This study has shown that the potency of this biculturality can be well

---

13   Félix Castan, 'Pas de nation sans pluralité', *Hopala!*, 7 (2001), 11. The piece was originally entitled 'Contre la pensée unique, contre le Centralisme français', and refused by *Le Monde* in summer 2000, to be published in *Hopala!*, after his death, with an introduction by Sèrgi Javaloyès.

14   Félix Castan, 'Pas de nation sans pluralité', p.13.

15   On this fear, see Ager, *Identity, Insecurity and Image*, Chapman, *The Celts*, p.136, and Anne-Marie Thiesse, who sums it up: 'Enracinement: le thème revient de manière de plus en plus lancinante à mesure que décline la position internationale de la France', *Écrire la France*, p.13.

observed on the level of the detail of the text. The evolution and revolution in representations of Brittany was the result of writers working with, manipulating and subverting 'Bretagne', or 'le mythe breton'. The tensions implicit in such a project rise to the verbal surface, and tracing the trajectory of individual words, through close reading of selected texts shows how they can become highly charged. The word 'chêne', for instance, travels from Balzac's descriptions of prohibitive forests and the treachery concealed by them, through Brizeux's 'poussez bois défenseurs', to Corbière's Sainte-Anne, with her 'cœur de chêne'. The Breton expression 'tud kaled' (literally 'hard people'), used by Brizeux, must be read in the context of rocky imagery found in French-language evocations of Bretonness, such as the phrases found in Michelet: 'races de pierre', and 'peuple de granit',[16] and later in Renan: 'La pierre, en effet, semble le symbole naturel des races celtiques'.[17] Most of all, the example of the word 'sauvage' shows how potentially explosive individual lexical items can be, and how they achieve new potency when taken to new contexts. A lexical approach to this relatively young, and largely neglected 'French-Breton' tradition allows new insight into bi-culturality, as well as giving us a fuller picture of the French tradition. French literature should not be seen as Paris-centred, any more than France should be; but equally, we cannot understand the French-language literature of Brittany without taking account of the ways in which it is written to Paris. Ultimately, this approach leaves us with *different* ways of seeing Frenchness and identities expressed through the medium of French, and that without looking as far afield as other Francophone corners of the globe.

---

16   For a synthesis of the imagery used by Michelet, see Jacques Landrin, 'La Bretagne de Michelet: mythe et réalité', *Ouest et romantismes*, pp.391–404 (esp. p.398).

17   Ernest Renan, 'La Poésie des races celtiques', in *Essais de morale et de critique* (Paris: Calmann-Lévy, 1928), pp.375–456 (p.404).

Bibliography

Primary sources

Arnold, Matthew, *On the Study of Celtic Literature* (London: Smith, Elder & Co, 1867)

Balzac, Honoré de, *Béatrix*, in *La Comédie humaine*, 12 vols, ed. by Pierre-Georges Castex, II, 637–941

—— *Les Chouans*, ed. by Maurice Regard (Paris: Garnier Frères, 1957)

—— *Les Chouans*, ed. by Pierre Gascar (Paris: Gallimard, 1972)

—— *Pierrette*, in *La Comédie humaine*, 12 vols, ed. by Pierre-Georges Castex, IV, 1–163

Banville, Théodore de, *Les Exilés* (Paris: Fasquelle, 1899), first publ. 1867

Borderie, Arthur de la, *La Bretagne et son histoire* (Rennes: Plihon, 1891)

Brizeux, Auguste [Anonymous] Mémoires de Madame de La Vallière, vol 2 of *Mémoires secrets et inédits sur les cours de France au XVe, XVIe, et XVIIe siècles* (Paris: Mame et Delaunay-Vallée, 1829)

—— [Anonymous] *Marie: roman* (Paris: Aug Auffray et Urbain Canel, 1832 [1831])

—— *Marie: poème* (Paris: Paulin et Eugène Renduel, 1836)

—— *Marie, poème*, par Auguste Brizeux (Bruxelles: Société Belge de Librairie, Hausnan-Cattois et Cie, 1837)

—— *Marie* (Bruxelles: Laurent, 1840)

—— *Marie*, par Auguste Brizeux, third edn (Paris: Paul Masgana, 1840)

—— *Barzonek pe kanaouen ar Vretoned*, 21 juin 1836, 100 printed in Quimper and Morlaix, distributed free to singers

—— *Aux Prêtres de Bretagne* (Paris: Dentu, 1840)

—— *Telen Arvor: la harpe d'Armorique* (Paris: Duverger, 1839)

—— *Telen Arvor: La harpe d'Armorique*, nouvelle édition (Lorient: Gousset, 1844)

—— *Les Ternaires: livre lyrique* (Paris: Masgana, 1841); deuxième édition 1842 [this becomes *La Fleur d'or*, 1853]

—— *Les Bretons: poème* (Paris: Masgana, 1845); second edn 1846; third edn 1848

—— *Primel et Nola* (Paris: Garnier, 1852)

—— *La Fleur d'or* (Paris: Garnier, 1853)

—— *Marie – La Fleur d'or – Primel et Nola* (Paris: Garnier, 1853)

—— *Histoires poétiques suivies d'un essai sur l'art ou poétique nouvelle* (Paris: Victor Lecou, 1855); second edn Hachette, 1855

—— *Furnez Breiz: Sagesse de Bretagne* (Lorient: Gousset, 1855)

—— *Œuvres: La Fleur d'or, histoires poétiques* (Paris: Alphonse Lemerre, 1884)

—— *Œuvres complètes de Auguste Brizeux*, précédées par une notice par Saint René Taillandier, 2 vols (Paris: Michel Lévy Frères, 1860)

—— *Œuvres choisies: Les Bretons, Marie, Telen Arvor, Furnez Breiz*, 2 vols (Paris: Lemerre, 1874)

—— *Œuvres d'Auguste Brizeux*, 4 vols (Paris: Lemerre, 1880–84)

—— *Choix de poésies* (Paris: Hatier, 1932)

—— *Œuvres de Auguste Brizeux*, 4 vols, ed. by Auguste Dorchain (Paris: Garnier Frères, 1910–1914)

—— *Marie*, (Quimperlé: La Digitale, 1980), reprint of 1832 [1831] Paris edn

Brizeux, A. and P. Busoni, *Racine: Comédie en un acte et en vers*, représentée pour la première fois sur le théâtre-français, par MM les comédiens du roi, le 27 décembre 1827 (Paris: Ponthieu, 1827) and (Paris: Barba, 1828)

Brizeux, Auguste, *Un Poète Romantique et ses amis: Auguste Brizeux. Correspondance (1805–1858)*, ed. by Jean-Louis Debauve (Brest: Centre de Recherche Bretonne et Celtique, 1989)

Brousmiche, Jean-François, *Voyage dans le Finistère en 1829, 1830 et 1831*, 2 vols (Quimper: Morvran, 1977)

Calvez, Léone, and Herri Caouissin, *'Bécassine' vue par les Bretons*, comédie dramatique en 4 actes (Pleyber-Christ: Ronan, 1937)

Cambry, Jacques, *Voyage dans le Finistère*, nouvelle édition accompagnée de notes historiques, archéologiques, physiques et de la flore et de la faune du département, par M. Le Chevalier de Fréminville (Brest: Lefournier, 1836); reprinted in facsimile, presented by Roger Dupuy (Geneva: Slatkine Reprints, 1979)

Caumery [pseudonym of Maurice Languereau] and Joseph P. Pinchon, *L'Enfance de Bécassine* (Paris: Gautier-Languereau, 1913)

Céard, Henry, *Terrains à vendre au bord de la mer* (Paris: Charpentier et Fasquelle, 1906)

Césaire, Aimé, *Cahier d'un retour au pays natal* (Paris: Présence africaine, 1971)

—— *Discours sur le colonialisme* (Paris: Présence africaine, 1955)

Chateaubriand, François de, *Mémoires d'outre-tombe*, 2 vols, ed. by Jean-Claude Berchet (Paris: Classiques Garnier, 1989)

—— *René* (Geneva: Droz, 1947)

—— *Œuvres romanesques et voyages*, 2 vols, ed. by Maurice Regard, Bibliothèque de la Pléiade (Paris: Gallimard, 1969)

Corbière, Edouard, *Le Négrier* (Saint-Malo: Édns L'Ancre de Marine, 1990)

Corbière, Tristan, *Les Amours jaunes* ed. by Élisabeth Aragon et Claude Bonnin (Toulouse: Presses universitaires Mirail, 1992)

—— *Armor, Gens de mer*, ed. by Gilles Plazy (Spézet: Coop Breizh, 2002)

Déguignet, Jean-Marie, *Mémoires d'un paysan bas-breton 1834–1905* (Relecq-Kerhuon: An Here, 1998)

Diderot, Denis, *Œuvres esthétiques*, ed. by Paul Vernière (Paris: Garnier Frères, 1968)

Durand, Philippe, *Breizh hiziv: Anthologie de la chanson en Bretagne* (Paris: Oswald, 1976)

Elégoët, Fanch, *'Nous ne savions que le Breton et il fallait parler français': mémoires d'un paysan du Léon* (Rennes: Breizh Hor Bro, 1978), trans. from Breton *Un Den, Ur Vro* (Douarnenez: Hor Yezh, 1975)

Elléouët, Yves, *Livre des rois de Bretagne* (Paris: Gallimard, 1974)

Flaubert, Gustave, *Bouvard et Pécuchet*, ed. by Jacques Suffel (Paris: Garnier-Flammarion, 1966)

Flaubert, Gustave, and Maxime DuCamp, *Par les champs et par les grèves*, ed. by Adrianne Tooke (Geneva: Droz, 1987)

Fromentin, Eugène, *Œuvres complètes,* ed. by Guy Sagnes, Bibliothèque de la Pléiade (Paris: Gallimard, 1984)

Geffroy, Gustave, *Nouveaux contes du pays d'Ouest* (Paris: Georges Crès, 1920)

Glanndour, Maodez, *Kregin-Mor* (Brest: Al Liamm, 1987)

Grall, Xavier, *La Fête de nuit* (Saint-Brieuc: Éditions Kelenn, 1972)

Hélias, Pierre-Jakez, *Le Cheval d'orgueil: mémoires d'un Breton du Pays bigouden* (Paris: Plon, 1975)

—— *Lettres de Bretagne* (Paris: Galilée, 1978)

—— *Un Pays à deux langues: inédits* I (Brest: Brud Nevez, 2000)

Huguenin, Jean-René, *La Côte sauvage* (Paris: Seuil, 1960).

Hugo, Victor, *Correspondance familiale et écrits intimes*, 2 vols, ed. by Jean Gaudon, Sheila Graudon, Bernard Leuillieot (Paris: Robert Laffont, 1991)

Huysmans, Karl-Joris, *A Rebours* (Paris: Garnier-Flammarion, 1978)

Jones, Dewi Morris and Mikael Madeg, eds, *Du a Gwyn /Gwenn ha du: Cerddi Cyfoes o Lydaw* (Talybont: Y Lolfa, 1982)

Keginer, Kristian, *Un dépaysement, précédé d'une Mise au point et suivi d'un Point de départ (Une poésie révolutionnaire bretonne existe)*, préface de Paol Keineg (Paris: Oswald, 1972)

Keineg, Paol, *Hommes liges des talus en transes, réédition augmentée de Le poème du pays qui a faim, et suivi de Vent de Harlem*, préface de Gwenc'hlan Le Scouëzec (Paris: Oswald, 1969)

—— *Chroniques et croquis des villages verrouillés, comprenant, en édition bilingue, Barzhonegou-trakt (poèmes-tracts)*, preface by Yves Rouquette (Honfleur: Oswald, 1971)

—— *Nevez-amzer ar Bonedoù Ruz/ Le printemps des Bonnets Rouges* play performed 9 December 1972, at the Cartoucherie de Vincennes

Keranflec'h, Charles de, *Voyage dans les montagnes du centre Bretagne en 1857* (Spézet: Keltia Graphic Editions, 1998); appeared in *La Revue de Bretagne et de Vendée*, 1857, under title 'Voyage dans les montagnes noires et les monts d'Arez'

Larzac, Jean, *L'étranger du dedans et autres poèmes politiques* (Paris: Oswald, 1972)

Lamartine, Alphonse de, *Souvenirs, impressions, pensées et paysages, pendant un voyage en Orient (1832–1833): ou, Notes d'un voyager* (Paris: C. Gosselin, 1835)

La Villemarqué, Hersart de la, *Le Barzhaz Breizh: trésor de la littérature orale de la Bretagne* (Spézet: Coop Breizh, 1997)

—— 'Un débris du bardisme', *l'Écho de la Jeune-France*, 1836

—— 'La Renaissance bretonne', epilogue to *La Bretagne contemporaine: sites pittoresques, monuments, costumes, scènes de mœurs, histoire, légendes, traditions et usages des cinq départements de cette province* (Paris: Charpentier, 1865)

—— *L'Avenir de la langue bretonne*, avant-propos d'Olivier de Gourcuff (Nantes: Éditions du Terroir Breton, 1904)

—— *Essai sur l'histoire de la langue bretonne*, reprinted in Bernard Tanguy, *Aux origines du nationalisme breton*, vol. 2 (Union Générale d'Éditions, 1977)

Le Mercier d'Erm, Camille, *Les Bardes et poètes nationaux de la Bretagne armoricaine* (Rennes: Plihon et Hommay, 1918)

Le Quintrec, Charles, *Les Grandes heures littéraires de Bretagne* (Rennes: Ouest France, 1978)

—— *Anthologie de la Poésie bretonne 1880–1980* (Paris: La Table Ronde, 1980)

—— *Littératures de Bretagne* (Rennes: Ouest France, 1992)

Lewis, Saunders, *Is There an Anglo-Welsh Literature?* (Cardiff: [Cardiff Branch of the Guild of Graduates, University of Wales], 1939)

Luzel, François-Marie, *Bepred breizad: toujours breton, poésies bretonnes, avec traduction française en regard* (Morlaix: J. Haslé, 1865)

—— *Gwerziou Breiz-Izel: chants populaires de la Basse-Bretagne*, 2 vols (Lorient: É. Corfmat, 1868–1874)

Mallarmé, Stéphane, *Œuvres complètes*, 2 vols, ed. by Bertrand Marchal, Bibliothèque de la Pléiade (Paris: Gallimard, 1998–2003)

Merimée, Prosper, *Correspondance générale*, 14 vols, ed. by Maurice Parturier (Paris: Plon, 1934)

—— *Notes d'un voyage dans l'Ouest de la France: extrait d'un rapport adressé à M. le Ministre de l'Intérieur* (Paris: Rournier, 1836)

Piriou, Yann-Ber, ed., *Défense de cracher par terre et de parler breton: poèmes de combat (1950–1970). Anthologie bilingue* (Honfleur: Oswald, 1971)

Proust, Marcel, *Contre Sainte-Beuve*, (Paris: Gallimard, 1954)

—— *A la recherche du temps perdu*, 4 vols, ed. by Jean-Yves Tadié, Bibliothèque de la Pléiade (Paris: Gallimard, 1989)

Quellien, Narcisse, *Breiz: Poésies bretonnes* (Paris: Librairie orientale et américaine J. Maisonneuve, 1898)

Renan, Ernest, 'La Poésie des races celtiques', *Revue des Deux Mondes*, n.s. 5 (1854), 473–506

—— 'La Poésie des races celtiques', in *Essais de morale et de critique* (Paris: Calmann-Lévy, 1928), pp.375–456

—— *Souvenirs d'enfance et de jeunesse*, ed. by Jean Balcou (Paris: Presses Pocket, 1992)

Romieu, Auguste, 'La Basse-Bretagne, ses mœurs, son langage et ses monuments', *Revue de Paris*, 2 (1829), 155–67

—— 'La Basse-Bretagne', *Revue de Paris*, 22 (1831), 13–20, 274–81

—— 'La Basse-Bretagne', *Revue de Paris*, 30 (1831), 145–54

Rouanet, Marie, ed., *Occitanie 1970: Les poètes de la décolonisation/Occitania 1970: los poètas de la descolonizacion: anthologie bilingue* (Paris: Oswald, 1971)

Rouquette, Yves, *Rouergue, si, précédé de Ode à saint Aphrodise et suivi de Messe pour les cochons, édition bilingue* (Paris: Oswald, 1972)

Rousse, Joseph, *La Poésie bretonne au XIXe siècle: ouvrage orné de 23 portraits* (Paris: Lethielleux, 1895)

Rousseau, Jean-Jacques, *Julie ou La Nouvelle Héloïse* (Paris: Garnier Frères, 1960)

—— *Les Confessions*, 3 vols, ed. by Ad. Van Bever (Paris: Garnier Frères, 1952)

—— *Les Rêveries du promeneur solitaire*, ed. by Samuel Silvestre de Sacy (Paris: Gallimard, 1972)

Saint-Pol-Roux, *La Rose et les épines du chemin*, (Paris: Gallimard, 1997)

Sainte-Beuve, *Volupté*, avec un appendice contenant les témoignages et jugements contemporains (Paris: Charpentier, 1919)

Sand, George, *Promenades autour d'un village*, new edn (Paris: Calmann Lévy, 1877)

Senancour, *Oberman*, ed. by Béatrice Didier (Paris: Livre de Poche, 1984)

Souvestre, Émile *Les Derniers Bretons*, 2 vols, ed. by Dominique Besançon (Rennes: Terre de Brume, 1997), first publ. in book form 1836

Stendhal, *Mémoires d'un touriste*, 2 vols (Paris: Calmann-Lévy, 1854)

Taylor, Justin, Charles Nodier and Alphonse de Cailleux, *Voyages pittoresques et romantiques dans l'ancienne France* (Paris: Didot, 1820)

Tiercelin, Louis, and J. Guy Ropartz, *Le Parnasse breton contemporain* (Paris: A. Lemerre/Rennes: H. Caillière, 1889)

Verlaine, Paul, *Les Poètes maudits*, ed. by Michel Décaudin (Paris: SEDES, 1982)

Villiers de l'Isle-Adam, *Contes cruels*, ed. by Pierre Citron (Paris: Garnier-Flammarion, 1980)

Yeats, W. B., 'The Celtic Element in Literature', in *Essays and Introductions* (London: Macmillan, 1961), pp.173–88

Secondary sources

[Anonymous], 'Marie, roman', *Le Globe: Journal de la doctrine de Saint-Simon*, 15 December 1831, 33–52

Aaron, Jane and Chris Williams, eds, *Postcolonial Wales* (Cardiff: University of Wales Press, 2005)

Abeozen, *Istor lennegezh vrezhonek an amzer-vreman* (Brest: Al Liamm, 1957)

Abrams, Meyer H., *The Mirror and the Lamp: Romantic Theory and the Critical Tradition* (Oxford: Oxford University Press, 1953)

Adams, Sam, ed., *Seeing Wales Whole: Essays on the Literature of Wales, in honour of Meic Stephens* (Cardiff: University of Wales Press, 1998)

Ager, Dennis, *Identity, Insecurity and Image: France and Language* (Clevedon: Multilingual Matters, 1999)

Anderson, Benedict, *Imagined Communities: Reflections on the Origins and Spread of Nationalism* (London: Verso, 1983), reprinted 1991

an Du, Klaoda, *Histoire d'un interdit: le breton à l'école* (Lesneven: Hor Yezh, 1991)

Angelet, Christian, 'A propos de la Rapsode foraine: Corbière et Hersart de La Villemarqué', *La Nouvelle Tour de Feu*, nos 11, 12, 13, special issue 1985

Ashcroft, Bill, Gareth Griffiths, and Helen Tiffin, eds, *The Empire Writes Back: Theory and Practice in Post-colonial Literatures* (London: Routledge, 1989)

—— *The Post-colonial Studies Reader* (London: Routledge, 1995)

Ashley, Scott, 'Primitivism, Celticism and Modernity in the Atlantic fin de siècle', in *Symbolism, Decadence and the 'fin de siècle'*, ed. by Patrick McGuinness (Exeter: Exeter University Press, 2000), pp.175–93

Augier, Éloi, *Brizeux et Mistral, Marie et Mireille*, conférence faite à la société académique de Brest le 18 mars 1888 (Brest: L'Océan, 1888)

Bajon, Bernard, 'Le Romantisme de Saint-Pol-Roux et la Bretagne', *Ouest et romantismes, actes du colloque des 6,7,8 et 9 décembre 1990*, ed. by Georges Cesbron (Angers: Presses de L'Université d'Angers, 1991), pp.417–28

Balcou, Jean and Yves Le Gallo, eds, *Histoire littéraire et culturelle de la Bretagne*, 3 vols, Centre de recherche bretonne et celtique (Paris/Geneva: Champion-Slatkine, 1987)

Balcou, Jean, 'Les Bretons, ce sont nos indiens', in *Ouest et romantismes, actes du colloque des 6,7,8 et 9 décembre 1990*, ed. by Georges Cesbron (Angers: Presses de L'Université d'Angers, 1991), pp.43–51

Barbey d'Aurévilly, Jules, 'M. Brizeux', in *Les Œuvres et les hommes, III, Les poètes (première série)*, 26 vols (vol 3) (Geneva: Slatkine reprints, 1968), reprint of 1862 Paris edition, pp.75–98

Barbier, Auguste, *Souvenirs personnels et silhouettes contemporaines* (Paris: Dentu, 1883)

Barlow, Norman, *Sainte-Beuve to Baudelaire* (Durham, N.C.: Duke University Press, 1964)

Barnes, Helen Elcessor, *A Study of the Variations between the Original and the Standard Editions of Balzac's 'Les Chouans'* (Illinois: The University of Chicago Press, 1923)

Bassnett, Susan, and Harish Trivedi, eds, *Post-colonial Translation: Theory and Practice* (London: Routledge, 1999)

Beer, William R., *The Unexpected Rebellion: Ethnic Activism in Contemporary France* (New York: New York University Press, 1980)

Belmont, Nicole, ed., *Aux sources de l'ethnologie française: l'académie celtique* (Paris: Éditions du CTHS, 1995)

Bénichou, Paul, *L'Écrivain et ses travaux* (Paris: Corti, 1967)

—— *Nerval et la chanson folklorique* (Paris: Corti, 1970)

—— *Le Temps des prophètes: doctrines de l'âge romantique* (Paris: Gallimard, 1977)

Bérest, Eugène,'Les voyageurs français en Bretagne', in *Histoire littéraire et culturelle de la Bretagne*, 3 vols, ed. by Jean Balcou and Yves Le Gallo, Centre de recherche bretonne et celtique (Paris/Geneva: Champion-Slatkine, 1987), II, 177–218

Berger, Marianne Renate, *Sprachkontakt in der Bretagne: Sprachloyalität versus Sprachwechsel* (Tübingen: Niemeyer, 1988)

Bertho, Catherine, 'La naissance des stéréotypes régionaux en Bretagne au XIXe siècle' (unpublished doctoral thesis, 1979)

—— 'L'invention de la Bretagne: Genèse sociale d'un stéréotype', *Actes de la recherche en sciences sociales*, 35 (1980), 45–62

Besnier, Patrick, 'L'entre-deux mondes des "Contes cruels"', *Annales de Bretagne et des Pays de l'Ouest*, 76 (1969), 531–39

Bhabha, Homi K., ed., *Nation and Narration* (London: Routledge, 1990)

—— *The Location of Culture* (London: Routledge, 1994)

Bohata, Kirsti, *Postcolonialism Revisited* (Cardiff: University of Wales Press, 2004)

Bothorel, Jean, *La Bretagne contre Paris* (Paris: La Table Ronde, 1969)

Bourdieu, Pierre, and Luc Boltanski, 'Le fétichisme de la langue', *Actes de la Recherche en Sciences Sociales*, 4 (1975), 2–32

Bretagne = colonie (Rennes: Union Démocratique Bretonne, 1972)

Bretagne et romantisme, mélanges offerts à Louis Le Guillou, ed. by Bernard Duchatelet (Brest: Université de Bretagne Occidentale, 1989)

Broudic, Fañch, *La Pratique du breton de l'Ancien Régime à nos jours* (Rennes: Presses universitaires de Rennes, 1995)

—— *A la recherche de la frontière: la limite linguistique entre Haute et Basse-Bretagne aux XIXe et XXe siècles* (Brest: Ar Skol Vrezoneg, 1995)

—— *L'Interdiction du breton en 1902: la IIIe. République contre les langues régionales* (Spezet: Coop Breizh, 1997)

—— *Qui parle Breton aujourd'hui? Qui le parlera demain?* (Brest: Brud Nevez, 1999)

Brown, Terence, ed., *Celticism* (Amsterdam: Rodopi, 1996)

—— 'Cultural Nationalism, Celticism and the Occult', in *Celticism*, ed. by Terence Brown (Amsterdam: Rodopi, 1996), pp.221–30

Burch, Francis F., *Sur Tristan Corbière* (Paris: Nizet, 1975)

Caerléon (pseydonym of R. Caouissin), *La Révolution bretonne permanente* (Paris: La Table Ronde, 1969)

Cahiers d'Iroise, Peintres et Poètes en Bretagne, Cahiers d'Iroise, 22e année, No 4 (Nouvelle Série), Octobre–Décembre 1975/4

Cairns, David and Shaun Richards, *Writing Ireland: Colonialism, Nationalism and Culture* (Manchester: Manchester University Press, 1998)

Calin, William, *Minority Literatures and Modernism: Scots, Breton, and Occitan, 1920–1990* (Toronto: University of Toronto Press, 2000)

Calvet, Louis-Jean, *Linguistique et colonialisme: petit traité de glottophagie* (Paris: Payot, 1974)

Cassard, Jean-Christophe, 'Comment peut-on être Pierre-Jakes Hélias?', *Le Peuple Breton*, 328 (April 1991), pp.21, 24

Castan, Félix, 'Pas de nation sans pluralité', *Hopala!*, 7 (2001), 11–5

Catani, Damian, *The Poet in Society: Art, Consumerism, and Politics in Mallarmé* (Oxford: Peter Lang, 2003)

Certeau, Michel de, Julia Dominique and Jacques Revel, *Une Politique de la langue. La Révolution française et les patois: l'enquête Grégoire* (Paris: Gallimard, 1975)

Cerquiglini, Bernard, 'La Charte européenne des langues régionales ou minoritaires', in Clairis, Christos, Denis Coastaouec, and Jean-Baptiste Coyos, eds, *Langues et cultures régionales de France: état des lieux, enseignement, politiques* (Paris: L'Harmattan, 1999), pp.107–10

Cesbron, Georges, ed., *Ouest et romantismes, actes du colloque des 6,7,8 et 9 décembre 1990*, (Angers: Presses de L'Université d'Angers, 1991)

Champaud, Claude, *Le Séparisianisme* (Rennes: Armor-Editeur, 1977)

Champion, Timothy, 'The Celt in Archaeology', in *Celticism*, ed. by Terence Brown (Amsterdam: Rodopi, 1996), pp.61–78

Chapman, Malcolm, *The Gaelic Vision in Scottish Culture* (London: Croom Helm, 1978)

—— *The Celts: The Construction of a Myth* (London: Macmillan, 1992)

Charles-Merrien, Ghyslaire, 'Jean-René Huguenin: un héros romantique des années 60', in *Ouest et romantismes, actes du colloque des 6,7,8 et 9 décembre 1990*, ed. by Georges Cesbron (Angers: Presses de L'Université d'Angers, 1991), pp.143–53

Chassé, Charles, 'Mallarmé dans le Finistère', in *Lueurs sur Mallarmé* (Paris: Editions de la Nouvelle Revue Critique, 1947), pp.79–84

Clairis, Christos, Denis Coastaouec, and Jean-Baptiste Coyos, eds, *Langues et cultures régionales de France: état des lieux, enseignement, politiques* (Paris: L'Harmattan, 1999)

Collini, Stefan, *Matthew Arnold: A Critical Portrait* (Oxford: Clarendon Press, 1994)

Conley, Tom, and Steven Ungar, eds, *Identity Papers: Contested Nationhood in Twentieth-Century France* (Minneappolis and London: University of Minnesota Press, 1996)

Constantine, Mary-Ann, *Breton Ballads* (Aberystwyth: Cambrian Medieval Celtic Studies, 1996)

—— 'Ballads Crossing Borders: La Villemarqué and the "Breton Lenore"', *Translation and Literature*, 89:2 (1999), 197–216

Crawford, Robert, *Devolving English Literature* (Oxford: Clarendon Press, 1992)

Croix, Alain, and Jean-Yves Veillard, eds, *Dictionnaire du patrimoine breton* (Rennes: Apogée, 2000)

Cronin, Michael, *Across the Lines* (Cork: University of Cork Press, 2000)

Crossley, Ceri, 'P.-T. Cailleux, celtomane extraordinaire', *Romantisme*, 37 (1982), 53–64

—— *French Historians and Romanticism: Thierry, Guizot, The Saint-Simonians, Quinet, Michelet* (London: Routledge, 1993)

Crystal, David, *Language Death* (Cambridge: Cambridge University Press, 2000)

Dakyns, Janine R., *The Middle Ages in French Literature 1851–1900* (Oxford: Clarendon Press, 1973)

Davies, R. R., *The First English Empire: Power and Identities in the British Isles, 1093–1343* (Oxford: Oxford University Press, 2000)

Debauve, Jean-Louis, 'Autour d'un cénacle romantique: Brizeux et quelques-uns de ses amis', *Cahiers d'Iroise*, 1 (1961)

—— 'Autour de la publication des Amours jaunes', *La Nouvelle Tour de feu*, 11–13 (1985), 55–77

Débray, Régis, *La République expliquée à ma fille* (Paris: Seuil, 1998)

Deleuze, Gilles and Félix Guattari, *Kafka: pour une littérature mineure* (Paris: Minuit, 1975)

Delouche, Denise, 'Rencontres de peintres et de poètes en Bretagne au XIXe siècle', *Cahiers d'Iroise*, 22e année, (1975), 175–83

—— *Peintres de la Bretagne: découverte d'une province* (Paris: Klincksieck, 1977)

—— 'Le Mot et l'image dans la vision romantique picturale de la Bretagne', in *Ouest et romantismes, actes du colloque des 6,7,8 et 9 décembre 1990*, ed. by Georges Cesbron (Angers: Presses de L'Université d'Angers, 1991), pp.253–63

Denez, Per, 'Modern Breton Literature', in *Literature in Celtic Countries*, ed. by J. E. Caerwyn Williams [Taliesin Congress Lectures] (Cardiff: University of Wales Press, 1971), pp.113–36

Déniel, Alain, *Le Mouvement breton 1919–1945* (Paris: Maspero, 1976)

Derrida, Jacques, *Le Monolinguisme de l'autre* (Paris: Galilée, 1996)

Dietler, Michael, '"Our Ancestors the Gauls": Archaeology, Ethnic Nationalism and the Manipulation of Celtic Identity in Modern Europe', *American Anthropologist*, 96 (1994), 584–605

Dugalès, Nathalie, Ronan Le Coadic and Fabrice Patez eds, *Et la Bretagne?: héritage, identité, projets* (Rennes: Presses universitaires de Rennes, 2004)

Duhamel, Maurice, *La Question bretonne dans son cadre européen* (Paris: André Delpeuch, 1929) and (Rennes: Breiz Atao, 1929)

Dujardin, Louis, *La Vie et les œuvres de Jean-François-Marie-Maurice-Agathe Le Gonidec, grammairien et lexicographe breton 1775–1838* (Brest: Imprimerie commerciale & administrative, 1949)

Durand-Le Guern, Isabelle, 'Province et passé: la représentation de la Bretagne dans Béatrix', in *Province ⇔ Paris: topographies littéraires du XIX siècle*, ed. by A. Djourachkovitch and Y. Leclerc (Mont-Saint-Aignan: Publications de l'Université de Rouen, 2000), pp.83–96

Eagleton, Terry, *Exiles and Emigrés* (London: Chatto and Windus, 1970)

Ehrard, Jean, and Paul Viallaneix, eds, *Nos ancêtres les Gaulois, actes du colloque international de Clermont-Ferrand* (Clermont-Ferrand: Association des Publications de la Faculté des Lettres et Sciences Humaines, 1982)

Eliot, T. S., 'What is minor poetry?', (1944), in *On Poetry and Poets* (London: Faber and Faber, 1957), pp.39–52

—— *The Varieties of Metaphysical Poetry* ed. by Ronald Schuchard (London: Faber and Faber, 1993)

Evans, D. Ellis, 'Celticity, Celtic awareness and Celtic Studies', *Zeitschrift für celtische Philologie*, 49–50 (1997), 1–27

Favereau, Francis, *Littérature et écrivains bretonnants depuis 1945* (Morlaix: Skol Vreizh, 1991), trans. into English as *Breton Literature and Writers since 1945* (Morlaix: Ar Falz, 1992)

—— ed., Pierre-Jakez Hélias, *Bigouden universel* (Rennes: Presses universitaires de Rennes, 2001) [Plurial 9]

—— *Anthologie de la littérature bretonne au XXe siècle: Le premier 'Emzao' 1900/1918*, vol. 1 (Morlaix: Skol Vreizh, 2002)

—— *Anthologie de la littérature bretonne au XXe siècle: Breiz Atao et les autres en littérature 1919/1944*, vol. 2 (Morlaix: Skol Vreizh, 2003), with two further volumes in preparation

Finistère, Henri, *Auguste Brizeux et l'idée bretonne* (Rennes/Paris: Caillière/Lemerre, 1888)

Ford, Caroline, *Creating the Nation in Provincial France: Religion and Political Identity in Brittany* (Princeton: Princeton University Press, 1993)

Forsdick, Charles, 'Between "French" and "Francophone": French Studies and the Postcolonial Turn', *French Studies*, 59:4 (2005), 523–30

Forsdick, Charles, and David Murphy, eds, *Francophone Postcolonial Studies: A Critical Introduction* (London: Arnold, 2003)

Fouéré, Yann, *La Bretagne écartelée (1938–1948)* (Paris: Nouvelles éditions latines, 1962)

—— *En prison pour le FLB* (Paris: Nouvelles éditions latines, 1977)

—— *Histoire résumée du mouvement breton du XIXe s. à nos jours (1800–1976)* (Quimper: Nature et Bretagne, 1977)

Furman, Nelly, *La Revue des Deux Mondes et le Romantisme (1831–1848)*, (Geneva: Droz, 1975)

Galand, René, *L'Ame celtique de Renan* (New Haven: Yale University Press, 1959 [c. 1958])

Garavini, Fausta, 'Province et rusticité: esquisse d'un malentendu', *Romantisme*, 35 (1982), 73–89

Garlick, Raymond, 'Is there an Anglo-Welsh Literature?', in *Literature in Celtic Countries: Taliesin Congress Lectures*, ed. J. E. Caerwyn Williams [Taliesin Congress Lectures] (Cardiff: University of Wales Press, 1971), pp.195–213

Gaskill, Howard, ed., *Ossian Revisited* (Edinburgh: Edinburgh University Press, 1991)

Gaskill, Howard, and Fiona Stafford, *From Gaelic to Romantic: Ossianic Translations* (Amsterdam/Atlanta, G.A.: Rodopi, 1998)

Gerson, Stéphane, 'Parisian littérateurs, provincial journeys and the construction of national unity in post-Revolutionary France', *Past and Present*, 151 (1996), 141–73

—— 'Town, Nation, or Humanity? Festive delineations of place and past in Northern France, ca. 1825–1865', *The Journal of Modern History*, 72 (2000), 628–82

—— 'La représentation historique du "pays", entre l'État et la société civile', *Romantisme*, 110 (2000), 39–49

Gibson, Jacqueline, 'Cofiant Bécassine', *Keleier Breizh*, 32 (2002), 12–6

—— 'Bécassine, 'C'hoazh hag Adarre', *Breizh* [formerly Keleier Breizh], 40 (2005), 21

Gildea, Robert, *The Past in French History* (London: Yale University Press, 1994)

Glon, Thierry, 'Écrivains de la "recouvrance" (de 1960 à 1980)', in Hue, Bernard, and Marc Gontard, eds, *Écrire la Bretagne 1960–1995, Plurial 5* (Rennes: Presses universitaires de Rennes, 1995)

—— *Pierre-Jakez Hélias et la Bretagne perdue* (Rennes: Presses universitaires de Rennes, 1998)

—— 'Xavier Grall et la recouvrance', Gontard, Marc, ed., *Bretagne: L'autre et l'ailleurs, Plurial 8* (Rennes: Presses universitaires de Rennes, 1999), 58–75

Gontard, Marc, *De Sable et de sang* (Paris: L'Harmattan, 1982)

—— 'Effets de métissage dans la littérature bretonne', *Métissage du texte: Bretagne, Maghreb, Québec Plurial 4* (Rennes: Presses universitaires de Rennes, 1994), 27–39

—— 'Pour une littérature bretonne de langue française', *Écrire la Bretagne: 1960–1995, Plurial 5* (Rennes: Presses universitaires de Rennes, 1995), 17–31

—— 'Tristan Corbière et l'imaginaire celtique', in *Tristan Corbière en 1995: Lire 'Les Amours jaunes' 150 ans après la naissance du poète* (Morlaix: Comité Tristan Corbière et Bibliothèque Municipale de Morlaix, 1996), pp.19–34

Gontard, Marc, and Bernard Hue, eds, *Écrire la Bretagne: 1960–1995* (Rennes: Presses universitaires de Rennes, 1995)

Gourvil, Francis, *Théodore-Claude-Henri Hersart de La Villemarqué (1815–1895) et le 'Barzaz Breiz' (1839–1845–1867): origines, éditions, sources, critique, influences* (Rennes: Impr. Oberthur, 1959 [i.e. 1960])

Grall, Xavier, *Le Cheval couché: réponse au cheval d'orgueil* (Paris: Hachette, 1977)

Gracq, Julien, *En lisant en écrivant*, 2 vols (Paris: Corti, 1981)

Granet, M., 'La Nostalgie de l'Ouest dans le livre IV des Mémoires d'outre-tombe de François de Chateaubriand, une figure de l'intellectuel', in *Ouest et romantismes, actes du colloque des 6,7,8 et 9 décembre 1990*, ed. by Georges Cesbron (Angers: Presses de L'Université d'Angers, 1991), pp.371–80

Gravier, Jean-François, *Paris et le désert français en 1972* (Paris: Flammarion, 1972), first publ. 1947, significantly revised 1958

Guillermin, J. 'Brizeux', in *Biographies du XIXe siècle* (Paris: Bloud et Barral, 1888), pp.205–21

Guiomar, Jean-Yves, 'Quand les bretonistes répudièrent la Gaule (1840–1850)', in *Nos ancêtres les Gaulois, actes du colloque international de Clermont-Ferrand*, ed. by Jean Ehrard and Paul Viallaneix (Clermont-Ferrand: Association des Publications de la Faculté des Lettres et Sciences Humaines, 1982), pp.195–201

—— *Le Bretonisme: les historiens bretons au XIXe siècle* (Mayenne: Imprimerie de la Manutention, 1987)

—— 'Le Barzaz-Breiz de Théodore Hersart de La Villemarqué', in *Les Lieux de mémoire*, ed. by Pierre Nora, 3 vols (Paris: Gallimard, 1992), II, 527–65

Gwalarn, 'Premier et dernier manifeste de Gwalarn en langue française', March 1925, *Gwalarn*, 1; facsimile in *Francis Favereau, Anthologie de la littérature bretonne au XXe siècle: Breiz Atao et les autres en littérature 1919/1944*, vol. 2 (Morlaix: Skol Vreizh, 2003), p. 239

Gwegen, Jorj, *La Langue bretonne face à ses oppresseurs* (Quimper: Nature et Bretagne, 1975)

Hale, Amy, and Philip Paynton, eds, *New Directions in Celtic Studies* (Exeter: Exeter University Press, 2000)

Hargreaves, Alec G., and Mark McKinna, eds, *Post-colonial Cultures in France* (London: Routledge, 1997)

Heaney, Seamus, 'The Regional Forecast', in *The Literature of Region and Nation*, ed. by R. P. Draper (London: Macmillan, 1989), pp.10–23

Hechter, Michael, Internal Colonialism: *The Celtic Fringe in British National Development, 1536–1966* (London: Routledge & Kegan Paul, 1975)

Hincks, Rhisiart, *I Gadw Mamiaith Mor Hen: Cyflwyniad i Ddechreadau Ysgolheictod Llydaweg* (Llandysul: Gomer, 1995)

Hoare, Rachel, 'An integrative approach to language attitudes and identity in Brittany', *Journal of Sociolinguistics*, 5:1 (2001), 73–84

—— 'Linguistic competence and regional identity in Brittany: attitudes and perceptions of identity', *Multilingual and Multicultural Development*, 21:4 (2000), 324–46

—— *L'Identité linguistique des jeunes en Bretagne* (Brest: Brud Nevez, 2003)

Hobsbawm, Eric, and Terence Ranger, eds, *The Invention of Tradition* (Cambridge: Cambridge University Press, 1983)

Hoffet, Frédéric, *Psychanalyse de l'Alsace, avant-propos de Germain Muller* (Colmar: Éditions Alsatia, 1973), first publ. 1951

Hue, Bernard, ed., *Métissage du texte: Bretagne, Maghreb, Québec, Plurial* 4 (Rennes: Presses universitaires de Rennes, 1994)

—— 'Du mythe à la réalité', *Métissage du texte: Bretagne, Maghreb, Québec*, ed. by Bernard Hue, *Plurial* 4 (Rennes: Presses universitaires de Rennes, 1994), 5–6

—— '*Le temps des évidences*', *Écrire la Bretagne 1960–1995*, ed. by Bernard Hue and Marc Gontard, *Plurial* 5 (Rennes: Presses universitaires de Rennes, 1995), 11–3

—— '*De Bohême en Rennanie: L'aventure bretonne de Milan Kundera*', *Écrire la Bretagne 1960–1995*, ed. by Bernard Hue and Marc Gontard, *Plurial* 5 (Rennes: Presses universitaires de Rennes, 1995), 57–61

Hughes, Alex and Keith Reader, eds, *Encyclopaedia of Contemporary French Culture* (London: Routledge, 1998)

Iknayan, Marguerite, *The Concave Mirror: From Imitation to Expression in French Esthetic Theory 1800–1830* (Stanford: Anma Livre, 1983)

J. M., 'Quand la "Renaissance celtique" gêne, à Paris', *Le Peuple breton*, 349 (1993), 21

Jenkyns, Richard, *Virgil's Experience* (Oxford: Clarendon Press, 1999)

Jones, Mari C., 'At what price language maintenance?: standardization in modern Breton', *French Studies*, 49:4 (1995), 424–38

—— 'Death of a language, birth of an identity: Brittany and the Bretons', *Language Problems and Language Planning*, 22 (1998), 129–42

Jones, R. M., *Ysbryd y Cwlwm: Delwedd y Genedl yn ein Llenyddiaeth* (Cardiff: University of Wales Press, 1998)

Jourdan, Annie, 'The Image of Gaul during the French Revolution: Between Charlemagne and Ossian', in *Celticism*, ed. by Terence Brown (Amsterdam: Rodopi, 1996), pp.183–206

Kiberd, Declan, *Inventing Ireland: The Literature of the Modern Nation* (London: Vintage, 1996)

Kidd, William, and Siân Reynolds, eds, *Contemporary French Cultural Studies* (London: Arnold, 2000)

King, Stewart, 'Catalonia and the Postcolonial Condition', in Stewart King and Jeff Browitt, eds, *The Space of Culture: Critical Readings in Hispanic Studies* (Newark, DL: University of Delaware Press, 2004), pp.39–53

Kristeva, Julia, *La Révolution du langage poétique: l'avant-garde à la fin du XIXe siècle: Lautréamont et Mallarmé* (Paris: Seuil, 1974)

Lachuer, Valérie, *L'Etat face à la langue bretonne* (Rennes: Klask, 1998)

Lacombe, Philippe, 'Corps, culture, religion: la dimension profane des pardons bretons', *Ethnologie française*, 30 (2000), 109–18

Lafont, Robert, *Mistral ou l'illusion* (Paris: Plon, 1954)

177

—— *La Révolution régionaliste* (Paris: Gallimard, 1967)

—— *Clefs pour l'Occitanie* (Paris: Seghers, 1971)

—— *La Revendication occitane* (Paris: Flammarion, 1974)

Landrin, Jacques, 'La Bretagne de Michelet: mythe et réalité', in *Ouest et romantismes, actes du colloque des 6,7,8 et 9 décembre 1990*, ed. by Georges Cesbron (Angers: Presses de L'Université d'Angers, 1991), pp.391–404

Laroche, Hugues, *Tristan Corbière ou les voix de la corbière* (Saint-Denis: Presses universitaires de Vincennes, 1997)

Larzac, Jean, ed., *Le Petit livre de l'Occitanie, par une équipe du COEA* (Paris: Maspéro, 1972)

Lasserre-Vergne, Anne, *Les Pyrénées centrales dans la littérature française entre 1820 et 1870* (Toulouse: Éché, 1985)

Laurent, Donatien, 'Savoir et mémoire du peuple: Introduction', in *Histoire littéraire et culturelle de la Bretagne*, 3 vols, ed. by Jean Balcou and Yves Le Gallo, Centre de recherche bretonne et celtique (Paris/Geneva: Champion-Slatkine, 1987), II, 247–49

—— *Aux sources du Barzaz-Breiz: la mémoire d'un peuple* (Douarnenez: Ar Men, 1989)

Le Berre, Yves, 'Langue et littératures bretonnes depuis la révolution: une aculturation paradoxale', *Beiträge zur Romanischen Philologie*, 28 (1989), 271–78

—— *La Littérature de langue bretonne: livres et brochures entre 1790 et 1918*, 2 vols (Brest: Ar Skol Vrezoneg, 1994)

Le Cam, Jean-Luc, ed., *Hélias et les siens/Hélias hag e dud, KREIZ* 15 (Brest: CRBC, 2001)

Le Clech, Marthe, and François Yven, *Tristan Corbière: la métamorphose du crapaud* (Morlaix: Bretagne d'Hier, 1995)

Le Coadic, Ronan, *L'Identité bretonne* (Rennes: Terre de Brume, 1998)

Le Coadic, Ronan, and Christian Demeuré-Vallée, *Identités & démocratie: diversité culturelle et mondialisation: repenser la démocratie* (Rennes: Presses universitaires de Rennes, 2003)

Le Disez, Jean-Yves, 'Mes filles expliquées à la République', *Noir/Blanc* [i.e. *Hopala!*], 1 (1999), 14–24

—— review in *Hopala!* [actually entitled *Noir/Blanc* at this time], 1 (1999), 85–7

—— *Étrange Bretagne: récits de voyageurs britanniques en Bretagne 1830–1900* (Rennes: Presses universitaires de Rennes, 2002)

Le Dû, Jean, and Yves Le Berre, 'Un siècle d'écrits en langue bretonne: 1790–1892', in *Histoire littéraire et culturelle de la Bretagne*, 3 vols, ed. by Jean Balcou and Yves Le Gallo, Centre de recherche bretonne et celtique (Paris/Geneva: Champion-Slatkine, 1987), II, 251–91

Le Gars, Annaig, *Les Bretons par eux-mêmes: essai sur la condition bretonne* (Relecq-Kerhuon: An Here, 1998)

Le Guillou, Louis, 'Images littéraires de la Bretagne au XIXe siècle: Introduction', in *Histoire littéraire et culturelle de la Bretagne*, II, 7–15

—— 'Romantisme et christianisme bretons', in *Histoire littéraire et culturelle de la Bretagne*, 3 vols, ed. by Jean Balcou and Yves Le Gallo (Paris/Geneva: Champion-Slatkine, 1987), II, 17–78

Le Hir, Marie-Pierre, 'Balzac's Bretons: Racism and National Identity in *Les Chouans*', in *Peripheries of Nineteenth-Century French Studies: Views from the Edge*, ed. by Timothy Raser (Newark: University of Delaware Press, 2002), pp.197–216

Le Quéau, Jean-René, ed., *Per-Jakez Hélias* (Morlaix: Skol Vreizh, 1997)

Le Sidaner, Jean-Marie, ed., special issue of *Europe*, 625 (1981)

Le Stum, Philippe, *Le Néo-druidisme en Bretagne: origine, naissance et développement 1890–1914* (Rennes: Éditions Ouest-France, 1998)

Lebesque, Morvan, *Comment peut-on être breton?: essai sur la démocratie française, preface de Gwenc'hlan Le Scouëzec* (Paris: Seuil, 1970)

Lehning, James R., *Peasant and French: Cultural Contact in Rural France During the Nineteenth Century* (Cambridge: Cambridge University Press, 1995)

Lemaire, Yannick, *Le Peuple breton*, 351 (1993), 20

Lecigne, L'abbé C., *Brizeux, sa vie & ses œuvres d'après des documents inédits* (Paris: Poussielgue, 1898) and (Lille: Morel, 1898)

Leerssen, Joep, 'Outer and Inner Others: The Auto-Image of French Identity from Mme de Staël to Eugène Sue', *Yearbook of European Studies*, 2 (1989), 35–52

—— 'Celticism', in *Celticism*, ed. by Terence Brown (Amsterdam: Rodopi, 1996), pp.1–20

Lexandre, A. [pseudonym of Alexandre Tisseur], *Un Pèlerinage au pays de Brizeux: la Bretagne et son poète* (Paris: Dentu, 1879)

Lloyd, Rosemary, *Baudelaire's World* (Ithaca: Cornell University Press, 2002)

Lloyd-Morgan, Ceridwen, 'Les Fonds bretons à la Bibliothèque nationale du Pays de Galles', *Mercator Media Forum*, 1 (1995), 88–95

Looten, C. *Brizeux et son dernier critique* (Arras/Paris: Sueur-Charruey, 1898), extrait de la Revue de Lille, 1898

Lough, John, *The Writer and Public in France: From the Middle Ages to the Present Day* (Oxford: Clarendon Press, 1978)

Lunn-Rockliffe, Katherine, 'Corbière and the poetics of irony' (unpublished doctoral thesis, University of Oxford, 2002)

Luzel, François-Marie, *Deux bardes bretons du XIXe siècle: Auguste Brizeux et Prosper Proux* (Quimperlé: Clairet, 1888)

McDonald, Maryon, *'We are Not French!': Language, Culture and Identity in Brittany* (London-New York: Routledge, 1989)

McPhee, Peter, 'A Case of Internal Colonization: The Francisation of Northern Catalonia', *Review*, 3:3 (1980), 399–428

Mahé, Georges, 'Quelques lettres inédites de La Villemarqué à Brizeux', *Cahiers d'Iroise*, 16 (1969), 154–59

—— *Brizeux: essai de Biographie (d'après des documents inédits)* (Paris: Klincksieck, 1969)

—— 'Essai de bibliographie des œuvres bretonnes de Brizeux', *Cahiers d'Iroise*, 21 (1974), 214–20

Malaurie, Jean, 'Histoire de la naissance du Cheval d'orgueil et révélation d'un écrivain', in *Hélias et les siens/Hélias hag e dud, KREIZ* 15, ed. by Jean-Luc Le Cam (Brest: CRBC, 2001), pp.219–24.

Martin, Anne-Denes, *Itinéraire poétique en Bretagne: de Tristan Corbière à Xavier Grall* (Paris: l'Harmattan, 1995)

—— 'Actualité de Tristan Corbière', in *Tristan Corbière en 1995: Lire 'Les Amours jaunes' 150 ans après la naissance du poète* (Morlaix: Comité Tristan Corbière et Bibliothèque Municipale de Morlaix, 1996), pp.94-101

Martin-Fugier, Anne, *Les Romantiques: figures de l'artiste 1820–1848* (Paris: Hachette, 1998)

Maurice, René, 'Autour d'un Brizeux ignoré', *Cahiers d'Iroise*, 15 (1968), 145–53;

Maurice, René, 'Loti et Brizeux', *Cahiers d'Iroise*, 1967/3, pp.145–53

Mc Cormack, W. J., *Ascendancy and Tradition in Anglo-Irish Literary History from 1789–1939* (Oxford: Clarendon Press, 1985)

Mordrel, Olier, *La Bretagne dans la littérature* (Geneva: Famot, 1980)

—— *Le Mythe de l'hexagone* (Paris: Jean Picollec, 1981)

Morgan, Prys, 'Thomas Price (1748–1848) et les Bretons', *Triade: Galles, Écosse, Irlande*, 1 (1995), 5–13

Morvan, Françoise, *Le Monde comme si: nationalisme et dérive identitaire en Bretagne* (Arles: Actes Sud, 2002)

Morvannou, Fañch, 'Carnavalesque!', *Le Peuple breton* (Août 1977), p.21

—— 'La littérature de langue bretonne au XXe siècle', in *Histoire littéraire et culturelle de la Bretagne*, 3 vols, ed. by Jean Balcou and Yves Le Gallo, Centre de recherche bretonne et celtique (Paris/Geneva: Champion-Slatkine, 1987), III, 175–249

Mozet, Nicole, 'Yvetot vaut Constantinople: littérature et géographie en France au XIXème siècle', *Romantisme*, 35 (1982), 91–114

Nisard, Désiré, 'Marie, Roman', *Journal des Débats politiques et littéraires*, 22 avril 1832, pp.3–4

Nouvelle Revue de Bretagne, numéro spécial du 150e anniversaire de sa naissance, Mélanges Brizeux (juillet–août 1953)

O'Callaghan, Michael John, *Separatism in Brittany* (Cornwall: Dyllansow Truran, 1983)

Ozouf, Mona, *L'École de la France: essais sur la Révolution, l'utopie et l'enseignement* (Paris: Gallimard, 1984)

Pailleron, Marie-Louise, *François Buloz et ses amis: la vie littéraire sous Louis Philippe* (Paris: Firmin-Didot, 1930)

Pelletier, Yannick, ed., *Histoire générale de la Bretagne et des Bretons*, 2 vols, (Paris: Nouvelle Librairie de France, 1990)

—— *La Bretagne chez Chateaubriand* (Spézet: Coop Breizh, 1998)

Perazzi, Jean-Charles, *Diwan: vingt ans d'enthousiasme, de doute et d'espoir* (Spézet: Coop Breizh, 1998)

Picard, Jeanine Picard, *Hélias, Le Cheval d'orgueil*, Glasgow Introductory Guides to French Literature, 44 (Glasgow: University of Glasgow French and German Publications, 1999)

Piriou, Yann-Ber, 'Barzhed er Gorventenn', *Al Liamm*, 88, pp.339–47

—— 'Une lettre de L. Sauvé à Luzel', in *Études sur la Bretagne et les pays celtiques: mélanges offerts à Yves le Gallo*, *Cahiers de Bretagne Occidentale* 6 (Brest, 1987), pp.407–10

Postic, Fañch, 'La Villemarqué et le Pays de Galles (1837–1838): deux lettres inédites de Thomas Price', *Triade: Galles, Ecosse, Irlande*, 1 (1995), 15–32

Poupinot, Yann, *Les Bretons à l'heure de l'Europe* (Paris: Nouvelles Éditions Latines, 1961)

Pratt, Mary Louise, *Imperial Eyes: Travel Writing and Transculturation* (London: Routledge, 1992)

Prémel, Gérard, *Hopala!* 14 (2003), 77

Prendergast, Christopher, *Balzac: Fiction and Melodrama* (London: Edward Arnold, 1978)

—— *Paris and the Nineteenth Century* (Oxford: Blackwell, 1996), first publ. 1992

Press, Ian J. 'Breton speakers in Brittany, France and Europe: constraints on the search for an identity', in *The Changing Voices of Europe: Social and Political Changes and their Linguistic Repercussions, Past, Present and Future, papers in honour of Professor Glanville Price*, ed. by M. Mair Parry, Winifred V. Davies, and Rosalind A. M. Temple (Cardiff: University of Wales Press, in conjunction wth the Modern Humanities Research Association, 1994), pp.213–26

Queffélec, Henri, *La Bretagne intérieure, suivi de La Bretagne des pardons* (Quimper: Calligrammes, 1992)

Quentel, Yves, and Daniel Yonnetf, eds, *Nos années Breizh, La Bretagne des années 70*, (Rennes: Apogée, 1998)

Raoul, Lukian, *Geiriadur ar skrivagrerien ha yezheurien vrezhonek aet da annen a-raok mis Meurzh 1992* (Brest: Al Liamm, 1992)

Rannou, Pascal, 'Littérature et bretonnité', *Le Peuple Breton*, issues 278–79 (1987)

—— 'De l'histoire littéraire et culturelle de la Bretagne à l'histoire générale de la Bretagne et des Bretons', *Le Peuple breton*, [in several parts] 324–28 (1990–91)

—— *Guillevic: du menhir au poème* (Morlaix: Skol Vreizh, 1991)

—— 'Approche du concept de littérature bretonne francophone à travers des textes de Villiers de l'Isle-Adam, Yvon le Men, Kristian Keginer et Youenn Coïc' (unpublished thesis, University of Rennes, 1991)

——— 'Approche du concept de littérature bretonne de langue française', in *Métissage du texte: Bretagne, Maghreb, Québec*, ed. by Bernard Hue (Rennes: Presses universitaires de Rennes, 1994), pp.75–86

——— *Inventaire d'un héritage: essai sur l'œuvre littéraire de Pierre-Jakez Hélias* (Relecq-Kerhuon: An Here, 1997)

——— 'Julien Gracq: visiteur de la Bretagne', in Gontard, Marc, ed., *Bretagne: L'autre et l'ailleurs, Plurial* 8 (Rennes: Presses universitaires de Rennes, 1999), pp.129–43

Rannou, Pascal and Pierre Bazantay, eds, *Visages de Tristan Corbière* (Morlaix: Skol Vreizh, 1995)

Rearick, Charles, *Beyond the Enlightenment: Historians and Folklore in Nineteenth-Century France* (Bloomington and London: Indiana University Press, 1974)

Reece, Jack E., *The Bretons against France: Ethnic Minority Nationalism in Twentieth-century Brittany* (Chapel Hill: The University of North Carolina Press, 1977)

Richard, Jean-Pierre, *Pages/Paysages: Microlectures* II, (Paris: Seuil, 1984)

Richardot, Jean-Pierre, *La France en miettes* (Paris: Pierre Belfond, 1976)

Riffaterre, Michael, *The Semiotics of Poetry* (Bloomington and London: Indiana University Press, 1978)

Rigney, Ann, 'Immemorial Routines: The Celts and their resistance to history', in *Celticism*, ed. by Terence Brown (Amsterdam: Rodopi, 1996), pp.159–81

Rio, Joseph, 'Brizeux: les Bretons, une épopée nationale?', proceedings of conference: *Le monde kalévaléen en France et en Finlande* (Paris: Klincksieck, 1987)

——— *Mythes fondateurs de la Bretagne: aux origines de la celtomanie* (Rennes: Editions Ouest-France, 2000)

Ripoll, Roger, 'Bouvard et Pécuchet à la recherche des Gaulois', in *Nos ancêtres les Gaulois, actes du colloque international de Clermont-Ferrand*, ed. by Jean Ehrard and Paul Viallaneix (Clermont-Ferrand: Association des Publications de la Faculté des Lettres et Sciences Humaines, 1982), pp.331–37

Rousselot, Jean, *Tristan Corbière: un essai par Jean Rousselot* (Paris: Seghers, 1951)

Rudel, Yves-Marie, *Panorama de la littérature bretonne des origines à nos jours: écrivains de langue bretonne & de langue française* (Rennes: Imprimerie Bretonne, 1950)

Said, Edward W., *Orientalism* (London: Penguin, 1995), first publ. 1978

Sainte-Beuve, 'Marie, Roman, Iambes, par M Auguste Barbier', *Revue des Deux Mondes*, 1:4 (1831), 524–34

——— *Revue de Paris*, 34 (1832), 210–22

——— 'Poètes et romanciers modernes de la France, XLV, M. Brizeux (Les Ternaires, Livre lyrique)', *Revue des Deux Mondes*, 4: 3 (1841), 779–90

——— *Causeries du lundi, portraits de femmes et portraits littéraires*, 16 vols, ed. by Ch. Pierrot (Paris: Garnier, 1926–1949)

—— *Correspondance générale*, ed. by Jean Bonnerot, 15 vols (Paris: Didier, 1966)

—— *Le Cahier vert 1834–1847*, ed. by Raphaël Molho (Paris: Gallimard, 1973)

—— *Port-Royal*, 5 vols (Paris: Hachette, 1860)

Salomé, Karine, LesÎles *bretonnes: une image en construction (1750–1914)* (Rennes: Presses universitaires de Rennes, 2004)

Schor, Naomi, 'Domestic Orientalism: on the road with Gustave and Maxime', in *Corps/decors: femmes, orgie, parodie*, ed. by Catherine Nesci, Gretchen Van Slyke and Gerald Prince, (Amsterdam: Rodopi, 1999), pp.57–65

Schwab, Raymond, *La Renaissance orientale* (Paris: Payot, 1950)

Ségalen, Auguste-Pierre, 'Stéphane Mallarmé en Bretagne (Août–Septembre 1873)', *Cahiers d'Iroise*, 22e année, No 4 (Nouvelle Série), Octobre–Décembre 1975/4, pp.211–17

—— *Géographie littéraire de Bretagne* (Rennes: Institut Culturel de Bretagne, 1995)

Senghor, Sédar, L, *Anthologie de la nouvelle poésie nègre et malgache de langue française, précédée de Orphée noir par Jean Paul Sartre* (Paris: Presses universitaires de France, 1972), first publ. 1948

Simon, Jean-Pierre, *La Bretonnité: une ethnicité problématique* (Rennes: Terre de Brume, 1999)

Sims-Williams, Patrick, 'The Visionary Celt: the construction of an ethnic pre-conception', *Cambridge Medieval Celtic Studies*, 11 (1986), 71–96

—— 'The Invention of Celtic Nature Poetry', in *Celticism*, ed. by Terence Brown (Amsterdam: Rodopi, 1996), pp.97–124

—— 'Celtomania and Celtoscepticism', *Cambrian Medieval Celtic Studies*, 36 (1998), 1–35

—— 'How are you finding it here?', *London Review of Books*, 28 October 1999, p.30 [review of Simon James, The Atlantic Celts: Ancient People or Modern Invention? (London: British Museum, 1999)]

Sonnenfeld, Albert, *L'Œuvre de Tristan Corbière* (Paris: Presses universitaires de France, 1960)

Souriau, Maurice 'Les cahiers d'écolier de Brizeux', in *Moralistes et poètes* (Paris: Vuibert et Nony, 1907), pp.197–225

Stafford, Fiona, *The Sublime Savage: James Macpherson and the Poems of Ossian* (Edinburgh: Edinburgh University Press, 1988)

—— *The Last of the Race: The Growth of a Myth from Milton to Darwin* (Oxford: Clarendon Press, 1994)

—— 'Primitivism and the "primitive" poet: a cultural context for Macpherson's Ossian', in *Celticism*, ed. by Terence Brown (Amsterdam: Rodopi, 1996), pp.79–96

Stephan, Andrée, 'Pouldreuzic et Péribonka: les communautés rurales du Cheval d'orgueil et de Maria Chapdelaine', *Études canadiennes/Canadian Studies*, 21:1 (1986), 227–34

Stückemann, Franck, 'Tristan Corbière et la Jeune Belgique: ou le mystérieux auteur de la première critique des Amours jaunes', in *Tristan Corbière en 1995: Lire 'Les Amours jaunes' 150 ans après la naissance du poète* (Morlaix: Comité Tristan Corbière et Bibliothèque Municipale de Morlaix, 1996), pp.122–29

Sven-Myer, Gwenno, 'Digwyddiadau 1940–1944 a'r Llydaweg', (unpublished doctoral thesis, University of Wales Aberystwyth, 2003)

Tanguy, Bernard, *Aux origines du nationalisme breton*, 2 vols (Paris: Union générale d'éditions, 1977)

——'De la gallomanie au nationalisme breton', in *Nos ancêtres les Gaulois, actes du colloque international de Clermont-Ferrand*, ed. by Jean Ehrard and Paul Viallaneix (Clermont-Ferrand: Association des Publications de la Faculté des Lettres et Sciences Humaines, 1982), pp.187–93

Tanner, Marcus, *The Last of the Celts* (New Haven MA:Yale University Press, 2004)

Thiesse, Anne-Marie, *Écrire la France: le mouvement littéraire régionaliste de langue française entre la belle époque et la libération* (Paris: Presses universitaires de France, 1991)

—— *Ils apprenaient la France* (Paris: Edns maison des sciences de l'homme, 1998)

—— *La Création des identitiés nationales: Europe, XVIIIe–XXe siècle* (Paris: Seuil, 1999)

—— 'Des fictions créatrices: les identités nationales', *Romantisme*, 110 (2000), 51–62

Thomas, M. Wynn, ed., *Internal Difference: Twentieth-Century Writing in Wales* (Cardiff: University of Wales Press, 1992)

—— *DiFfinio Dwy Lenyddiaeth Cymru* (Cardiff: University of Wales Press, 1995)

—— *Corresponding Cultures: The Two Literatures of Wales* (Cardiff: University of Wales Press, 1999)

Thompson, Christopher W., *Walking and the French Romantics: Rousseau to Sand and Hugo* (Bern: Peter Lang, 2003)

Tiercelin, Louis, *Bretons de Lettres* (Paris: Honoré Champion, 1905)

Tristan Corbière en 1995: *Lire 'Les Amours jaunes' 150 ans après la naissance du poète* (Morlaix: Comité Tristan Corbière et Bibliothèque Municipale de Morlaix, 1996)

Vallerie, Erwan, *Nous barbares locaux: théorie de la nation et autres textes de Sav Breizh* (Relecq-Kerhuon: An Here, 1997); collection of his earlier writing from Sav Breizh, 1971–5

Jeanjean, Henri, *De l'utopie au pragmatisme? (le mouvement occitan, 1976–1990)* (Perpignan: Trabucaire, 1992)

Hamon, Kristian, *Les nationalistes bretons sous l'occupation* (Relecq-Kerhuon: An Here, 2001)

Van Tieghem, Paul, *Ossian en France*, 2 vols (Paris: Rieder, 1917)

Vetter, Eva, *Plus de breton? Conflit linguistique en Bretagne rurale* (Relecq-Kerhuon: An Here, 1999), original German title, Nicht mehr Bretonisch?

Sprachkonflikte in der ländlichen Bretagne (Frankfurt am Main: Peter Lang, 1997), trans. by Gérard Cornillet

Vier, Jacques, 'Le romantisme en Bretagne: dans le sillage des maîtres', in *Histoire littéraire et culturelle de la Bretagne*, 3 vols, ed. by Jean Balcou and Yves Le Gallo (Paris/Geneva: Champion-Slatkine, 1987), II, 79–102

Vigny, Alfred de, *Lettres à Brizeux*, ed. by Éric Lugin (Paris: Nouvelles Éditions Latines, 1954)

Williams, Daniel, 'Pan-Celticism and the Limits of Post-Colonialism: W. B. Yeats, Ernest Rhys, and Williams Sharp in the 1890s', in *Nations and Relations: Writing Across the British Isles*, ed. by Tony Brown and Russell Stephens (Cardiff: New Welsh Review, 2000), pp.1–29

Williams, Heather, 'Diffinio dwy lenyddiaeth Llydaw', *Tu Chwith*, 12 (1999), 51–56

—— 'Diffinio Llydaw', *Y Traethodydd*, 157 (2002), 197–208

—— 'Le voyage transculturel de Brizeux', in *Seuils et traverses: enjeux de l'écriture de voyage*, 2 vols, ed. by Jean-Yves Le Disez (Brest: CRBC, 2002), I, 275–85

—— 'Séparisianisme: or internal colonialism', in *Francophone Postcolonial Studies: A Critical Introduction*, ed. by Charles Forsdick and David Murphy (London: Arnold, 2003), pp.102–11

—— 'Une sauvagerie très douce', in *Visions/Revisions: Essays on Nineteenth-Century French Culture*, ed. by Nigel Harkness, Paul Rowe, Tim Unwin, Jennifer Yee (Oxford: Peter Lang, 2003), pp. 99–106

—— 'Writing to Paris: poets, nobles, and savages in nineteenth-century Brittany', *French Studies* (2003), 57:4 (2003), 475–90

Williams, Jane 'Ysgafell', *Literary Remains of the Rev. Thomas Price, Carnhuanawc, Vicar of Cwmdû, Breconshire; and Rural Eean*, 2 vols (Llandovery: William Rees, 1854 55)

Zumthor, Paul, *La Mesure du monde* (Paris: Seuil, 1993)

Journals

Al Liamm
Ar Bed Keltiek
Breiz atao
Bretagne révolutionnaire
Bretagnes
Gwalarn
Hopala! Débats de Bretagne et d'ailleurs
Lutte occitane: organe d'information et de combat de "lucha occitana", rédigé par des équipes militantes

Le Peuple breton
Plurial
Sav Breizh

Works of reference

Anglo-Norman Dictionary, ed. by Louise W. Stone and William Rothwell (London: Modern Humanities Research Association, 1977–92)

Dictionnaire de l'Académie française (Paris: Hachette, 1932), earlier editions consulted online

FRANTEXT www.frantext.fr

Französisches Etymologisches Wörterbuch: eine Darstellung des galloromanischen Sprachshatzes, 24 vols and unbound parts, ed. by Walther von Wartburg (Bonn: Klopp, 1928–)

Godefroy, Frédéric, ed., *Dictionnaire de l'ancienne langue française et de tous ses dialectes du IXe. auXVe. siècle* (Paris: Vieweg, 1881–1902)

Lewis, Charlton T., and Charles Short, *A Latin Dictionary* (Oxford: Clarendon Press, 1975)

Lommatzsch, Erhard, ed., *Altfranzösisches Wörterbuch*, Adolf Toblers nachgelassene Materialien, 10 vols and 5 unbound parts (Berlin: Weidmannsche, 1925–)

Niermeyer, Jan Frederik, and C. van de Kieft, eds, *Medieval Latin Dictionary*, édition remaniée par J. W. J. Burgers (Leiden: Brill, 2002)

Oxford Latin Dictionary, ed. by P. G. W. Glare (Oxford: Clarendon Press, 1982)

The Oxford Book of French Verse, XIIIth century – XIXth century, chosen by St. John Lucas (London: Clarendon Press, 1908)

The Oxford Book of French Verse, XIIIth century – XIXth century, ed. by St. John Lucas and Percy Mansell Jones (Oxford: Clarendon Press, 1957)

The Oxford Companion to French Literature, ed. by Paul Harvey and J. E. Heseltine (Oxford: Clarendon Press, 1959)

The Oxford Companion to Literature in French, ed. by Peter France (Oxford: Clarendon Press, 1995)

Robert, Paul, ed., *Dictionnaire alphabétique et analogique de la langue française*, 9 vols (Paris, 1985)

Trésor de la langue française: dictionnaire de la langue du XIXe et du XXe siècle (1879–1960), vols 1–10 (Paris: Éds. du CNRS), vol. 11 (Paris: Gallimard, 1971–1994)

Index

191

Cultural Identity Studies

Edited by
Helen Chambers

This series aims to publish new research (monographs and essays) into relationships and interactions between culture and identity. The notions of both culture and identity are broadly conceived; interdisciplinary and theoretically diverse approaches are encouraged in a series designed to promote a better understanding of the processes of identity formation, both individual and collective. It will embrace research into the roles of linguistic, social, political, psychological, and religious factors, taking account of historical context. Work on the theorizing of cultural aspects of identity formation, together with case studies of individual writers, thinkers or cultural products will be included. It focuses primarily on cultures linked to European languages, but welcomes transcultural links and comparisons. It is published in association with the Institute of European Cultural Identity Studies of the University of St Andrews.

Vol. 1   Helen Chambers (ed.)
          Violence, Culture and Identity: Essays on German and
          Austrian Literature, Politics and Society. 436 pages. 2006.
          ISBN 3-03910-266-4 / US-ISBN 0-8204-7195-X

Vol. 2   Heather Williams
          Postcolonial Brittany: Literature between Languages. 191 pages. 2007.
          ISBN 978-3-03-910556-4 / US-ISBN 978-0-8204-7583-7

Lightning Source UK Ltd.
Milton Keynes UK
UKHW021826060722
405478UK00005B/117